WOOD MAGAZINE

D1490176

FINISH CARPENTRY & TRIMWORK

Meredith® Books
Special Interest Media

WOOD Finish Carpentry & Trimwork
Editors: Benjamin Allen, Larry Johnston
Senior Associate Design Director: Tom Wegner
Copy Chief: Doug Kouma
Copy Editor: Kevin Cox
Publishing Operations Manager: Karen Schirm
Edit and Design Production Coordinator: Mary Lee Gavin
Editorial Assistant: Diana Meinders
Book Production Managers: Marjorie J. Schenkelberg,
    Mark Weaver
Imaging Center Operator: Chris Sprague
Contributing Copy Editor: David Rosetti
Contributing Proofreaders: Cheri Madison, Julie Collins
Contributing Indexer: Donald Glassman
Other Contributors: Janet Anderson

Additional Editorial Contributions from
    Greenleaf Publishing, Inc.
Editor: Dave Toht
Designer: Rebecca Anderson
Contributing Writer: Jeff Day
Contributing Copy Editor: Barbara McIntosh Webb
Contributing Photographer: Dan Stultz, Stultz Photography
Studio Assistants: Mike Anderson, Jonathan Anderson
Contributing Illustrator: Ian Worpole

Meredith® Books
Editorial Director: Gregory H. Kayko
Art Director: Gene Rauch
Managing Editor: Kathleen Armentrout
Brand Manager: Mark Hetrick

Director, Marketing and Publicity: Amy Nichols
Executive Director, Sales: Ken Zagor
Director, Operations: George A. Susral
Director, Production: Douglas M. Johnston
Business Director: Janice Croat

Vice President and General Manager, SIM: Jeff Myers

Meredith Publishing Group
President: Jack Griffin
Executive Vice President: Doug Olson

Meredith Corporation
Chairman of the Board: William T. Kerr
President and Chief Executive Officer: Stephen M. Lacy

In Memoriam: E.T. Meredith III (1933–2003)

Thanks to
Photos, bottom left and right of page 62, courtesy of
    Rockler Woodworking and Hardware
Photo bottom left of page 75 courtesy of Grizzly
    Industrial
Photo bottom left of page 74 and top left of page 75
    courtesy of Ryobi Power Tools
Photo right of page 75 courtesy of Ridgid Tool Company

All of us at Meredith® Books are dedicated to providing
you with the information and ideas you need to enhance
your home and garden. We welcome your comments and
suggestions. Write to us at:
Meredith Books
Home Improvement Books Department
1716 Locust St.
Des Moines, IA 50309–3023

Note to the Readers: Due to differing conditions, tools,
and individual skills, Meredith Corporation assumes
no responsibility for any damages, injuries suffered, or
losses incurred as a result of following the information
published in this book. Before beginning any project
review the instructions carefully, and if any doubts or
questions remain, consult local experts or authorities.
Because codes and regulations vary greatly, you always
should check with authorities to ensure that your project
complies with all applicable local codes and regulations.
Always read and observe all of the safety precautions
provided by manufacturers of any tools, equipment,
or supplies, and follow all accepted safety procedures.

QUICK GUIDE TO PROJECTS

CONTENTS

CHAPTER 1
PLANNING YOUR PROJECT
6

CHAPTER 2
CHOOSING MATERIALS
24

CHAPTER 3
CARPENTRY AND WOODWORKING TOOLS
42

CHAPTER 4
WOODWORKING BASICS
82

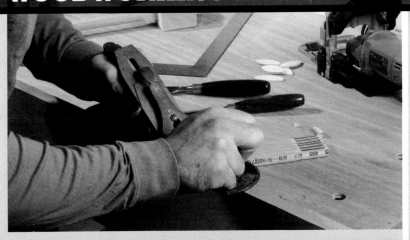

CHAPTER 5
MOLDINGS
130

CHAPTER 6
PROJECTS
162

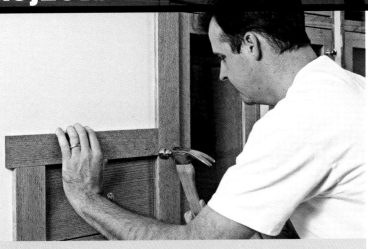

PLANNING YOUR PROJECT

WHETHER YOU GET YOUR INSPIRATION FROM A MAGAZINE, the Internet, or classical architecture, the time will come to put it all down on paper and begin to plan. Sometimes the best projects take more time to think about and draw than

DEVELOPING A DESIGN

Here is valuable information on standard dimensions and how to choose appropriate materials. . . . 8

GETTING THE BIG PICTURE

Planning out how you will put things together—and assessing your site— are essential first steps toward a successful project. 12

MOLDING

This gallery shows just a few of the many uses of molding. 14

PANELING AND BEAMS

Here are some ideas for upgrading your walls and ceilings. 18

SHELVES AND BOOKCASES

Enjoy this collection of goodlooking, functional built-ins 20

KITCHEN UPGRADES

Add beautiful detail to the hardest-working room in the house.. 22

to actually build. Being able to build fast is often the result of good planning too. This chapter guides you through the fundamentals of proportion, measuring, and layout, and includes a gallery of great project ideas.

DEVELOPING A DESIGN

WHETHER YOU WILL BUY A READY-MADE PLAN OR START FROM SCRATCH, YOU HAVE TO THINK DESIGN. AND DESIGN IS ABOUT TWO THINGS: WILL IT WORK AND WILL IT LOOK GOOD? MAKE SURE THAT YOUR PROJECT DOES BOTH BEFORE YOU START.

Despite the oft-heard saying, form might not always follow function. What, after all, is the function of an ornamental molding on a door? For practical purposes you can live by a far simpler rule: Whatever you build should look good.

You already know what appeals to you. The challenge is drawing it on paper and then building it in the shop. Most beginners find their first projects by thumbing through plans in magazines or books or browsing online. Even for many experienced woodworkers, this is enough. The joy for them is in the building. For others woodworking is like painting a picture—they like to sketch out the project first, move things around, and play with the composition before they make a commitment.

Whichever type you are look at projects that others have built; doing so will improve your own work. Even

the most basic piece of furniture requires some design work. Go to an auction, read a book on furniture history, and wander through antiques shops, furniture stores, and museums. Get a feel for what things look like and why they look that way. Seeing what's available helps you decide what you like.

Sooner or later every woodworker runs into the same problem: A favorite design is too big, too small, or too tall to go where it's meant to. If it's a matter of lopping off an inch or two, the Fibonacci gauge on pages 10–11 will help you adjust the proportions without ruining the looks.

But there are limits. You can make a dinner table 25 percent shorter; but if you make it 25 percent lower, it becomes a coffee table. And you can make a table as long as you'd like, but if it is too wide you won't be able to pass the gravy across it. The charts on

Dressers, chests, and cabinets

The size of a dresser or chest depends on what will go in it, how things will be stored, and who will use it.

Take a blanket chest, for example. The width depends on the size that your blankets fold to. The height depends on both the length of your arms and the stacking problem: How far can you reach, and how many blankets do you feel like moving to get to the one on the bottom? Practical limits put both the depth and height at about 24 inches.

Dressers solve the stacking problem with drawers, but drawers have their limits too. A drawer wider than 3 or 4 feet will rack and jam as you pull it open or push it closed. If you make the drawers deeper than 2 feet or higher than 1 foot, things will get lost in them. A height of 29 to 34 inches for the

dresser keeps the drawers below eye level, making it easy to look into them. The upper height limit for a drawer is about 5 feet 8 inches—eye level for a 6-foot person. Keep upper drawers shallow so that they're easy to reach into. As for the cabinet consider any part above 6 feet to be decorative.

TYPICAL CABINET SIZES

	DEPTH	WIDTH	HEIGHT
Blanket chest	12"–24"	30"–60"	15"–24"
Dresser	18"–24"	36"–48"	29"–34"
Tall dresser/Highboy	12"–24"	36"–48"	72"–84"
Wardrobe	24"	40"–70"	72"–84"
Hutch	18"–24"	40"–60"	80"–85"

Bookcases

Bookcases present three practical concerns: the distance between shelves, the depth of the shelf, and the length of the shelf. The first two depend on the size of the books, though adjustable-height shelves give you a lot of leeway with regard to book size. You also have some flexibility on shelf length: Hardwood sags less than plywood, allowing you to design a longer shelf. The charts here list typical book sizes and allowable shelf spans for different materials.

MAXIMUM SPAN

¾" hardwood	48"
¾" plywood	36"
¾" particleboard	28"
½" acrylic	22"

BOOK SIZES

	BETWEEN SHELVES	SHELF DEPTH
Children's books	8"	8"
Paperbacks	8"	10"
Large hardcovers	15"	12"
General reading	11"	12"
Reference	10"	14"

these pages give you the outer limits of both what works and what looks right.

If you start from scratch or redesign a plan radically, you can test your design and save yourself a lot of headaches by building a full-scale prototype. A prototype is anything but fancy—you can make the whole thing from sheets of foam insulation or from 2×4s and construction-grade plywood. Don't spend more than a morning on it. Get the size right, but approximate the details. Any joinery more sophisticated than a drywall screw wastes time.

The advantage of a prototype is that you can put it in place to see if the size and proportions are right. You can also test out details that don't show up on

paper. Is the table apron so low that it scrapes your knees? Does the dresser cover an outlet you really need? Can you reach across the desk to the bookshelf?

Unlike wood, which is measured in thickness, width, and length, furniture is measured in depth, width, and height. The difference can be confusing.

Here's how furniture dimensions are given: Height is the distance from the floor to the top of a piece; depth is the distance from the front edge to the cabinet back or wall; when you're looking at the cabinet front, length is the distance from left to right. The charts on these two pages show some common dimensions for various projects.

Desks and tables

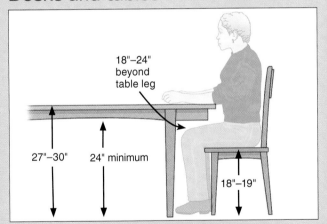

18"–24" beyond table leg

27"–30"   24" minimum

18"–19"

TYPICAL DESK AND TABLE SIZES

	DEPTH	WIDTH	HEIGHT
Desk	24–30"	48–72"	28–30"
Rectangular side table	19–28"	21–48"	17–28"
Square side table	15–32"	15–32"	17–28"
Round side table	16–30"	16–30"	18–22½"
Rectangular coffee table	15–24"	21–86"	12–18"
Square coffee table	32–42"	32–42"	15–17"
Round coffee table	30–42"	30–42"	15–16½"
Dining table	24–42"	24–36" per person	27–30"

Desk and table design depends on leg and arm length. To be comfortable a table obviously needs to clear your legs. A dinner spent with the table apron digging into your thighs will be miserable, no matter how good the food. Less obvious is arm length. If the center of the table is much farther away than the distance from your shoulder to your wrist, it becomes difficult to pass food across. Elbow room counts too. If everyone around the table is squeezed between two others, no one is going to be happy. Your best bet when designing a table is to allow each person 24–36 inches from side to side and 12–18 inches from front to back.

The guidelines change when it comes to designing a desk. You'll need to allow space for in/out trays or papers, books, a phone and address book, probably a computer monitor and other electronics, and the inevitable knickknacks and memorabilia.

Design side tables, coffee tables, and end tables with their purpose in mind. Will they hold the books you're reading, the light you read them by, or both? If the table will be tall to match something it's next to, make it wide enough to be stable. If it's low make it sturdy enough to rest your feet on. If it will be outside, make it stout enough to hold the ice chest that someone will inevitably set on it.

DETERMINING PROPORTIONS

FOR THOUSANDS OF YEARS ARCHITECTS AND ARTISTS HAVE FOLLOWED THE PRINCIPLE OF THE GOLDEN MEAN TO MAKE DESIGNS LOOK JUST RIGHT.

All the best carpenters and woodworkers seem to have one thing in common—a natural eye for proportion. From sketch to finished project, they never lose their sense for balanced proportions. Those lacking this natural gift can rely on the Golden Mean.

Believed to have originated in ancient Greece, the Golden Mean is a mathematical formula for proportioning one dimension to another for eye-appealing balance. A furnituremaker can calculate the proper size for a coffee-table top in relation to its total height to arrive at a pleasing proportion.

Mathematically he or she would utilize the Golden Mean ratio of 1:1.618, which determines the length of the long side in relation to the short side of a rectangle. Here's how it works:

Let's say the rectangular coffee table you want to make will stand 18 inches high (a standard height and the short side of the rectangle). To calculate the top's length (the long side of the rectangle), multiply 18 inches by 1.618 to arrive at about 29 inches, which represents the top's width. (No need for fractional exactness.) See **DRAWING 1** for how it's done.

The Fibonacci gauge lets you determine proportions at a glance, without the math.

MATERIALS LIST

Part		FINISHED SIZE			Qty.
		T	W	L	
A	outside arms	¹⁄₁₆"	½"	6¾"	2
B	inside arm	¹⁄₁₆"	½"	4¼"	1
C	cross arm	¹⁄₁₆"	½"	3"	1

The Fibonacci gauge—named after 13th-century Italian mathematician Leonardo Fibonacci—is an adjustable design tool that holds constant the Golden Mean ratio even if it's compressed or expanded. The shorter span between the centerpoint (B) and outer point (C) represents a unit that's 0.618 of the span length between the centerpoint (B) and the other outer point (A).

1 To make your own start by cutting the arms (A, B, C) to width and shape from ¹⁄₁₆-inch dense hardwood stock, using the dimensions shown in **DRAWING 2**. (The one shown is figured maple, but any wood will do.)

2 Mark the hole centerpoints on the arms. Drill the ⁷⁄₃₂" holes where marked and add finish to each arm.

3 Join the pieces in the configuration shown on the exploded view and accompanying side view drawings with binder posts and screws, using Loctite to prevent the screws from loosening over time.

You can use the Fibonacci gauge to find the proportional dimensions for a piece of furniture or built-in project (or its parts) shown in a photo. For example perhaps you like the looks of a tall drop-front secretary and storage cabinet featured in a magazine, but no dimensions are given. Using the Fibonacci gauge you can work out its approximate proportional height.

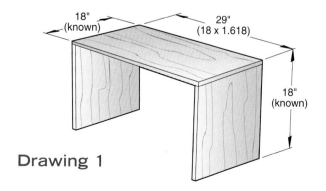

18" (known) 29" (18 x 1.618) 18" (known)

Drawing 1

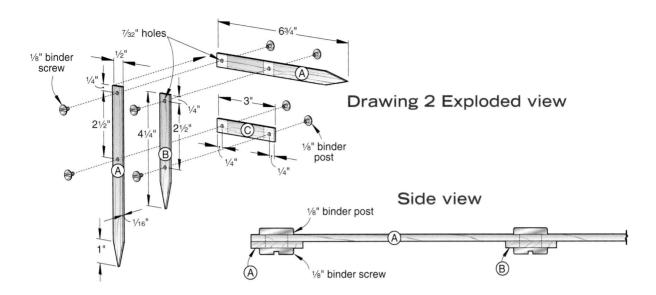

Drawing 2 Exploded view

⅛" binder screw

7/32" holes

6¾"

½"

¼"

2½"

4¼"

2½"

¼"

3"

C

⅛" binder post

B

A

A

¼"

¼"

1/16"

1"

Side view

⅛" binder post

A

A

⅛" binder screw

B

To do this, start by assuming that the distance from the floor to the desk's writing surface is a fairly standard 30 inches. Place the gauge on the photo so that the longer span (B to A) represents the 30 inches. If the piece were built proportionately, the outer point (C) should rest at or close to the top of the pigeonholed center section, as you can see in **PHOTO A.** Since the shorter span (B to C) represents .618 of 30 inches, the center section's height would be about 18½ inches. To find the height of the upper

cabinet, reverse the gauge so that the smaller span (B to C) spreads across the center section. The point of the larger span (B to A) should rest at the cabinet top, showing that its height is close to 30 inches, as shown in **PHOTO B.** The total height of the unit equals the sum of the parts: 30 + 18½ + 30 inches = 78½ inches. Use the same method to find widths.

A Fibonacci gauge isn't a tool for making precise measurement. But using one will always get you close to pleasing proportions.

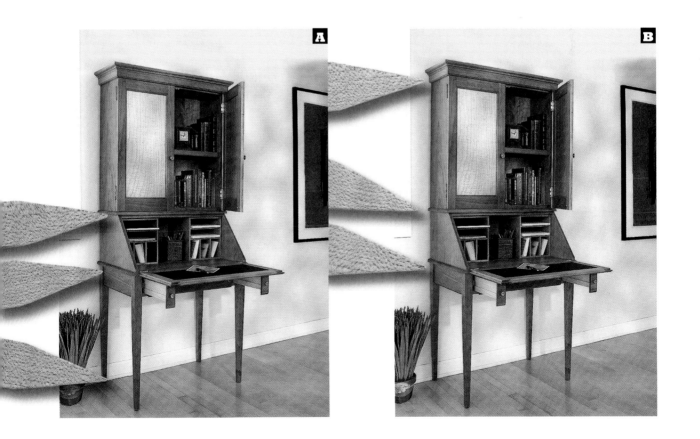

A

B

GETTING THE BIG PICTURE

PLANNING OUT HOW YOU WILL PUT THINGS TOGETHER—AND ASSESSING YOUR SITE—ARE ESSENTIAL FIRST STEPS TOWARD A SUCCESSFUL PROJECT.

Any project starts with a good drawing and a good cutting list. Even a master builder doesn't just grab some tools and start work. Good builders draw plans and know every construction detail in advance— joinery, structure, and the size of every part. You should too. Always plan out how you will tackle your project to ensure success.

ORDER OF WORK

Once your plans are done, sketch out how you want to use each board, either on a piece of paper or in chalk on the board itself. Next rough-cut the pieces, leaving everything about ¼ inch longer and wider. Make the cuts with a circular saw, bandsaw, or chop saw. Don't cut rough-sawn wood on the tablesaw unless you have good, solid hold-downs (see page 71).

Cut boards to length first, then to width so that the pieces are easier to handle. Start with a cut along the end of the board to look for defects and keep cutting until they're gone. Measure from the cut end, add the ¼ inch, and cut the piece to approximate length.

If you're working with rough-sawn lumber, plane or joint a face once you've cut the pieces to approximate length and width, then plane the boards to thickness. Running a board through the planer without jointing it first will give you a board with parallel sides but not necessarily flat sides.

If you're cutting plywood cut the widest dimension first. If a piece is 2×4 feet, for example, make the first cut to give you a piece that's 4 feet wide. Then run the 4-foot edge against the fence to cut the 2-foot dimension, giving you a long, reliable edge as a guide.

Make finish cuts slowly, using your best blade.

Ensure the blade is square to the table. Rip or joint a straight flat surface, still leaving the piece wide. Then reset the rip fence, double-checking the position with your tape measure. Rip all pieces that are the same width (regardless of length) before moving the fence, so that your pieces will be uniform. When you've ripped all the pieces, check to make sure the miter gauge is square with the blade and cut one end square on each piece. Cut the pieces to final length with a stop block, as shown below, cutting all the pieces of the same length before resetting the stop.

Stop block

Cutting pieces the same length

Cut two pieces the same length by clamping a stop block to a fence on the miter gauge. Position the block to give you a piece that's the desired length and cut all the pieces that are that length before moving the stop.

Follow the drawing as closely as you can for as long as you can during assembly. But when it comes time to cut doors, drawers, and shelves, make them fit the cabinet, not the drawing.

WHAT'S INSIDE A WALL?

When you attach something to a wall you should almost always connect with a framing member. Screw a cabinet to the studs and you can expect it to stay there, come what may. If you plan to insert something in a wall (like the clever built-in cabinets and drawers shown on pages 182–189), knowing what's inside the wall becomes even more important. Be sure you are not going to run into any wiring, plumbing, or HVAC ducting. Learning what is inside your wall is an important part of project planning.

Studs are the 2×4s that run up and down behind the plaster or drywall. They're usually 16 inches on center (o.c.), meaning that the studs are 16 inches apart measured from center to center. The bottom of a stud is nailed to a 2×4, called a sole plate, that is nailed to the subfloor. The top is nailed to another 2×4 nailed to the ceiling joists, called a top plate. If the wall supports the roof or a floor above it, there are usually two top plates for strength, one on top of the other.

The framing around doors and windows is modified to create the necessary openings. An exterior wall has insulation between the studs, along with plywood or some other sheathing on the outside surface. Some exterior walls are 2×6s, to allow for extra insulation, as are some interior walls. Studs in 2×6 walls are generally 24 inches o.c.

Regardless of size or spacing, you can find studs easily with an electronic stud finder, which beeps or lights up as it passes over a stud. But you'll also have to watch out for plumbing, vents, and wiring. If there's a sink, toilet, or bathtub on either side of the wall, or one above it, expect water pipes immediately above and below. Air-conditioning or heating (known as HVAC—heating, ventilating, air-conditioning) vents require ducts in the wall, usually running up and down, that you don't want to puncture. Fortunately the

Whether you are attaching chair rail or hanging kitchen cabinets, you'll need to fasten to framing members. An electronic stud finder will help you locate studs and headers.

most dangerous item, wiring, can be detected with a voltage detector sold as a "sniffer," which lights when it passes over an electrified wire. (Some stud finders even have built-in sniffers.) If tests—or logic—indicate live wires, turn off the power before you work on the wall.

Studs are spaced evenly throughout a wall. Doors and windows have a header above them to support shortened studs. Windows have a sill with shortened studs below them. Carpenters have given each stud a name to describe its function.

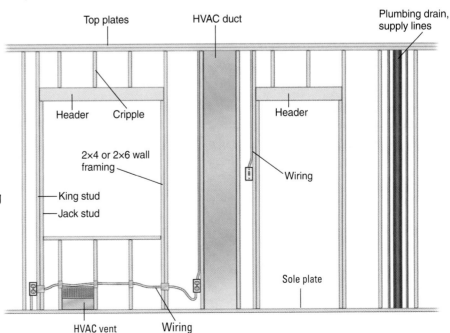

Top plates · HVAC duct · Plumbing drain, supply lines · Header · Cripple · Header · 2×4 or 2×6 wall framing · Wiring · King stud · Jack stud · Sole plate · HVAC vent · Wiring

MOLDING

MOLDING EXISTS TO CREATE BEAUTIFUL SHADOWS, ARCHITECTS SAY. HERE ARE SOME EXAMPLES OF HOW MOLDING CAN ADD DETAIL AND DEFINITION TO A ROOM, WHETHER THE FINAL STYLE STATEMENT IS SUBTLE OR BOLD.

Even simple wall frames can set a room apart (left). This design combines the virtues of chair rail and wainscoting and has a Shaker-like simplicity that bridges traditional and contemporary styles. (See how to build similar wall treatments on pages 156–157 and 160–161.) A custom combination of moldings crowns a bank of cabinets (above) for an eye-catching feature. This example also shows the benefits of leaving molding unpainted. Letting the grain show through can be a design feature in itself.

Even the blandest interior gains classic style with these subtle molding touches on the walls and a built-in (above). Add a generous baseboard, and you'll make it clear that your house isn't fresh out of the box. On the more elaborate end of the scale, the lacelike arrangement at left turns a plain wall into a stunning feature.

Floor to ceiling this beautiful landing (above) is a study in understated detailing. It would be an exciting challenge for a woodworker. The alcove, something that typically might be simply framed and drywalled, is made more welcoming with the addition of vertical molding.

The stairway at left demonstrates how combining molding profiles can lead to a one-of-a-kind arrangement. The beaded-board wainscoting is a goodlooking, hardworking surface that's ideal for a staircase. Both examples show that a little woodgrain can go a long way. It really shines when contrasted with painted molding.

A fireplace with mantel is an enviable feature for any room, but with the addition of the gablelike pediment (opposite), it is a stunner.

Wall frames, whether in a Craftsman style (above left) or a more traditional approach (below), are an affordable and easy-to-install addition to a wall. Hardwood molding (above) is more expensive and more difficult to work with but beautiful when completed.

PANELING AND BEAMS

DECORATING WALLS AND CEILINGS CAN GO BEYOND A NEW PAINT JOB. ADD TEXTURE AND STYLE TO PLAIN SURFACES WITH PANELING, WAINSCOTING, AND BEAMS.

Beams made of 1-by hardwood (above) are just a way to set a room apart for a modest cost. (See pages 168–169 for how to build and install faux ceiling beams.)

Painted wall paneling (left) can be made of inexpensive materials such as Medium Density Fiberboard (MDF) and hardboard but still remain an upscale feature. The shelf for pictures is a welcome bonus.

Oak panels executed in a Craftsman style (above) make a magnificent addition to a room. The plate shelf underlines the Craftsman goal that things be functional as well as beautiful. (See pages 164–167 for how to add similar panels to your own home.)

The beam-and-plaster look of a cottage ceiling (right) can be replicated with 1-by stock.

SHELVES AND BOOKCASES

EVERYONE HAS BOOKS OR COLLECTIONS OF ITEMS BUT TOO FEW PLACES TO PUT THEM. THESE PROJECTS ADD MUCH-NEEDED STORAGE, OFTEN IN OTHERWISE WASTED SPACE.

Shelf-cabinet combos offer display and storage. When they wrap a window (above), the walls seem to be stone-cottage thick.

Built-in shelves are an ideal way to put odd nooks and crannies to work. This tall beauty (left) fits within a room divider. A mirror backing the glass display shelves shows off collectibles.

Most bookshelves run floor-to-ceiling, but they don't have to. The colorful example above starts where the sofa leaves off. Instead of having to keep the furniture a couple of feet out from the bottom shelves, wasting valuable floor space, furnishings can be pushed right up against the built-in.

These out-of-the-way shelves (left) top a bank of windows, putting otherwise unused space to attractive use. Even though the shelf is plain 1-by stock, the addition of small, arched brackets produces a custom look.

KITCHEN UPGRADES

THE KITCHEN IS THE MOST COMPLICATED ROOM IN THE HOUSE, AND THAT MEANS IT CAN BENEFIT FROM A WIDE RANGE OF IMPROVEMENTS. HERE ARE SOME IDEAS TO GET YOUR PLANNING STARTED.

Open shelving (opposite) is simple to build and an attractive way to store essentials.

Crown molding, a boxed-in sink, and custom corner shelves like those shown above can be combined with your existing cabinetry to give your kitchen a high-impact upgrade.

For open plan kitchens, attractive areas for display are even more important. The kitchen at right boasts glass-fronted cabinets, shelves, and niches, all of which make the kitchen as eye-catching as it is functional.

CHOOSING MATERIALS

THE RAW MATERIALS FOR YOUR PROJECT CAN OFTEN BE found at your local home center, but you'll find better variety at a good contractor-oriented lumberyard. If you need something beyond poplar, oak, and birch, look to

WOOD-BUYING BASICS

Understanding species, grades, and board feet

MANUFACTURED LUMBER AND SHEET GOODS

A guide to the stuff sheet goods are made of and the new materials that offer alternatives to wood

CHOOSING HARDWARE AND FASTENERS

The right hardware selections make a huge difference in how your project goes together and holds together.

specialty hardwood dealers. Online sources offer huge variety, if you are willing to pick up the shipping costs. For hardware, home centers have good basics, but you'll need to turn to specialty woodworking sources for something really different.

WOOD-BUYING BASICS

HERE'S HELP IN DECIDING WHAT HARDWOOD OR SOFTWOOD TO BUY AND HOW MUCH YOU NEED.

The right wood for any project is the straightest, flattest, most knot-free board you can find. The species you choose is a matter of taste. Hardwoods, such as walnut and cherry, have always been popular for furniture and trimwork. Oak is used in many historic styles. Softwoods such as pine and fir have seen wide use, especially for trimwork.

Hardwood lumber comes from deciduous trees, those that lose their leaves each fall. Softwood, on the other hand, is produced from cone-bearing, needle-leaved trees called conifers. Neither term has anything to do with the physical hardness or strength of the wood, although the wood from deciduous trees generally proves to be harder than that from coniferous trees. But always remember, balsa is a hardwood and hard fir is a softwood.

Hardwood is the choice for most furnituremaking because of its beauty, stability, strength, predictability for working, and resistance to denting. Few softwoods offer the same characteristics.

HARDWOOD GRADES

When trees are cut into lumber, any piece less than 2 inches thick is called a board. Any given tree yields boards of varying quality. The boards taken from the outside of the tree are narrow; those taken toward the center are wider. The boards taken from the bottom of the tree generally have fewer knots than those taken farther up. Boards are crosscut and ripped to yield cuttings, which are graded and eventually become the stock we purchase. In making a cutting the sapwood is trimmed off the edge of the board and it is crosscut into a manageable length. When crosscutting the choice is made to cut out major knots for a higher grade or leave them in and accept a lesser grade.

The National Hardwood Lumber Association (NHLA) assigns specific quality grades to hardwood boards. Each grade reflects a classification according to the percentage of clear material that the grade is expected to yield. The greater the percentage, the higher the grade and value of the board. Let's look at the top four standard grades of hardwood lumber.

• **Firsts & Seconds (FAS)** measure 6 inches and wider by 8 feet and longer. Graded from the poorer side, FAS boards can be cut to yield pieces at least 4 inches × 5 feet or 3 inches × 7 feet. Clear-face cuttings must yield no more than 16 percent waste.

• **FAS 1-Face (FAS1F) or Selects.** FAS1F is graded like FAS, except that the boards are graded from the better side or the clearer face of the board. The backside of the board will grade no lower than No. 1 Common grade.

• **No. 1 Common** is graded from the poorer side. Boards are 3 inches and wider, 4 feet and longer, providing minimum cuttings of 4 inches × 2 feet or 3 inches × 3 feet. Clear-face cuttings must yield two-thirds or more usable wood.

• **No. 2A Common** is most often found in flooring. Boards of this grade yield at least 50 percent clear wood in cuttings at least 3 inches wide and 2 feet long.

SOFTWOOD GRADES

Like hardwood furniture-quality softwood is graded on the number of cuttings a board will yield. Softwood grades fall into three main categories— select, shop, and common. A board's best side determines the grades for all but 5/4 (1¼") and thicker shop grades. One-inch lumber generally is sold in 2-inch width increments (1×2, 1×4, etc.), and 1¼" lumber comes in random widths and lengths. Several rules and regulations govern softwood grades. Following is a simple rundown.

• **C and Better Select** is the clearest grade available from most American mills.

• **D Select** is suitable for many projects. D Selects have only minor defects, such as small, tight knots.

• **Molding Stock** is a grade intended for making molding. This grade gives more than 70 percent clear rippings 1 inch and wider, 6 feet and longer.

• **Shop-Grade** includes four subdivisions. The highest shop grade, No. 3 Clear, has only a few well-placed defects, allowing a high yield of clear, two-faced stock. The rest of shop-grade falls into three categories: No. 1 Shop, No. 2 Shop, and No. 3 Shop. Widths are 5 inches and wider with lengths from 6 to 16 feet. No. 1 Shop yields 50 percent clear cuttings, and No. 2 Shop yields one-third clear cuttings.

• **Common-Grade** is the lowest grade. No. 1 Common is no longer graded and sold separately; instead it's included with No. 2 Common and sold as No. 2 & Better Common. Sometimes referred to as knotty or shelving grade, No. 2 Common is the most popular utility grade. No. 3 Common includes boards of less uniform appearance. Common grades are S-Dry, meaning they have 18 to 20 percent moisture content. More expensive softwood grades are kiln-dried to less than 10 percent.

BOARD FEET AND THICKNESS

The thickness of furniture-grade wood is measured in quarters. Two-quarter wood (2/4) is ½" thick; 3/4 wood is ¾" thick, and 4/4 is a full 1" thick. Furniture-grade lumber is generally sold as unplaned rough lumber and is priced by the board foot.

A board foot is a piece of lumber 1×12×12 inches, or 144 cubic inches. In practice the 144 inches can be in any shape or form: An 8-foot board that is 1×9 inches is 6 board feet, as is a 2×9-inch board 4 feet long. The box, above right, shows how to calculate board feet.

Both hardwoods and softwoods are sold by their thickness before planing. If you buy wood planed, you'll pay for both the machining and the sawdust in the waste bin. A piece of 4/4 rough-cut stock becomes a ¾" board when planed, but you'll still be charged as if it were an inch thick.

NOMINAL VS. ACTUAL THICKNESS

Like hardwoods, construction lumber (2×4, 2×6, etc.) is sold by its size before planing. Unlike hardwoods construction lumber is usually sold after it's been planed. The 2×4 that started out at 2×4 inches measures 1½×3½ inches after planing. A 1×6 actually measures ¾"×5½".

Calculating board feet

A board foot is 144 cubic inches. Calculate board feet by multiplying a board's thickness by its width and then by its length. If length is in inches, divide by 144; if length is measured in feet, divide by 12.

$\frac{T'' \times W'' \times L''}{144}$ = board feet	$\frac{T'' \times W'' \times L'}{12}$ = board feet
1" × 6" × 96" = 576	1" × 6" × 8' = 48
576 ÷ 144 = 4 board feet	48 ÷ 12 = 4 board feet

GUIDE TO KEY WOODS AND USES

		PRIMARY USES	OTHER USES
HARD	Alder (red)	cabinets, simple furniture	
	Ash (white)	cabinets	sporting goods
	Basswood	carved items	
	Birch (yellow)	cabinets, furniture	flooring
	Butternut	carved items	
	Cherry	cabinets, fine furniture	moldings
	Hickory	chairs	tool handles, cabinets
	Mahogany	classic furniture	outdoor furniture
	Maple (hard)	durable tables & chairs	cabinets, moldings
	Oak (red)	cabinets, furniture	moldings
	Oak (white)	outdoor & indoor furniture	barrels
	Poplar	utility furniture	painted items
	Teak	furniture	boat decks & trim
	Walnut (black)	fine furniture	moldings
SOFT	Bald Cypress	outdoor & indoor furniture	
	Cedar (western red)	outdoor furniture	decks, fences
	Pine (ponderosa)	country furniture	
	Pine (southern yellow)	flooring	treated for outdoor use
	Pine (white)	country furniture	
	Redwood	outdoor furniture	decks, fences

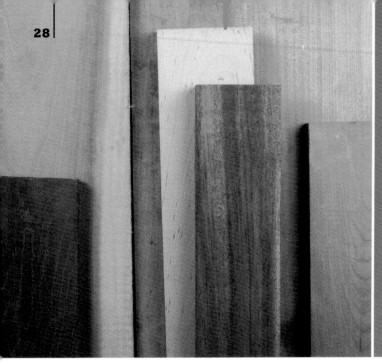

TYPES OF WOOD

WOOD IS A NATURAL MATERIAL, AND EVERY SPECIES HAS A UNIQUE PERSONALITY. YOU'LL GET TO KNOW THEIR QUIRKS THE MORE YOU USE THEM.

After you work with a wood for a while, you get to know its characteristics. How it looks. How it works. You even come to recognize the smell as you work it. A pass with the plane, or your first crosscut, will teach you much of what you need to know. Each species not only has its unique appearance—it reacts differently too. Not only is oak harder than pine, it chips more easily.

During assembly you can let glue dry on most woods, except walnut. But why gamble? Let the glue dry a bit until it turns rubbery and then slide a chisel along the seam to remove it.

Light woods sometimes benefit from staining; dark woods seldom do. (Leave cherry alone, and it will darken as it ages.) Unfortunately pine and maple turn blotchy when stained. You can avoid the problem by applying gel stain, which doesn't blotch.

WHITE PINE

White pine

You'll run into both red and white pine when you're making furniture. Of the two, white pine is harder and has less pitch. With either wood, however, pitch can build up on your power tools and cause the cut to wander. Clean the cutting edge occasionally with acetone or another solvent. A Teflon-coated blade or cutter also works well. Because of the pitch drilling can also cause burning. Drill pine at a faster speed than you would hardwood, and be sure to back the bit out of the hole often.

Sap pockets in a joint will hinder adhesives. If you can't avoid them, wipe the pocket or knot with acetone before gluing. Before finishing seal knots

with shellac. To reduce chances of blotchy staining, rely on gel stains for even coloring. Under a clear finish red pine will darken and yellow with age.

POPLAR

Poplar

Poplar, also known as yellow poplar, is an underappreciated wood and with reason: The grain isn't particularly striking, and the yellow heartwood is often streaked with dark grain. But poplar is one of the few woods still available in wide boards— boards up to 20 inches are not uncommon. Poplar sands to a smooth, almost-perfect painting surface. The wood is stable, generally straight-grained, and uniform in texture. It planes with less tear-out than most woods and usually with less effort.

BIRCH

Birch

Yellow birch and sweet birch are the two most important birch species used in woodworking. Yellow birch has white sapwood and light reddish brown heartwood. Sweet birch has light-colored sapwood and dark brown heartwood with reddish tones. Both are heavy, hard, and strong. The grain is fine and uniform but prone to tear-out during planing.

RED AND WHITE OAK

Two kinds of oak are used in making furniture: red and white oak. They look similar, though white oak is less porous and lacks the pinkish tinge of red oak. In the shop they both tend to chip.

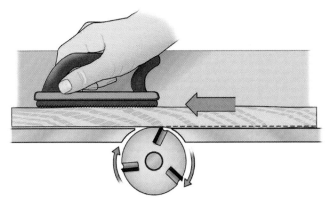

To minimize chipping on the jointer, feed oak so that the knife rotation follows the direction of the grain. Make shallow router passes and light cuts on the jointer or planer.

Mahogany

HONDURAN MAHOGANY

Honduran mahogany's long, straight grain is easy to work and finishes beautifully. Don't be waylaid by "Philippine mahogany," which looks like mahogany and is easy to work but is not a true mahogany and is too soft for furniture work.

Mahogany surfaces with minimal tear-out. It cuts equally well with steel or carbide-tipped blades, but rip blades with more than 28 teeth might cause burning. It cuts beautifully on a jigsaw or scroll saw. Feed figured stock into a planer slowly and at a slight angle.

Rout with sharp bits (and don't forget the dust mask) for mark-free results. The grain "frizzes" with dull bits. All types of glue work well on mahogany.

Red oak

White oak

Red oak quickly dulls anything other than a carbide blade. Too fast a feed rate on the tablesaw or radial arm saw, or with the router, can cause burning, although burns sand off easily. Put a backing board on the exit side during crossgrain work to minimize chipping.

Clamp bars and other metals stain the wood if they touch the glue squeeze-out.

When white oak is used for outdoor projects, its high tannic acid will turn ordinary screws black and stain the wood. Use brass or stainless-steel fasteners.

MAPLE

Maple is a clear, close-grained wood. The grain can be nearly invisible or beautifully wild, as in curly or bird's-eye maple. Rock maple (not surprisingly) is hard, while soft maple is not.

Maple

Always use carbide cutters and blades. When ripping use a rip blade with fewer than 28 teeth. Take light cuts at the jointer and planer; use sharply honed knives. With figured stock plane at a slight (15-degree) angle and never to finished thickness; always leave some for sanding or use a cabinet scraper after planing.

If slippage occurs when gluing, switch to white glue with a longer open time. Coat both sides, then rub together and let the glue set up slightly before clamping. Use gel stains to avoid occasional blotching.

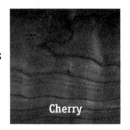
Cherry

BLACK CHERRY

Black cherry, the only one of the cherries used in furniture, planes extremely well because of its fine, close grain, but take light cuts in jointing. Dull blades burnish it. High-speed steel blades burn black cherry less than carbide-tipped blades. Avoid burning by feeding the stock without hesitation. In crosscutting carbide blades outperform steel. Except for the common twist drill, any type of bit does well. However use slower drill-press speeds (about 250 rpm). A pause will burn the wood. In routing black cherry doesn't chip or tear, but it will burn during a split-second hesitation. Take light passes without stopping.

Squeeze-out mars a clear finish more jarringly than on other woods. To check, highlight the glue lines by wiping joints with lacquer thinner.

Walnut

BLACK WALNUT

Black walnut works easily and finishes to a beautiful dark brown with little effort. Any glue works well on walnut, but keep glue squeeze-out to a minimum and skim off skinned-over glue. White and yellow glues in particular discolor the wood and show up in the finish. When finishing straight-grain walnut, you usually don't need to fill the grain. Figured walnut, especially burls and crotch wood, has an irregular, open grain that you should fill.

MOLDING PROFILES

INSTALLING MOLDING IS THAT ENJOYABLE FINAL STEP ON A PROJECT WHEN YOU ADD DETAIL AND DECORATION. HERE IS A SELECTION OF PROFILES.

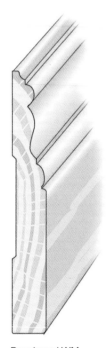
Baseboard WM

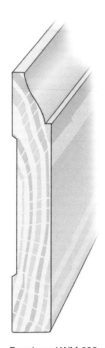
Baseboard WM 623

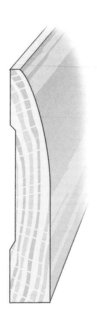
Baseboard WM 713

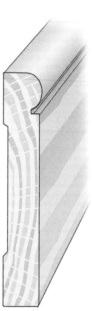
Baseboard WM 753

Baseboard WM 258

Base cap WM 172

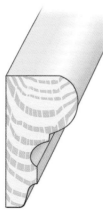
Base cap WM

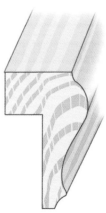
Base cap WM 292

Base shoe 127

Quarter round WM 105

Once you get past the astragals and the ogees, the nomenclature for molding is pretty straightforward. Often you can use a number assigned by the Wood Moulding & Millwork Producers Association, prefaced by WM (paint-grade, softwood molding) or HWM (hardwood molding). These numbers are shown here as a starting point, but be forewarned that not every supplier uses these numbers. Many have numbers and profile charts of their own.

BASEBOARD bears the brunt of anything that might slide across the floor and into the wall—not to mention baseboard's all-important function of covering the gap between the wall and the flooring.

BASE CAP combines with S4S stock (see page 33) to make a custom baseboard.

QUARTER ROUND AND BASE SHOE, along with casing, are the basic workhorses of molding profiles. A common mistake is using quarter round along the baseboard where the wall meets the floor. That's the job for base shoe; reserve quarter round for inside corner trim.

CASING is applied to bridge the gap between door or window jambs and the surrounding wall.

CROWN, COVE, AND BED MOLDINGS top off walls or cabinets. Crown is the ornate granddaddy of the group. Cove is slightly concave; bed is smallish and so named because other molding rests above it. Some crowns (see the first example below, WM48) have an ogee—that elegant elongated S profile.

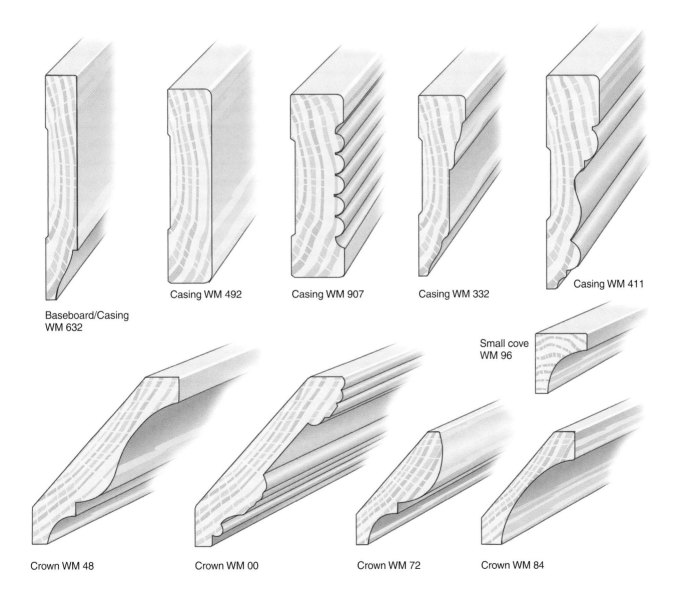

Baseboard/Casing
WM 632

Casing WM 492

Casing WM 907

Casing WM 332

Casing WM 411

Small cove
WM 96

Crown WM 48

Crown WM 00

Crown WM 72

Crown WM 84

MOLDING PROFILES *(CONTINUED)*

CHAIR RAILS were originally installed to keep the backs of chairs from pocking plaster walls. They can still do that job today but are installed more often as a decorative feature.

ASTRAGAL molding looks similar to some symmetrical chair rails but was originally attached to one of a pair of cabinet doors to keep the other from swinging through the opening. (The T-shaped version makes for a firmer attachment.) The astragal can also cover the joint between two shelf uprights.

MULLION CASING covers jambs where two windows or a door and a sidelight meet.

PANEL MOLDING is applied directly to walls to make ornamental frames.

Like chair rail **PICTURE RAIL** originally served in the cause of plaster defense. Applied a foot or so beneath the ceiling, it is a rim from which pictures can be hung, eliminating the need for pounding a nail in the wall.

HALF-ROUND AND SCREEN MOLDING are handy choices for shelf edging or as a surface-mounted detail—and of course for repair jobs on old window screens.

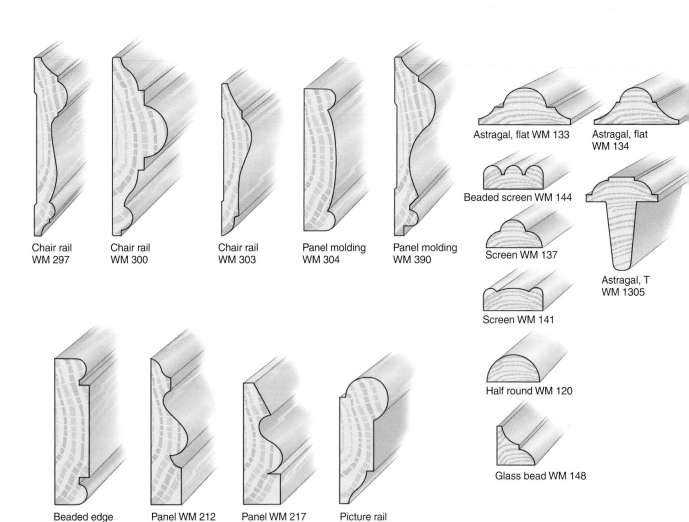

Chair rail WM 297

Chair rail WM 300

Chair rail WM 303

Panel molding WM 304

Panel molding WM 390

Astragal, flat WM 133

Astragal, flat WM 134

Beaded screen WM 144

Screen WM 137

Screen WM 141

Astragal, T WM 1305

Half round WM 120

Glass bead WM 148

Beaded edge mullion WM 956

Panel WM 212

Panel WM 217

Picture rail WM 273

GLASS BEAD holds glass within a window or door muntin—a useful item when making your own glass-fronted cabinet doors.

CORNERS AND CAPS finish off wainscoting and paneling. **BACKBANDS** have a similar function but typically attach to other moldings to add an ornamental touch and cover end grain.

STOP is the handy stuff against which doors close and along which double-hung windows slide. Some types can be used to bridge gaps or make wall frames.

LATTICE was once used primarily to make the lacy panels on arbors and along porch skirts, but today most people buy such things prefabbed. Lattice is handy as a decorative element.

STOOL molding is what most of us know as windowsill. Some are rabbeted. All have a finished front edge. In regions where newer housing predominates, stool can be hard to find.

S4S STOCK is clear lumber that is Surfaced 4 Sides. S4S is a handy element for making your own custom combinations of molding. Fine woods can be purchased S4S, S2S (surfaced 2 sides), or even S1S (surfaced 1 side).

ROSETTES are handy ways to avoid miter joints and are in keeping with the architectural style of homes 70 years old or more. On doorways they are combined with plinths (see page 137).

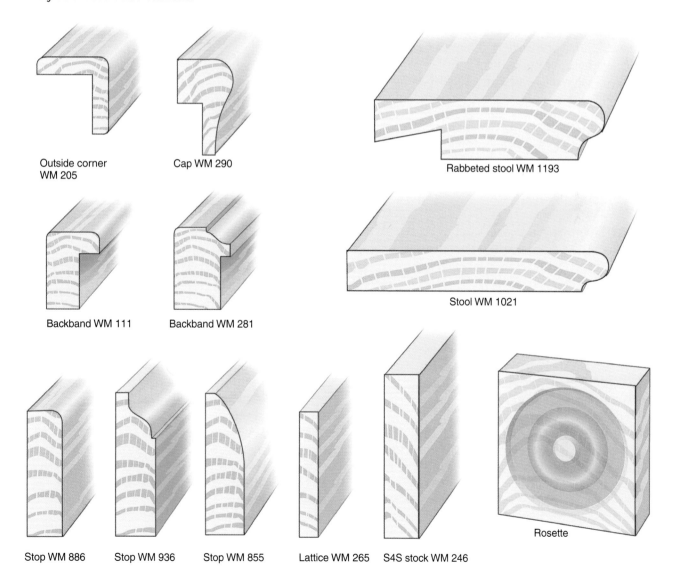

Outside corner
WM 205

Cap WM 290

Rabbeted stool WM 1193

Backband WM 111

Backband WM 281

Stool WM 1021

Stop WM 886   Stop WM 936   Stop WM 855   Lattice WM 265   S4S stock WM 246

Rosette

Plywood

MDF

Hardboard

Particleboard

MANUFACTURED LUMBER AND SHEET GOODS

USING PLYWOOD, PARTICLEBOARD, HARDBOARD, AND MEDIUM-DENSITY FIBERBOARD IN THE RIGHT PLACES SAVES TIME AND MONEY, AND NO ONE WILL BE THE WISER.

Plywood, particleboard, and other sheet goods are often thought of as cheap materials that lack romance. But factory-made materials can save you money and hours of work. There is little point in putting valuable solid wood on a cabinet back that no one will ever see, for instance, or gluing up wide panels for drawer bottoms and planing them to fit.

Sheet goods have countless uses. They are stable, offer a variety of surfaces, are reliably square, and are easy to work with. Most are readily available at home centers and lumberyards.

PLYWOOD

Manufacturers divide plywood into two classes: hardwood plywood and construction plywood. Ironically construction plywood, which is manufactured for strength, is made almost entirely out of softwoods. At the same time the interior layers of hardwood plywood are often softwood.

Whether hardwood or construction-grade, plywood is essentially a sandwich. Typically it's made of layers of veneer laminated (glued together under pressure) to form a flat, stable sheet. The face layers in hardwood plywood are a top-grade veneer, such as walnut, oak, or cherry, and give the sheet its name. These veneers may be either slip matched or book matched (see photos above right). The inner layers, or plies, are another wood.

The grain alternates direction from layer to layer to create a sheet that stays flat and expands and contracts very little with changes in humidity. There are always an odd number of plies in a sheet of plywood, with the grain in center and face plies running the length of the sheet. Some plywood called

Slip-match

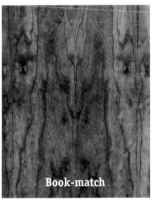
Book-match

"lumber-core" has a center ply made of narrow pieces of solid wood. This can minimize sagging in applications such as shelves. (You can glue the face of a 1×2 to each of the long edges of standard plywood to stiffen it.)

Sheet goods with veneer faces over a particleboard or medium-density fiberboard core are also plywood, technically speaking. They're fine as far as they go, but the limitations of fiberboard and particleboard don't disappear just because they are covered with veneer. (See Medium-Density Fiberboard and Particleboard, opposite page.)

Plywood is usually available in 4×8-foot sheets in thicknesses of $\frac{1}{8}$, $\frac{1}{4}$, $\frac{3}{8}$, $\frac{1}{2}$, $\frac{5}{8}$, and $\frac{3}{4}$ inch. Larger sheets are available by special order. Price depends on the quality of the facings (see box, opposite).

Panels can vary from their nominal thickness by $\frac{1}{64}$ to $\frac{1}{32}$ inch, which means you can't count on a $\frac{3}{4}$-inch panel fitting perfectly into a $\frac{3}{4}$-inch groove. Special router bits are available to rout slightly smaller grooves for snug fit. U.S.–made hardwood plywood has face veneers averaging $1/30$ inch in thickness. Some species, such as black walnut, are sliced to $1/32$ inch. Foreign veneers are thinner still. They can be difficult to cut without splintering and hard to sand without going through the veneer.

MEDIUM-DENSITY FIBERBOARD

Medium-density fiberboard (MDF) is made of strands of wood fiber mixed with glue and compressed to form a flat sheet. The pressure produces an almost perfectly smooth surface that is somewhat harder than the core. Because the fibers run randomly through the sheet, it has no grain, making MDF equally strong in all directions. It is not, however, as strong as wood, in which the fibers run parallel to each other. MDF is more prone to sagging, and joints such as tenons, tongues, and sliding dovetails will sheer off. MDF is best assembled with glue and screws or housed in a full-width groove. The panels are an inch wider and longer than 4×8 feet because the edges damage easily. Panels are exactly as thick as stated: A $3/4$-inch piece of MDF will fit perfectly in a $3/4$-inch groove. Use MDF for small projects, nonstructural pieces, or flat surfaces in jigs, and as patterns. MDF is available in 4×8-foot sheets and in thicknesses of $1/4$, $3/8$, $1/2$, $5/8$, and $3/4$ inch.

HARDBOARD

Hardboard is made by several manufacturers but is best known by one of its brand names—Masonite. Hardboard begins as wood fibers like those in MDF, but little or no glue is applied. Instead the fibers are soaked in water before they're pressed, and the natural glue that holds wood together—lignum—holds the fibers together once they're compressed. Unlike regular hardboard tempered hardboard has been treated with an oil such as linseed or tung oil and then heat-treated for strength. Both are available in 4×8-foot sheets and in $1/8$- and $1/4$-inch thicknesses.

PARTICLEBOARD

Particleboard was developed as a way of using the sawdust created during the manufacture of other wood products. It consists of relatively coarse sawdust mixed with glue and dried into a sheet. Because the fibers in sawdust are short, particleboard has less internal strength than MDF. It's typically used as an underlayment for laminate countertops and as the core for plywood in inexpensive furniture. It can swell and break down if it gets wet. It's available in 4×8-foot sheets and thicknesses from $3/8$ to $1^3/16$ inch; $5/8$- and $3/4$-inch thicknesses are the most common.

Nonwood millwork

If you plan to paint your molding anyway, MDF and polyurethane moldings will do the job just as well as wood. While both are easy to cut and shape, you have to work them a bit differently than wood. For example thin edges on MDF will chip easily and MDF is heavy. Long pieces bend and can break if you are not careful. Polyurethane is more rigid and less prone to chipping. However heat from a circular saw blade can create a crust along the cut edge. If you drop a piece onto concrete, it can shatter. Some nonwood moldings are pretty good representations of woodgrain and tone, though imitation wood is not to everyone's taste.

Grading plywood

The veneer on the face of a plywood sheet is graded—A through D for the front side and 1 through 4 on the back. A1 has the best veneer on both sides; A3 is prime on one side but has some open defects on the back. An additional grade, called shop-grade, is made of high-quality plywood that has a cosmetic defect. Not all stores and lumberyards carry every grade; but if you can get it, A4 is considerably cheaper than A1 and is perfectly suited to cabinet backs, lower shelves, and drawer bottoms. Some yards use the letter designation to describe both sides of a sheet.

FACE GRADE	BACK GRADE
A — Veneers are matched for grain and color. A limited number of small repairs allowed.	1, 2 — Sound surfaces. Repaired knotholes, etc., allowed. Vertical wormholes not larger than $1/16$" allowed without repair.
B — Matched for color only. Pieces of veneer are narrower; more small repaired defects allowed.	3 — Some open defects.
C, D — Sound surfaces; unlimited color variation. Larger repairs allowed.	4 — Open splits and some knotholes up to 4" in diameter allowed.
Shop-Grade — High-quality seconds suited to making jigs and shop furniture.	

CHOOSING HARDWARE AND FASTENERS

GOOD HARDWARE ISN'T CHEAP, BUT IT CAN MAKE OR BREAK YOUR WORK. SHOP CAREFULLY, BUY THE BEST, AND IF YOU CAN'T FIND WHAT YOU'RE LOOKING FOR, MAKE YOUR OWN.

Hardware is an important part of furniture design. You can experiment by swapping a cabinet knob with something different. Slender knobs on a small cabinet make it look delicate, for example. Replace them with medium-size knobs and the piece looks utilitarian. Large knobs might make it look as if the cabinet is in danger of falling over. Choosing hardware is as important a part of design as shape, proportion, and the wood you use.

KNOBS AND PULLS

Woodworking tool catalogs have lots of knobs and pulls. But don't stop there. Check to see if they have a separate hardware catalog too. Then search the Internet for businesses that specialize in hardware. (For classic hardware try horton-brasses.com and ballandball-us.com.) Search the Internet by style too. Searches for Art Deco knobs, Mission knobs, or Shaker knobs, for example, turn up a variety of hardware.

CATCHES

A catch keeps the door firmly closed when it should be closed and lets you open it easily when needed. Magnetic catches pull the door shut for the last fraction of an inch and open with a gentle pull. Ball catches, mortised into the door, require a bit more authority, which might be what you need. Double-ball catches screw to the cabinet and have a door-mounted keeper that snaps between the balls. You can adjust the pressure on the balls to make the door easier or harder to open. Roller catches, though not adjustable, do the same thing, using cylinders instead of balls.

BRACKETS

Shelf supports can be utilitarian metal strips, called pilasters, that hold a small shelf support. You can also buy clips or pins that fit inside small holes that you've drilled in the cabinet. Or check catalogs for Victorian cast-brass or cast-iron brackets.

Make your own knobs

Hardware can be as individual as your woodwork if you make your own. A simple way to make hardware is to pour casting epoxy into commercially made molds. Some molds are specifically for knobs. Others, made for jewelry, work just as well.

Polymer clay is a stiff, colorful putty that hardens with time or heat, depending on the brand. You can shape it, carve it, apply other shaped pieces, or stack layers to get stripes. Make a knob in two steps. In the first step you make the knob but leave an oversize recess for the mounting screw. When the knob is dry, insert the screw with more clay. Let it dry completely before installation.

Both epoxy and polymer clay are available in art or craft stores. If you want to make metal pulls, drill two small holes into an old piece of silverware, such as a spoon handle. Shape the silverware by bending it over a coffee can filled with sand. Screw it in place.

To make a wooden knob, cut a plug with a hole saw and glue a dowel into a hole in the back. Chuck it in your drill and shape it with wood files.

CHOOSING FITTINGS

Ready-made fittings and slides are available to help deal with details that are otherwise difficult to build. For example easily attached drawer slides (right) will spare you hours of handcrafting wood slides that typically work less well than their manufactured substitutes. Other useful fittings include a variety of pin-type shelf brackets that hold shelves by means of a few well-placed holes.

Home centers and hardware stores carry some of these, but the best selection is found in specialty woodworking shops or online (see Resources, pages 236–237).

You'll need a place for pens, pencils, scissors, and tape. This complete, ready-to-install pencil drawer mounts with just four screws.

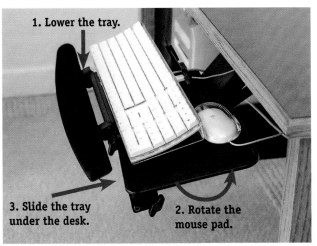

1. Lower the tray.

3. Slide the tray under the desk.

2. Rotate the mouse pad.

An easy-to-install keyboard tray saves desk space and is adjustable for typing comfort. When it's not in use, slide the assembly under the desktop.

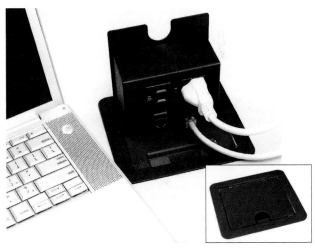

Ideal for laptop users this flip-up power station saves you from crawling under your desk every time you need to connect to power and the Internet.

1. Slide out.

2. Rotate.

Fastened to the desktop a swiveling holder holds your CPU above the dusty floor. To connect or disconnect cables, slide the CPU forward and rotate it.

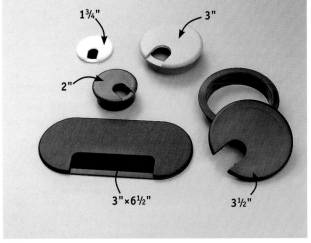

1³⁄₄"   3"

2"

3"×6½"   3½"

Essential for routing wires through a desktop, grommets come in a wide range of shapes, sizes, and colors. Materials include plastic, wood, and metal.

CHOOSING HARDWARE AND FASTENERS (CONTINUED)

COMMON CABINET HINGES AND THEIR APPLICATIONS

HINGE TYPE					
110° European edge-mount	107° European full-overlay clip-on	Piano (continuous)	Butt	No-mortise (ball-tip)	Adjustable-mount (ball-tip)
USES					
For overlay doors (up to ¾" overlay for this one) where concealed frame-face mounting is preferred.	Use on full-overlay or half-overlay doors. The clip mounts inside a cabinet on the side surface.	Extra length supports large or heavy doors. Can be cut to the length of a door edge.	Traditional choice for cabinet doors.	Suitable for most inset cabinet doors, especially where minimal gap is wanted.	General-purpose hinge for all but the smallest projects.
COMMENTS					
Allows 110° door swing. Adjusts for raising, lowering, and plumbing door.	Other versions offer 120° and 170° openings. Mounting plates might be sold separately from hinges.	Most lack a swag and require a mortise to reduce gaps on inset doors. Specialty suppliers offer swagged styles.	Must be mortised for inset doors. Not adjustable.	Several finishes are available. Used on many WOOD® magazine projects because of its ease of installation.	Several finish options. Use without mortises for 3⁄32" gap or mortised on one or both leaves for smaller gaps.
COST					
Medium price, varies according to finish.	Medium price, varies according to finish.	Low to high price, varies by length, leaf width, and finish.	Low to high price, varies with size and finish.	Low to medium price; sometimes sold in pairs.	Medium price, varies according to finish.

HINGE TYPE					
Offset (ball-tip)	Partial-wrap inset (ball-tip)	Double-offset knife (or pivot)	Strap (5" zinc-plated)	3⁄8" inset overlay	Surface-mounted ornamental
USES					
Use on partial inset doors with a 3⁄8" rabbet around the back outside edge.	A general-purpose hinge for inset doors. No-mortise design leaves minimal gap.	Mounts on top and bottom door edges to become inconspicuous when the door is closed.	A heavy-duty hinge suitable for outdoor use; typically surface-mounted.	By mounting on the frame face, this hinge allows variation in the amount of door overlay.	Use as decorative hinges on projects with small or lightweight doors.
COMMENTS					
Several finish options. Shape helps ensure uniform mounting position without mortising.	Full-wrap version mounts around the cabinet frame edge. Several decorative tip and finish options.	Variations work with overlay doors. Mortising is required for minimal gaps.	Sizes range from 3" to 24". Some types might have too much play for precision work.	Might incorporate a spring to make the door self-closing. Several finishes available.	No built-in adjustability. Might be less sturdy than other styles. Many design variations exist.
COST					
Medium price, varies according to finish.	Medium price, varies according to finish.	Medium to high price, varies with size and finish.	Low to high price, varies by size and finish.	Low to medium price; sometimes sold in pairs.	Low to high price, varies with size and finish.

SELECTING FASTENERS

Finish nails or pneumatic brads are ideal for trimwork and the final application of surface pieces to your project. Framing and attachments to walls and ceilings require stronger fasteners. Here is a range of likely choices for finish carpentry and trimwork. (See pages 116–117 for more information.)

NAILS

Framing and finish nails are sold in penny sizes, abbreviated by the letter "d," which stands for *denarius,* a Roman coin. The penny size used to relate to the cost of a nail, the larger nails being more expensive. Today penny sizes translate to the following approximate lengths: 4d, 1⅜ inches long; 6d, 1⅞ inches; 8d, 2⅜ inches; 10d, 2⅞ inches; 12d, 3¼ inches; 16d, 3½ inches, and 20d, 4 inches. (There are no 14d or 18d nails.)

Cement-coated

Ringshank

Brite

Spiral-shank

Framing nails have large heads for holding power. They won't be seen because they'll be covered by wall or flooring material or trim. They are typically cement-coated (CC) for extra grab, though uncoated (brite) ones are also available.

Variations on headed nails include spiral- and ringshank, both of which have tremendous holding power. Subflooring and drywall nails have ringshanks. Galvanized nails, coated with zinc to resist rust, are intended for exterior use.

The heads of finish nails are barely wider than the nail's shank and are meant to be set beneath the surface and puttied over. Casing nails have slightly larger heads for greater holding power and are useful for heftier molding. Other finish nails include brads, which are simply small finish nails, and colored paneling nails, which are ringshanked for holding power.

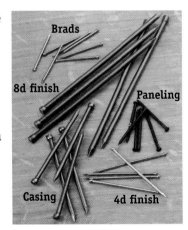

Brads

8d finish

Paneling

Casing

4d finish

NAIL GUN FASTENERS

Framing, roofing, and other types of nails are available for nail guns; for finish-carpentry purposes you'll likely only use finish nails and brads. Both come in clips and are made for specific nailers. Their lengths are designated in inches and their diameters are expressed as wire gauges.

Nail clips

Brad clips

SCREWS

Screws you can drive with a drill/driver are a versatile way to assemble projects. They are easy to work with, hold tightly, and if you goof up they can be backed out. For framing deck screws are strong and a fail-safe choice. The gold-tinted general-purpose screws are less strong but fine for jigs and light assemblies. Both can split wood if you don't drill pilot holes. One exception is self-tapping screw tips. They have a groove on the tip that drills its own pilot hole. Square-drive trim screws have a ³⁄₁₆-inch head—great holding power but a bit large for some finishing jobs.

General-purpose

Finish

Self-tapping particleboard

Deck

TOGGLES AND ANCHORS

For hanging objects too heavy for a picture hook but light enough to be held by the wall material instead of the framing, toggles and anchors are a handy choice. Such items as heavy mirrors and light shelves are good candidates for this type of fastener; kitchen cabinets (even medicine cabinets) are not. Some anchors screw into the wall without boring a hole first; others have a mechanism that, once pushed into a hole, grabs behind the wall.

Self-boring

Clip

Expanding

Toggle

CHOOSING HARDWARE AND FASTENERS *(CONTINUED)*

GUIDE TO CHOOSING AND USING WOODWORKING GLUES

	ADHESIVE TYPE	BEST USE	TOTAL ASSEMBLY TIME	MINIMUM CLAMP TIME	FULL-STRENGTH TIME	STRENGTH RATING	WATER RESISTANCE	HEAT RESISTANCE	GAP-FILLING
POLYVINYL ACETATE (PVA)	YELLOW	Interior woodworking projects.	15 minutes	½ hour	24 hours	3,600 psi	Good	Good	No
	YELLOW (extended assembly time)	Interior woodworking projects where long open time is desired. Recommended for bent laminations and larger, more involved assemblies.	20–25 minutes	½ hour	24 hours	3,510 psi	Good	Excellent	No
	DARK WOOD	Ideal for dark hardwoods, such as walnut and mahogany. Interior use only.	15 minutes	½ hour	24 hours	3,600 psi	Good	Good	No
	WEATHERPROOF	Exterior woodworking projects where water resistance is important. Interior projects that might come in contact with food and water.	15 minutes	½ hour	24 hours	3,750 psi	Excellent	Good	No
	WEATHERPROOF (extended assembly time)	Exterior woodworking projects where long open time is desired. Good choice for gluing bent laminations. Interior projects subjected to water.	20–25 minutes	½ hour	24 hours	3,840 psi	Excellent	Good	No
	MOLDING AND TRIM	Ideal for hard-to-clamp joints. Interior use only. Strong initial grip.	15 minutes	½ hour	24 hours	3,000 psi	Good	Poor	Yes
	WATERPROOF	Exterior projects requiring longer assembly time or lower application temperature than nonextended cross-linking PVAs.	20–25 minutes	½ hour	24 hours	4,000 psi	Excellent	Good	No
OTHER	POLYURETHANE	Exterior projects requiring long working time and waterproof joinery.	20–25 minutes	2–4 hours	4 hours	3,500 psi	Excellent	Excellent	No
	POLYURETHANE HOTMELT	Any project requiring quick-setting bonds. Needs little or no clamping. Bonds well when fit is marginal and with end grain. Bonds wide variety of materials.	30 seconds	1–2 minutes	24 hours	1,480 psi	Excellent	Excellent	Yes
	HIDE GLUE	Ideal for authentic repairs in antiques and musical instruments that you might want to disassemble later. Will expand and contract with wood.	Approx. 5 minutes	10 minutes	24 hours	500 psi	Poor	Poor	No
	HIDE GLUE—PREMIXED	Ready-to-use formula. Long assembly time. Sensitive to moisture (easy to disassemble later). Latex paint applied over dried glue will provide a crackled paint surface.	20–30 minutes	1 hour	24 hours	3,590 psi	Poor	Excellent	No
	5-MINUTE EPOXY	Excellent for repairs and joints that don't mate tightly. Cures quickly to any thickness. Fills gaps. Easily colored. Won't shrink. Bonds dissimilar materials.	Approx. 3 minutes	1 hour	24 hours	5,000 psi	Good	Good	Yes
	STRUCTURAL EPOXY	Like 5-minute epoxy but creates waterproof joint that can be used underwater. Easily colored. Won't shrink. Excellent for oily exotic woods.	1 hour	24 hours	7 days	7,500 psi	Excellent	Excellent	Yes
	CYANOACRYLATE (instant glue)	Strengthens weak areas and thin, delicate parts. Available in thin and thick (gap-filling) viscosities. Thin CA best used with tight-fitting parts.	Bond is immediate	*not applicable*	24 hours	2,900 psi	Excellent	Poor	Some types

MINIMUM APPLICATION TEMPERATURE	CLEANUP BEFORE SET	CLEANUP AFTER SET	SHELF LIFE (YEARS)	NONWOOD MATERIAL IT ALSO BONDS	COST	COMMENTS
50°F	Water	Scrape or sand	2	Leather, cloth, paper	Low	Fast grab. Best general-purpose interior glue. Least expensive. Good sandability. Long shelf life.
40°F	Water	Scrape or sand	1	Leather, cloth, paper	Low	Good sandability.
50°F	Water	Scrape or sand	2	Leather, cloth, paper	Low	Minimizes visibility of glue line in dark hardwoods. Dyed version of yellow glue.
55°F	Water	Scrape or sand	2	Leather, cloth, paper	Low	Approved for indirect food contact for projects such as cutting boards. Great general-purpose glue. Paintable. Dries and cures through chemical reaction. Long shelf life. Good for wet-use applications.
60°F	Water	Scrape or sand	2	Leather, cloth, paper	Low	Approved for indirect food contact for such projects as cutting boards. Paintable. Good for wet-use applications.
55°F	Water	Scrape or sand	1	Leather, cloth, paper	Low	Thick formula fills some thin gaps. Power sanding not recommended. Doesn't run or drip.
47°F	Water	Scrape or sand	1	Leather, cloth, paper	Medium	Best option for most outdoor projects. Less messy than polyurethanes or epoxies.
50°F	Mineral spirits	Scrape or sand	1	Most materials except some plastics	High	Triggered by contact with moisture; can be applied to damp surface. Polyurethane adhesives foam up and are tough to remove from hands; wear gloves during application. Relatively long clamping time.
250°F	*not applicable*	Scrape or sand	1	Most materials except some plastics	Medium	Requires specialty heat gun. WW30 (30-second) sets up quickly; WW60 (60-second) has gap-filling properties; WW75 (75-second) also bonds nonporous materials. Gloves recommended to protect from hot adhesive.
120°F	Water	Scrape or sand	Indefinite	Leather, cloth, paper	High	Dissolves in water. Use in glue pot/warming device (some use slow cooker) at about 145°F. May be stored in refrigerator between uses. Disassemble joints with steam and heat. Water-base finishes could affect hide glue.
50°F	Water	Scrape or sand	1	Leather, cloth, paper	Medium	Requires no mixing, heating, or stirring. Has the crackled appearance of traditional hide glues.
35°F	Alcohol or lacquer thinner	Scrape, sand, or water	1	Most materials except some plastics	High	Two-part adhesive. Resin and hardener react with each other, producing heat. Bonds many plastics. Gloves recommended. Three different hardeners are available for various temperature ranges.
35°F	Alcohol or lacquer thinner	Scrape or sand	1	Most materials except some plastics	Medium	Two-part adhesive. Resin and hardener react with each other, producing heat. For bonding oily woods (such as teak), sand, wipe with lacquer thinner, and apply epoxy within 60 minutes. Bonds many plastics. Gloves recommended.
-65°F	*not applicable*	Scrape, sand, or solvent	1	Most materials except some plastics	High	Accelerator reduces cure time; 75% strength at end of cure. Specialty solvents debond joints. Little glue required; use one drop per square inch. Gloves recommended because it bonds to skin instantly.

CARPENTRY AND WOODWORKING TOOLS

chapter 3

THERE IS A TOOL FOR EVERY CARPENTRY TASK. IF YOU HAVE the right tool of reasonable quality, your job will go much easier. Covering everything from simple hand tools to benchtop and stationary power tools, this chapter will help

HAND TOOLS

Power tools save work, but good hand tools are indispensable. . . 44

PORTABLE POWER TOOLS

These workhorses are among the must-have tools for carpentry. . . 52

BENCHTOP AND STATIONARY POWER TOOLS

For precise cutting, drilling, and shaping, consider these tools. . . 68

SAFETY EQUIPMENT

How to protect yourself from dust, damaging noise, and debris . . . 80

you choose the tools you need and help you learn how to use them. Best of all this chapter provides you with many great reasons to buy some new tools.

HAND TOOLS

BIG SAWS DON'T DO THE TRICK WHEN YOU'RE CUTTING DOVETAILS, TRIMMING A TENON, OR MORTISING A HINGE. WHEN SOMETHING HAS TO BE JUST SO, WOODWORKERS REACH FOR THEIR HANDSAWS.

JAPANESE PULL SAWS

Unlike the familiar Western-style handsaws, a Japanese handsaw cuts on the pull stroke. This makes a significant difference: It's easier to keep a blade straight when you're pulling it than it is when you're pushing it. This allows the manufacturers to make a thinner blade. The cutting teeth are harder than on a Western-style saw (whose teeth must be softer to withstand the impact when the saw catches on the wood). In short, Japanese saws cut better and stay sharp longer. When the saw does get dull, you simply replace the blade, which is removable. There are three saws well worth considering for your tool kit.

DOZUKI SAW A dozuki saw (doh-ZOO-kee) has a thin blade reinforced by a stiffener (shown below). The blade has 16 to 25 teeth per inch (tpi) with less set than other saws—meaning they aren't bent outward as much. This produces a pencil-thin kerf

(often less than $1/64$ inch thick). With its rigid back a dozuki saw tracks well, even when cutting diagonally across the grain, although the stiffener limits the depth of cut to about 2 inches. When finetuning the fit of a joint, this saw excels in cutting both with and across the grain. It is perfect for cutting dovetails and is sometimes labeled as a dovetail saw.

KUGIHIKI SAW The kugihiki saw (koo-gee-HEE-kee, shown below) has a flexible blade with teeth that are set to only one side—marked the top. You can lay the saw against the wood and cut without scratching the wood surface. This lets you flex the saw against the surface and cut off dowels, screw plugs, or pegged tenons flush with the surface. Some saws are better than others however. Look for one that has a blade stiff enough to resist distorting during the cut but flexible enough to press flat against the workpiece. It is sometimes called a flush-cutting saw.

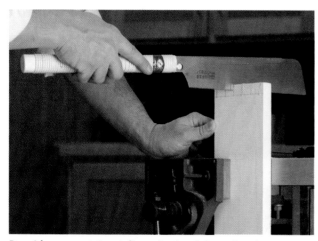

Dozuki saws cut dovetails and other joints cleanly.

Kugihiki saws are designed for flush-cutting.

Ryoba is a combination rip and crosscut saw. It cuts on the pull stroke, assuring a straight cut.

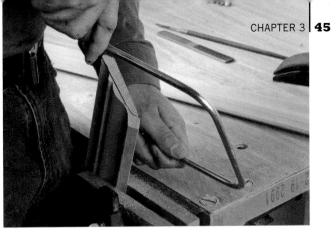

The coping saw handles tight curves. It is indispensable for joining molding where the corner is less than square.

RYOBA SAW The ryoba blade (ree-OH-buh, shown above) is slightly thicker than the dozuki. It has a double-edged blade—fine crosscut teeth on one edge and coarser ripping teeth on the other. The crosscut edge, with about 17 teeth per inch (tpi), makes a quick, fine cut—it can cut through a slab of ¾×4-inch hard maple more cleanly and in about one-fourth fewer strokes than a backsaw. Because it cuts on the pull stroke, it's easier to start the cut. The rip edge has about 8 tpi.

WESTERN-STYLE SAWS

Western handsaws include the rip, the crosscut, the backsaw, and the coping saw—all of which cut on the push stroke. Colonial America was built with these saws, but with the exception of the coping saw, they are rarely used today.

RIP AND CROSSCUT SAWS Rip and crosscut saws look similar—about 26 inches long, with a wooden handle that has an opening in it for the fingers. The ripsaw has only 4 tpi, however, so that it can cut aggressively between the wood fibers. The crosscut saw usually has 7 or 8 tpi in order to cut more smoothly across the fibers.

BACKSAW A backsaw has a stiffener running along the top of the blade to prevent flexing. Saws with blades about 4 inches wide with 12 to 14 tpi are used in miter boxes and for cutting tenons. Backsaws about 2 inches wide that have 18 to 22 tpi are dovetail saws for cutting joints.

COPING SAW A coping saw (shown top right) was the early jigsaw, a saw with a thin blade suitable for cutting curves. For carpenters it was, and still is, indispensable in installing crown molding, in which the ends are nested against each other instead of mitered together. The coping saw's narrow replaceable blade is gripped at each end in a U-shape metal frame. The blade should be inserted with the teeth pointing toward the handle so the saw cuts on the backstroke. On some saws turning the handle in one direction increases the blade tension; turning it the other direction loosens the blade so you can remove it. For more on using a coping saw, see page 92.

Miter boxes

Wood miter boxes are made of three pieces of wood joined together to make a U-shape channel 3 or 4 inches high and about 12 inches long. Grooves cut in the sides of the channel hold a backsaw at various angles, usually 45 degrees from left to right, 45 degrees from horizontal, and 90 degrees. A miter box is meant to be used with a backsaw, and the better the saw, the better the miter. Wood boxes can lead to problems, however, because the guide grooves wear, sometimes quickly, ruining the accuracy of the cut. You'll find inexpensive wood (or molded plastic) miter boxes at hardware stores and home centers. A simple miter box like the one below will serve for infrequent use, but there are better choices, including a power mitersaw, if you will be cutting a lot of miters for a project. (For more on miter boxes, see page 87.)

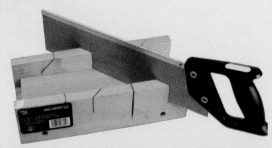

SHAPING TOOLS

WOOD IS SELDOM THE WAY YOU WANT IT WHEN IT COMES OFF THE SAW. BLADE MARKS AND BURN MARKS HAVE TO BE REMOVED. JOINERY MIGHT NEED FINETUNING. THAT'S WHEN SCRAPERS, SANDPAPER, FILES, AND PLANES COME INTO PLAY.

HAND PLANES A plane still comes in handy in these days of power tools and tablesaws. You might not need one often, but nothing else works as well in situations such as planing a cabinet door to fit or finetuning a drawer. A plane can also remove a step between two pieces of wood, shave a tenon that's too tight, or clean up a bevel.

Some inexpensive planes found at hardware stores or home centers are made with rough castings, soles that aren't flat, and low-quality blades poorly adjusted. Trying to use a dull, improperly adjusted plane will be unpleasant; the blade will alternately catch or not cut, gouging the wood or sending the plane skittering along the board.

If you're going to get a plane, seek out a good one. You can find good planes at some hardware stores and home centers or through woodworking specialty catalogs or on the Internet. The best planes have thick, sharp blades. If your blade isn't a full $\frac{1}{8}$ inch thick, check catalogs for replacement blades.

Of the many styles of planes available, the block plane is the most versatile. Originally meant for cleaning up end grain, it's a palm-size tool you can slip into your shop apron. It's easy to handle and cuts smoothly. Block planes are made with the blades set at one of two angles, either about 12 degrees or around 20 degrees. A 20-degree plane gives you the best all-around performance. A low-angle 12-degree plane is best for cutting end grain.

Block plane

CHISELS You'll use chisels to slice a peg flush with the surface, to square off a routed mortise, to clean out grooves, and to cut dovetails. Any good set of chisels will do, and often the best sets are available from mail order dealers. Look for chisels with beveled edges—square-edged chisels will keep you from getting into tight places. Either wooden or plastic handles are fine. You can hit plastic handles with a hammer, but use only a wood mallet to hit wood handles so you don't mash over the end of the handle. At the minimum you'll need a $\frac{1}{4}$-inch, $\frac{1}{2}$-inch, and $\frac{3}{4}$-inch chisel.

FILES, RASPS, SHAPING TOOLS

Files are for metalwork. You'll need them occasionally to file down a piece of metal or more often to sharpen a scraper. A 10-inch flat mill bastard file will do the trick. Bastard is a medium-cut file that falls between the coarse and second cut file.

Rasps are coarse files with sharp teeth, intended for removing wood quickly.

Shaping tools do the same work as rasps do,

Mill bastard

Rasp

Shaping tool

except that they cut with the sharpened edges of a series of teeth cut in a thin metal sole. They leave a smoother surface than rasps and cut as quickly. They come in a variety of shapes and sizes.

SANDING BLOCKS You'll do most of your sanding with an orbital sander. Going through a progression of grits—80, 120, 180, and 220— is typical. But even the best sander leaves swirl marks in the wood, which show up once you've applied finish. A second sanding with the final grit, this time by hand, removes the marks. Backing the paper with a sanding block not only gives you a firmer grip, it holds the paper completely flat, sanding out high spots and keeping you from accidentally sanding a groove in the surface. A wide range of commercially made blocks is available—soft rubber, wood blocks, and blocks with clips to hold the paper. All work well, as does a 2×4 with edges rounded to fit your hand.

SCRAPERS are thin, flexible pieces of metal with burrs on the long edges. Flexing and pushing the scraper shaves fine layers off the wood. Use the scraper before you sand to take off chatter marks left by the machine, and you'll cut your sanding in half.

A scraper edge has to be square to be sharp and smooth. Start by holding a mill bastard file flat on the edge and pushing it across the edge. Smooth out the filed edge and the faces of the scraper on a medium sharpening stone.

To form the burr on the edge, grip the scraper in a vise and hold the back of a chisel against the edge, with just the corner touching. Tilt the top of the chisel about 5 degrees toward the bench. Apply gentle pressure and pull the chisel along the edge, raising a burr along the point of the edge. Turn the scraper end for end and repeat.

Sharpening chisels and planes

If you want to be able to sharpen your chisels or plane blades, buy a grinder, get rid of the gray wheel, and get a white wheel. Gray wheels are vitrified—hardened enough to heat up and scorch tools, removing the temper from the metal. White wheels are friable—the wheel gives way as you sharpen, without overheating the metal.

Once you have the correct wheel, adjust the tool rest so the bevel sits flat on it. Gently grind away the chisel until you've ground the curve of the wheel into the face of the chisel. The chisel bevel is now "hollow-ground" and ready for hand-sharpening.

When you put the chisel on the bench stone, only two points—the heel and the edge—will touch it; you've ground away the space in between. With the extra metal out of the way, the chisel will almost snap into the correct angle on the stone. Push it across the stone until you've sharpened off any grinder marks at the tip of the bevel. Switch to a finer bench stone and give the chisel 10 to 20 pushes across the stone.

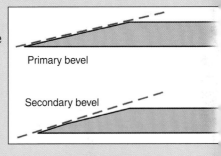

Primary bevel

Secondary bevel

Lift the chisel handle slightly and give it four or five more pushes across the stone. The exact angle doesn't matter. You're putting a secondary bevel on the edge, a finer edge sharp enough to shave with.

Having hollow-ground the bevel, you won't have to use the grinder next time the chisel gets dull. Keep sharpening by hand until the bevel has lost most of it's hollow and then regrind.

Lay the back of your chisel or plane blade flat on each stone every time you sharpen. Keep it flat and make a few passes along the stone. The factory grinder marks will disappear, creating an even smoother, sharper cutting point on the bevel.

The sharpening stones easiest to use are also the most expensive—ceramic stones. Get a medium- and a fine-grit stone. Japanese water stones are less expensive—a 1200-grit and a 6000-grit should do the job.

HAMMERS AND MALLETS

HAMMERS AND MALLETS ARE MADE WITH PARTICULAR JOBS IN MIND. YOU CAN OFTEN TELL THE PURPOSE OF A HAMMER BY THE SHAPE OF ITS HEAD.

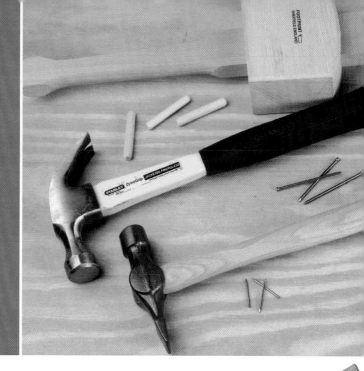

There once was a hammer for every trade from shoemaking to blacksmithing. A trip down the aisle of a hardware store or home center bears witness to the fact that many of them have survived. You don't just buy a hammer, you buy a hammer for the job at hand.

FRAMING HAMMERS weigh in the neighborhood of 20 to 30 ounces, have fairly straight claws, and have faces with a waffle pattern milled into them. The weight gives framing carpenters some heft for driving big nails, and the milled pattern keeps the head from sliding off the nail because of a glancing blow. The straightened claw does double duty as a pry bar.

FINISH HAMMERS weigh 10 to 20 ounces, with 16 ounces being the most common. A finish hammer's face is smooth and does far less damage than a waffle pattern if it accidentally strikes a finished surface. The curved claw pulls nails more quickly than the straight claw, though it isn't as strong. If there is a general-purpose hammer, this is it—you can frame a wall with it or tap brads into a piece of furniture.

WARRINGTON PATTERN HAMMERS are lightweight hammers designed with the cabinetmaker in mind. If you're going to build furniture, this is the hammer to use. The narrow end drives brads and the wide end drives finish nails.

Warrington pattern hammer

BALL PEEN HAMMERS are metalworkers' hammers. They were originally used to stress-harden metals by striking them, and the ball concentrates the weight of a blow on a single point. These days they're used for knocking out taper pins, dowel pins, and rusty bolts.

DEAD-BLOW HAMMERS AND RUBBER MALLETS are meant to prod an uncooperative piece of wood into place. Dead-blow hammers have a nonmarring surface, with loose shot inside the head. When you hit a piece of wood with it, the shot flies from the back of the head to the front, providing a little extra impact. Rubber mallets have a large solid rubber head. Get one with a nonmarring face.

Dead-blow hammer

Rubber mallet

CARVER'S AND JOINER'S MALLETS Carvers spin the mallet every time they hit the chisel so they won't wear a pockmark in the mallet. Joiner's mallets are wood so they don't smash the wood handle on the chisel.

Joiner's mallet

SETS, AWLS, AND KNIVES

ROLLING AROUND AT THE BOTTOM OF EVERY TOOLBOX ARE NAILS SETS, AWLS, AND KNIVES. THEY DON'T HAVE MUCH IN COMMON, EXCEPT THAT YOU CAN'T BUILD ANYTHING WITHOUT THEM.

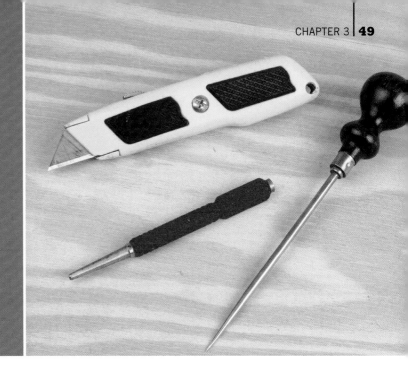

NAIL SETS are used to drive finish nails below the surface. They keep the hammer far away from the face of a board and leave a small hole that you fill to hide the nailheads. They come in four sizes for driving different sizes of nails—$1/32$, $1/16$, $3/32$, and $1/8$ inch.

AWLS are marking tools. Use an awl to mark a particular point—the center of a circle or the location of a screw.

When you drill a hole, mark the center with an awl and put the bit in the mark to keep it from wandering.

KNIVES A layout line made with a knife is more precise than a line drawn with anything else. Get a bright-colored knife with a retractable blade so that you can find it on your bench.

Prying, shifting, and demolition

Unfortunately nails that go in sometimes have to come out. There are a variety of ways to remove nails, but whichever way you choose, always put a piece of scrap wood between the puller and the surface to avoid marring it.

END CUTTERS, though designed for cutting cables, are perfect for pulling nails. Put the cutter down, grab the nail, and then roll the cutter along its curved jaws.

CAT'S PAWS are designed for pulling finish nails and for getting into narrow places.

PRY BARS are flat, wide levers, with a bend at one end and a flat at the other. They're meant largely for demolition work and are excellent for pulling nails, large and small. Miniature pry bars suit tacks and brads.

CROWBARS were originally used for opening boxes; their heft is handy in demolition work, but their thickness makes it hard to get under a nailhead.

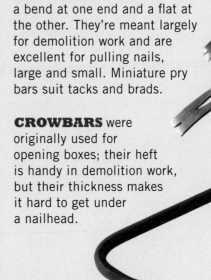

MUST-HAVE MEASURING AND MARKING TOOLS

HERE ARE THE TOP TOOLS THAT GIVE YOU RIGHT-ON-THE-MONEY RESULTS EVERY TIME, WITHOUT MAXING OUT YOUR CREDIT CARD.

Whether you're hanging pictures on a wall, building shelves, or planning a new kitchen, virtually every project you'll tackle requires accurate measurement and marking. Before you fill your shop with fancy machines, you need a handful of essential, high-quality marking and measuring tools. They might not be flashy, but you'll reach for them for nearly every shop project. (See Resources, pages 236–237.)

1 12-INCH COMBINATION SQUARE For accuracy and readability look for a matte or satin finish with etched markings on the steel rule (rather than stamped). Increments should go down to at least $\frac{1}{32}$ inch. The head of the square has two faces—one at 90 degrees to the blade and the other at 45 degrees—so you can lay out either angle.

2 FRAMING SQUARE Though intended for roof and wall framing, this simple tool is ideal for checking the squareness of cases.

3 FOLDING RULE For longer measurements a 6-foot wooden folding rule provides more reliable accuracy than a retractable steel tape measure because there's no hook on one end that can get bent and affect the accuracy. Get the kind with a sliding extension for dead-on measurement inside cases.

4 MACHINIST'S SQUARE A 4- or 6-inch machinist's square is ideal for tool setup and for marking crosscuts precisely. It slips easily into a tool-belt pocket. Good thing too, because you'll reach for this square more often than you might think.

5 SLIDING BEVEL GAUGE This simple device allows you to transfer or duplicate any angle without having to know the angle's numeric value in degrees.

6 MECHANICAL PENCIL Measurements to $\frac{1}{32}$ inch mean little if your pencil makes a line $\frac{1}{8}$ inch wide. A mechanical pencil's thin line is consistent and predictable.

7 RIGHT- AND LEFT-READING TAPES Most tape measures are easier for left-handers to use than for righties. That's because the numbers usually read left to right, forcing right-handers to read upside-down when marking with their right hand. You can purchase a tape measure printed right to left so that you can read it more easily. Jumbo tape measures—25 feet and longer—are great for building a garage but can be downright clumsy when you're working inside your shop. A 10- or 12-foot tape is easier to handle for most of your carpentry projects.

8 PENCIL COMPASS/ SCRIBE A piece of string is a last-ditch method for drawing arcs, and a child's school compass simply won't hold a precise

setting from the start of a circle to its end. An accurate pencil compass is inexpensive. Insert an ordinary wood pencil, and you'll get on-the-mark results. For an accurate and consistent line, substitute your mechanical pencil. The compass is also great for scribing countertops and cabinets to wavy walls.

9 STUD FINDER Modern stud finders are truly electronic marvels. Basic models eliminate guesswork by automatically finding the center of wood or steel studs and joints, then alerting you with both a beep and a beam of light. To eliminate other unpleasant surprises that hide inside walls, some sensors warn you of nonferrous metals (such as copper water pipes) in the wall, as well as the presence of electrical wires.

10 CONSTRUCTION CALCULATOR Unless you were the fraction champion back in grade school, you'll appreciate the push-button ease of calculating feet, inches, and fractions. You can add, subtract, multiply, and divide in one, two, or three dimensions. You can instantly figure equal spacing for pictures on a wall, calculate flooring in square feet or square yards, or compute cubic yards of mulch for your planting beds.

11 LAYOUT SQUARE This is a sensible tool that you'll reach for when you need to mark cutlines across deck boards, shelves, or other lumber. Clamp it to a fence post, and your circular saw's baseplate runs along the tool's edge to guide a square cut. The instruction book that comes with it outlines a wealth of other uses, including roof framing and stair building.

12 DRILL GAUGE AND SCREW GAUGE A fractional drill gauge quickly sorts out that jumbled pile of bits rattling around in your toolbox. The precision holes in the steel plate instantly identify bit sizes and also show

fractional equivalents so you don't have to search for a dog-eared paper chart. A companion tool is a screw gauge that identifies the gauge for screws, bolts, rivets, wires, and cotter pins. The threaded holes in the gauge also identify the pitch (threads per inch) for machine screws. (When you're gauging sheet metal and wood screws, insert the fasteners gently so you don't disturb the tapped machine screw threads.) You'll find this duo of gauges handy for woodworking, electrical repairs, mechanics, and more.

13 FRACTIONAL DIAL CALIPER

A dial caliper eliminates squinting at tiny vernier scales, and with its dual-scale display, you can easily read to the nearest $\frac{1}{64}$ inch on the inner ring and to .01-inch marks on the outer scale. Of course this setup also gives you instant conversions both ways between fractions and decimals. The caliper allows inside, outside, and depth measurements. A handy thumbscrew lets you lock down a measurement that you want to transfer.

On the level

Until recently levels and chalklines were the best way to install chair rail or kitchen cabinets. These days a laser level instantly projects accurate layout lines on the wall. Some laser levels project a single level line; others project two or three: a level line, plumb line, and a line at any angle you choose. Self-leveling models project a level line as soon as you turn them on. Others have adjusting knobs that you set with the help of built-in bubble vials. Check the accuracy before settling on a purchase: A typical model, accurate to within $\frac{3}{16}$ inch over 15 feet, is fine over short distances. If you're using it to wrap chair rail around a square 15-foot room, however, the end of the last piece could miss the beginning of the first by as much as $\frac{3}{4}$ inch.

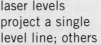
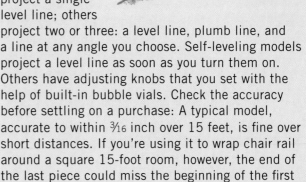

¼" hex drive

Three-jaw chuck

Right-angle chuck (optional)

Quick-connect chuck

Offset chuck (optional)

PORTABLE POWER TOOLS

DON'T JUDGE A TOOL ONLY BY ITS POWER. IT SHOULD BE ONE YOU CAN EASILY WORK WITH TOO.

CORDLESS DRILL/DRIVERS

Higher voltage equals more power. But judging a cordless drill by the voltage of its battery is like judging a book by its cover; you need to look a little closer. It is true that a 14.4-volt drill is usually more powerful than a 12-volt drill, and an 18-volt drill is usually more powerful yet. But that won't tell you if the drill feels good in your hand, how long it runs without recharging, and whether or not it holds a bit firmly. Here are the measures of a good drill:

TORQUE, not voltage, is the true measure of how much rotational force a drill can produce. Manufacturers rate their maximum torque in inch-pounds, and those ratings are a pretty good indication of the drill's true ability.

When you're shopping for a drill, read the box or go to the manufacturer's website and look for the torque numbers on the specifications page. If you don't find them there, many companies allow you to download the owner's manual, which might include the information. If you can't find it elsewhere, send the company an email or call its customer-service line.

CHUCK GRIP With ¼-inch hex-shank drill and driver bits available practically everywhere, a drill chuck's ability to hold fast on a round-shank bit means somewhat less than it used to. Still your drill must be able to grip a round-shank drill bit well enough to keep it from slipping. The top-performing chucks are a ratcheting style that actually increase their grip on the bit as torque increases.

Between the typical high and low gears, this drill adds a middle gear with enough torque to drive screws at a faster rate, drastically increasing run time.

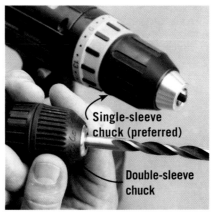

Single-sleeve chuck (preferred)

Double-sleeve chuck

A single-sleeve chuck tightens with only one hand. A double-sleeve chuck requires two hands in close proximity, resulting in a chuck that's finger-tight rather than hand-tight.

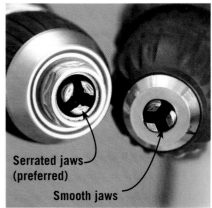

Serrated jaws (preferred)

Smooth jaws

Serrated jaws have a ridge or ridges along the length of each jaw to apply a more secure grip on round-shank bits. In our tests smooth jaws tended to slip.

For easy one-handed tightening, look for a big single-sleeve chuck. Serrated jaws that bite into the bit also help prevent slippage. Ideally you'll find all three features on the drill that you're considering. But if it has none and you buy it anyway, at least you'll know why your bits keep slipping.

CLUTCHES Most of the drill/drivers you'll see have an adjustable clutch between the chuck and the nose of the drill. A clutch stops the chuck from turning when it encounters a set amount of resistance, thus preventing the drill from shredding the screw head, breaking the screw, or driving it too deeply into the wood. Although manufacturers like to boast of how many clutch settings their drills have, experience shows there is little difference from drill to drill.

BATTERIES AND CHARGERS Drills run on one of three types of batteries. The original nickel cadmium–type cells (NiCad) are still in use. They're the least powerful, and the toxic cadmium can leach into the groundwater if they're not properly recycled at the end of their life. Nickel-metal hydride (NiMH) and lithium-ion run longer and are nontoxic—just throw them away when they fail. Lithium-ion (Li-Ion) in particular promises equal or better run time, lighter weight, and the ability to hold a full charge for more than a year while sitting on the shelf. They're expensive, but expect prices to drop as more manufacturers introduce more Li-Ion battery packs for cordless tools.

If your drill comes with two batteries, and most do, the speed at which they recharge might not be an issue. One battery can always be charging while the other is in use. Nonetheless charger speed is worth a look: Some chargers require 90 minutes to 2 hours for a full charge. Most require only an hour, and faster chargers are available for some drills as an accessory. If you're driving drywall screws nonstop, for example, you could easily drain the battery in an hour or less, and a 90-minute recharger won't be fast enough.

RUN TIME is something you can't compute in the store, because there are too many variables. The capacity of a battery pack is measured in amp-hours. Amp-hour capacity is comparable to gas-tank capacity in a car; some cars have larger tanks. But just as a Honda with a small tank will go farther than a Hummer that has a large one, a high amp-hour rating doesn't necessarily guarantee long run time. Run time depends on the efficiency of the motor and the work you're asking it to do.

If the run time on your drill seems low, shifting gears might extend it. Many drills have a high and low gear range, and some also have a third gear in the middle. If you usually run your drill in low gear at full speed, try using high gear and a slower trigger speed. This simple change could significantly boost the number of holes you can drill or the screws you can drive before needing to swap batteries.

The integrated LED work light on the belt hook of this drill helps you work in low-light situations. The hook rotates to five positions to direct the light.

This drill has a switch that disables the clutch in "drill" mode (above) for full-on power. Flipping to "drive" mode (top) reengages the clutch.

When to go corded

Once you're hooked on cordless drills, you might wonder why you would ever use a corded drill again. You might not. But then again you might have to drill some holes in concrete during an installation. You may want the firmness, heft, and power of a corded drill when using a hole saw to install a door lockset. You might be driving countless screws into maple and running down a cordless drill's battery faster than you can recharge it.

In fact you can use a corded drill anytime you like. Cordless drills haven't made cords obsolete; they've just made them avoidable. Anything a cordless drill does a corded drill can do, and sometimes better. If you compare prices you may find that you can pay a lot less too.

DRILLING ACCESSORIES

THE DRILL PROVIDES THE POWER, BUT THE BIT CREATES THE HOLE. AND THEY COME IN MORE VARIETIES THAN YOU MIGHT EXPECT.

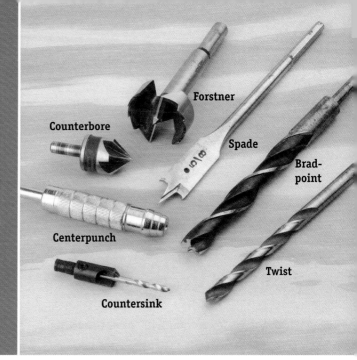

Counterbore

Forstner

Spade

Brad-point

Centerpunch

Twist

Countersink

TWIST DRILL The first bit anyone thinks of and the one most commonly found in a workshop is the twist drill. Originally designed for metalwork twist drills work well in wood too. Fractional sizes start at $\frac{1}{16}$-inch diameter and increase in $\frac{1}{64}$-inch increments. Twist drills are precise and work in both hand and power drills. Brad-point bits are twist drills adapted for the woodworker. Their daggerlike point extends past the cutting edges and keeps the bit from wandering when you start drilling.

SPADE BITS have a wide blade on a narrow shank, which means you can put a 1-inch diameter bit in a $\frac{3}{8}$-inch chuck. Spade bits work only in power drills and come in sizes of $\frac{1}{4}$ to $1\frac{1}{2}$ inches in $\frac{1}{8}$-inch increments. They fit in shank extensions so that you can drill deep holes, but the edge of the hole will always be a bit ragged.

AUGER The screw tip on an auger pulls the bit into the wood while the spiral flutes clear the chips. Some bits have a single cutting surface at the top; more expensive bits have double cutters. Augers were originally used by hand in a brace but can be used at slow speeds in a power drill. At high speeds the screw tip pulls the bit into the wood too quickly, heating up and burning the wood. Auger bits are available in diameters from $\frac{1}{4}$ to $1\frac{1}{2}$ inches in $\frac{1}{16}$-inch increments.

Drilling screw holes

Holes for screws should be the size and shape of the screw. The screw won't grab if the hole is too big, and the board might split if the hole is too small. But with the cone-shaped head, the threadless shank, and smaller threads that taper to a point, a wood screw is a complicated shape. Countersink bits come in several sizes that mimic the shape and drill a hole that is the perfect home for a screw in one pass. They will even drill a recess for a wooden plug that hides the screw.

If you want to you can drill the hole in three separate passes by following the chart below. The hole for the plug is called a counterbore, and a twist drill leaves a cone-shaped countersink for the head at the bottom. The clearance hole is the size of the shank; the pilot hole is the size of the shank minus the threads. Drill the counterbore and clearance holes in the first board and the pilot hole in the second.

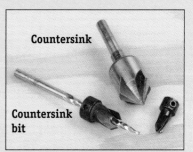

Countersink

Countersink bit

Screw size	#4	#6	#8	#10	#12
Counterbore	$\frac{15}{64}$"	$\frac{9}{32}$"	$\frac{11}{32}$"	$\frac{25}{64}$"	$\frac{7}{16}$"
Clearance hole	$\frac{7}{64}$"	$\frac{9}{64}$"	$\frac{5}{32}$"	$\frac{3}{16}$"	$\frac{9}{64}$"
Hardwood pilot hole	$\frac{5}{64}$"	$\frac{3}{32}$"	$\frac{7}{64}$"	$\frac{1}{8}$"	$\frac{9}{64}$"
Softwood pilot hole	$\frac{1}{16}$"	$\frac{5}{64}$"	$\frac{3}{32}$"	$\frac{7}{64}$"	$\frac{1}{8}$"

A multispur bit (left, with the toothed rim) or a Forstner bit (right, with the smooth rim) bores a large hole easily.

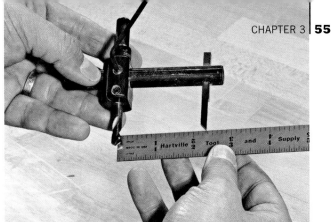

You can set the circle cutter to make any size hole. Measure the radius of the hole (half the diameter) from the center of the pilot bit to the outside of the blade.

BITS FOR LARGER HOLES

Big holes call for big bits—Forstner, multispurs, hole saws, or adjustable circle cutters.

Forstner bits and multispur bits look alike, but Forstners have smooth rims; multispur bits have teeth along the rims. Both are available in diameters up to 4 inches.

A hole saw is a cylindrical saw blade that attaches to a central arbor. If you want to change saw diameters, you remove the blade from the arbor and substitute a different one. Hole saws are available in sizes ranging from 9/16 to 6 inches.

An adjustable circle cutter cuts holes up to 8 inches in diameter with a single-tooth cutter attached to an arm that slides for adjustment. The quality of the cut usually won't equal that of the Forstner and multispur

bits but will be better than that of a hole saw. The tool's ability to bore any diameter is a plus.

Big cutters are not like other drill bits. They should be used in a drill press with the workpiece clamped to the table. Run the tool at a slow speed, 250 rpm or less, to minimize burning of the workpiece.

When boring dense hardwoods, such as hard maple, opt for a Forstner or multispur bit rather than the hole saw or circle cutter.

When boring deep with a Forstner or multispur bit or hole saw, clear the chips frequently by pulling the bit out. To prevent tear-out when boring with an adjustable circle cutter, cut most of the way through; then finish the cut from the other side, inserting the tool's pilot bit into the guide hole.

Drilling jigs for joinery

A doweling jig helps you drill the holes necessary for dowel joints. After you line it up where you want a dowel, this jig centers it on the workpiece as it is tightened. It holds the bit at a right angle to the wood while you drill. Some jigs require dowel centers that, once you're done drilling holes in the first piece, help you lay out corresponding holes in the second piece. The centers fit neatly in the existing holes and have a sharp point on the outer face. Pressing the points against the second board marks the centers of the holes you need to drill in it. (For more on doweling jigs, see page 93.)

A pocket-hole jig allows you to join two pieces of wood together without dowels or joinery. The secret is a hole that angles through the first piece of wood and screws that tap their way as they travel into the second piece of wood. Drill the pocket hole, put the second piece of wood against the first, and simply screw the pieces together. Pocket-hole screws are a great option for joints that will be hidden. (See Resources, pages 236-237.)

CIRCULAR SAW AND BLADES

YOU CAN BUILD WALLS, DECKS, OR EVEN A WHOLE HOUSE WITH A CIRCULAR SAW. FOR BEST RESULTS BUY A GOOD SAW AND USE THE RIGHT BLADE.

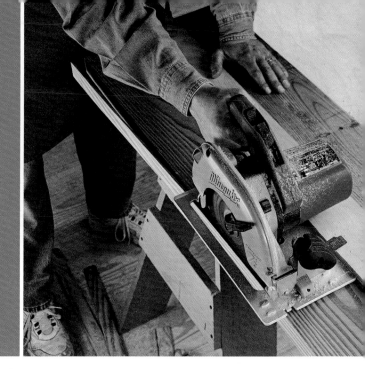

What do you want in a circular saw? Here's the short answer: a 13- to 15-amp corded saw with a 7¼-inch blade. Anything less runs the serious risk of being inadequate for some jobs. Now here's the long answer.

THE MOTOR The best way of gauging motor power is by measuring how much electrical power it uses. The horsepower rating isn't entirely helpful; it can be calculated in more than one way, and there's no standard approach.

A saw's ampere rating tells you how much electrical current the motor uses. Circular saws on the market range between 10 and 15 amps. While a 10-amp saw will cut through thin stock with no problem, the motor will bog down the first time you cut through a piece of hard maple or wet pressure-treated wood. If you're only buying one saw and want it to handle virtually any job, get one rated at 13 amps or more.

THE FEEL Pick up a circular saw, and you'll immediately appreciate handles with soft-grip material. In addition to comfort a slip-resistant grip can significantly reduce the amount of energy you expend to simply hold onto the tool. It might seem like a small point, but it can make a big difference at the end of a day of deck building.

CONVENIENCE Look at the depth adjustment and check its location and ease of operation. If you're like most people, you'll find a lever adjustment easier to manipulate than a thumbscrew. Many saws have a depth-of-cut scale, but some are easier to read than

others. If you work to metric specifications, you'll appreciate having a dual (metric/standard) scale.

On most saws you can set the blade at 90 degrees to the sole with the help of an adjustable stop. But adjustable stops for 45-degree bevels don't exist on some saws. It's a big impediment. If you cut lots of bevels, get a saw with a stop. Here too you'll probably find a lever adjustment more convenient than a thumbscrew. Check the bevel scale; some saws have single-degree markings, while others make you guess between 5-degree increments.

GOOD SIGHT LINES A blade mounted on the right side of the motor is the typical setup, although lefties might prefer one of the blade-left models. With a blade-right model, right-handers watch their layout line through a gap between the body of the saw and the blade guard. They'll get an even better view of the cut with a blade-left model. Getting the view, however, often requires placing the weight of the saw and the wide part of the sole on the waste piece, which can contribute to inaccurate cuts. Right-handed users are better off using blade-right saws; lefties should use blade-left models.

Some saws project a laser line to assist in guiding the saw freehand. Remember which side of the blade the laser line represents. It's far too easy to forget and make cuts that are one blade width too large or small. If you're working outdoors bright sunlight can wash out the laser beam.

18-tooth framing blade

40-tooth finishing blade

24-tooth rip/crosscut blade

Circular saw blades

The blades that come with circular saws usually dull quickly. Save yourself the disappointment by investing in a good blade when you buy your saw. The 18-tooth blade and the 24-tooth blade are both meant for cutting either with or across the grain. The 24-tooth blade makes a far smoother cut and is the better blade to use for finish work. The 40-tooth blade makes the smoothest cut of all, almost like a tablesaw cut. It is a good choice for finish carpentry.

CIRCULAR SAW BLADES

Not that many years ago, circular saw blades were simply high-speed steel discs with teeth ground around the rim. Today's blades have tough carbide teeth that stay sharp much longer, and the body of the blade often has laser-cut slots that combat friction, noise, and heat-induced distortion. Special coatings reduce friction even further.

Obtaining the cut you want is a matter of balancing quality against speed. Equipped with the right blade, a portable circular saw can cut tough jobs down to size in a hurry. When choosing a blade fewer teeth mean more aggressive cutting at the sacrifice of a smooth surface. A high tooth count often means a smooth cut when the blade is sharp; but when it's allowed to dull, you soon see burned edges. The practice of naming circular saw blades for their intended use helps sort out this contradiction.

For rough-cutting and framing jobs, choose a carbide-tipped framing blade with 18 to 24 teeth. (These blades are also referred to as rip/crosscut blades.) For demolition where the saw might run into nails, select a blade rated for nail-embedded wood.

When working with pressure-treated lumber that's still wet, reach for a deck blade with 18 to 24 special teeth that won't bog down. For finish cuts in solid wood, use a 36- to 40-tooth finishing blade. For finish cuts in plywood, use a high-speed steel plywood blade, with somewhere in the neighborhood of 100 to 140 teeth. Steel blades might be the oldest technology, but as long as they're kept sharp, they still do good work.

When you sense that a cut is beginning to require more effort than the previous cut, it's probably time to sharpen the blade or install a new one.

What about worm-drives?

Typical circular saws, often referred to as "sidewinders," have the blade on the end of the motor. Worm-drive saws place the motor at a right angle to the blade. The worm-drive gear for which the saw is named turns the blade. Worm-drive saws are popular with contractors because their slower speed (usually about 4,000 rpm, compared to the 5,000 to 5,800 rpm of sidewinders) means higher torque. The long, narrow body of the tool also gives the operator a longer reach and allows the saw to get into tight spots. A worm-drive saw usually weighs 3 to 8 pounds more than a sidewinder, and the price tag is heavier too. You'll probably pay about 30 percent more for a worm-drive saw.

The long, narrow worm-drive saw runs about 20 percent slower than other circular saws but has more power.

CORDLESS COMBO KITS

AS BATTERIES GET STRONGER MORE AND MORE CORDLESS TOOLS BECOME AVAILABLE. KITS THAT INCLUDE SEVERAL TOOLS CAN SAVE YOU MONEY.

Buying a combo kit is a great way to save money on cordless tools. You'll save about 25 percent of what the tools would cost individually, and you'll have batteries that run off one charger and fit in all your other tools. But kits are not without their pitfalls. Carefully consider whether each tool really meets your needs. Given the discount if three out of four tools meet your needs but the fourth is useless, you're just as well off buying the tools individually.

SOME POPULAR COMBINATIONS

The basic tool kit is usually a drill/driver (sometimes a hammer drill at higher power levels), a small circular saw, a reciprocating saw, and a flashlight. A larger kit might also include an impact driver, a right-angle drill, or a jigsaw.

Less common tools are available for some kits. These include power planers that take most of the hard work out of hanging and fitting doors or a handheld bandsaw for cutting a variety of materials.

POWER PACKS

Choosing the appropriate power level involves balancing four factors: power, run time, weight, and budget. Generally speaking high-voltage tools produce more power, but that doesn't mean they're the best. Although a 36-volt cordless saw will run a long time slicing through ¼-inch plywood, it's probably overpowered for the task. You'd also pay a lot for it, both in weight and in price.

Several manufacturers offer the option of buying the battery charger and tools separately. You can build your own combo kit and get exactly the tools you want—or add more tools without having to buy more batteries. But most manufacturers concentrate the widest choices in their product line at about the 18-volt level. That power plateau seems to satisfy the needs of both serious DIY enthusiasts and many pros, who count on their tools to make a living.

Cordless tools are powered either by nickel cadmium (NiCad) or lithium-ion (Li-Ion) batteries. NiCads do the job at a reasonable price. Newer Li-Ion batteries cost about 40 percent more but weigh less, last longer, and maintain their charge while stored. Expect the price to come down as they become more popular.

This Bosch combo kit features six pro-quality tools, including a flashlight, hammer drill/driver, 6½" circular saw, jigsaw, reciprocating saw, and planer. It also includes two 18-volt batteries with charger and a carrying bag.

JIGSAWS AND BLADES

BLADES AND JIGSAWS HAVE TAKEN GIANT LEAPS FORWARD. MAKE THE MOST OF IT.

Jigsaws cut curves, notches, openings for sinks, and holes for heat vents, pipes, and more. There isn't a cabinetmaker, carpenter, plumber, or electrician who doesn't have one in his or her truck.

In general jigsaws are simple tools that are safe and easy to use and easy to understand. The blade cuts while traveling up and down, and because it is narrow, it can cut curves. Some refinements are worth looking for: A chip blower puffs away the sawdust that collects in front of the cut, and a plastic shoe is less likely to scratch the surface you're cutting.

Orbital cutting action means the blade moves back and forth as well as up and down. The cut is faster but also rougher, so the orbital action can be turned off or set to different size orbits. Variable speed lets you adjust the speed of the blade—slow when cutting through brittle materials and faster for softer materials, such as wood.

Bimetal construction has forever changed jigsaw and reciprocal saw blades. Blade construction is no longer a choice between hard but brittle teeth and flexible but fast-wearing spring metal. Bimetal blades have hard teeth, electron- or laser-welded to a flexible metal backing. The combination means that bimetal blades typically outlast conventional ones by three to one.

Buy blades to match the job at hand: 6 tpi for rough cuts and 10 tpi for smoother cuts. For cutting a tight radius, choose a blade that has a narrower body—typically called a scrolling blade. When cutting plywood run the saw on the best face of the panel and use a blade that cuts on the downstroke. The chipping, which is unavoidable, will occur on the backside of the panel, where it's less likely to matter.

Reciprocating saws

A reciprocating saw is a remodeler's best buddy, rapidly chewing through demanding demolition tasks. A 6-inch blade with 6 tpi (teeth per inch) is a good choice for most jobs because it combines ample capacity, speed, and rigidity. For demolition jobs buy good-quality blades that will slice through nails without complaint.

Some blades use a progressive tooth spacing, where teeth are close together near the tang for thin stock and wide near the end for thick stock.

For jobs where you're attacking thicker material, move to a longer blade such as the 10-inch blade. Like the shorter version this blade also has 6 tpi.

A 10-tpi blade makes a smoother cut, but you'll rarely use a reciprocating saw for finished cuts.

For metal cutting select a blade that's engineered to handle the job. Choose a blade with 18 to 24 tpi depending on the thickness of the metal—the thinner the stock, the more teeth.

CHOOSING A ROUTER

WHETHER YOU GO FOR A FIXED-BASE, PLUNGE, OR DUAL-BASE MODEL, A ROUTER IS A VERSATILE TOOL THAT EXPANDS YOUR CAPABILITIES.

Plunge base   Fixed base

The router is arguably the most versatile tool in your shop. It can cut a wide variety of woodworking joints, shape edges, make signs, duplicate parts, joint edges, and much more.

At the heart of the router is its high-speed motor. Everything else plays a subordinate role: regulating the motor speed, holding the bit, or adjusting the depth of cut. The vast majority of router motors fall into the 1½- to 2¼-hp range. In practice however the difference between a given router and one that's ½ hp more powerful is negligible unless you push the motors to the maximum.

Routers come with one of two types of bases: fixed or plunge. On a fixed-base router, you adjust the depth of cut and lock it, and the depth stays constant during the cut. A plunge router, on the other hand, slides up and down on two metal rods. This lets you start the router with the bit above a board and then ease into it—to cut a mortise for example. If you're routing a groove in several passes—and you generally do in order to get a clean cut—you can make the first pass and move the router down for subsequent passes without having to stop the router.

Most woodworkers buy a fixed-base router first and then buy a plunge router when they need one. Some routers, however, come with interchangeable bases— a fixed base and a plunge base—giving you two routers, in effect, without investing a fortune. But the base isn't the only thing to consider.

THE SWITCH might seem like a small thing, but look for it in a convenient and logical location— you don't want to study your router every time you turn it on and off. An ideal location is one that you can reach while keeping both hands on the router's grips, but that's not always possible. Motors that get switched from a fixed to a plunge base, for example, sometimes compromise ideal switch location to achieve versatility. And ironically a switch location that's less than perfect in handheld mode is often perfectly situated when you turn the router upside down to mount it in a table.

THE COLLET is the part that grips the bit. Many incorporate a self-releasing mechanism that helps pop the bit free after you loosen the collet nut. Most midsize routers include both ¼- and ½-inch collets. Some, though, come with only a ½-inch collet and accommodate the smaller diameter bits by means of

½" collet

Motor shaft

Collet nut

¼" collet

½" collet

¼" reducer sleeve

These parts typify the collets you'll see on midrange routers. Separate ½" and ¼" collets thread onto the motor shaft at right. The other collet (left) is part of the shaft, and to use ¼"–shank bits, you insert a reducer sleeve into it.

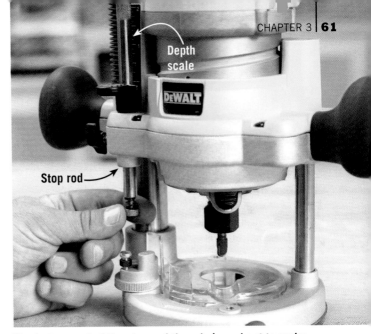

a reducer sleeve. The sleeve grips just as tightly as a dedicated collet but doesn't always release as quickly.

A SPINDLE LOCK helps when changing bits. Usually changing bits means holding the router shaft with one wrench while you loosen the collet nut with another wrench. Spindle locks keep the spindle from moving, without the help of a wrench. Not all routers have them, but changing a bit on those that do is simpler and faster. They're particularly handy in router tables.

SOFT-START CIRCUITRY makes it easier to control the router. Because the router reaches full speed so quickly, even the least powerful router will twist sharply in your hands when you start it. Soft-start circuitry brings the router up to operating speed without a jerk. It might seem like a minor refinement, but your hands, arms, and shoulders will appreciate the difference after an extended work session.

ELECTRONIC SPEED CONTROL helps maintain more consistent cutting by feeding more power to the motor when it's under strain. Tools that don't have an electronic feedback circuit typically take longer to recover speed after the bit enters the wood. The ability to maintain a smooth feed rate from the beginning of the cut promotes a uniform surface.

VARIABLE SPEED is another motor control that you might find useful. In fact the ability to dial down the speed is essential when you're using large-diameter bits. Without speed control using a panel-raising bit would be dangerous because the bit would develop extremely high rim speed.

If a router meets all your needs except for built-in speed control, don't worry. You can buy an accessory plug-in unit that provides an infinite dial-in range. It works with any single-speed router that doesn't have a soft-start feature. In fact you might even prefer this option to the limited number of speed steps offered on some routers.

HEIGHT ADJUSTMENT might not be a major concern, but setting cutting height can be a nuisance when you're working on a router table. Several companies have introduced routers with through-the-base height adjustment. As a bonus the collet on some of these routers rises completely through the base, which enables you to change bits from above the table.

The bottom end of the stop rod threads in and out to make minute adjustments on some plunge bases. Depth scales can vary in their ease of use. In this case the rod partially obscures the markings.

BATTERY POWER isn't out of the question. If you use a router outdoors, or anywhere else where electricity is tough to get, consider a cordless router. Cordless routers are available from some manufacturers in their higher-voltage tool lines. Both full-size and compact trim routers are available. Most come with a ¼" collet, but you can buy larger collets for some models.

Cordless routers weigh about the same as similar corded tools. Top-mounted batteries create a high center of gravity which makes them hard to maneuver in some situations. A corded router would be the best choice for a shop's only router, but a cordless one might be a good second machine to have around for special tasks.

This router has an extra access hole in the base for a wrench. Insert the wrench to easily adjust the bit height.

FIXED-BASE ROUTER

Power range: 1½–3¼ hp
Price range: $60–$340

You set the bit depth on a fixed-base router by raising or lowering the motor within the base. On some models you adjust the height by twisting the motor; others use a height-adjustment knob. So although the base isn't really fixed, the cutting depth must be locked in before making a cut.

Pros: Simple adjustment; easiest to mount in jigs, fixtures, and tables; low center of gravity enhances control; low-maintenance.

Cons: Can't easily or safely plunge the bit for routing mortises, stopped dadoes, and the like.

What to look for: Micro-adjustability of cutting depth; ability to add optional bases (such as D-handle and plunge), guide bushings, and accessories; height adjustment accessible from the underside of the router for table use; adjustable or replaceable handles.

PLUNGE ROUTER

Power range: 1¼–3¼ hp
Price range: $60–$400

Take the motor from a fixed–base router and mount it in a base with springs, and you have a plunge router. Because the motor slides up and down on spring-loaded posts, you adjust depth by unlocking the motor and pushing down on the handles to plunge the bit into the work. Locked, it functions like a fixed-base machine.

Pros: Easy to lower bit into work for mortises or stopped flutes and dadoes; ability to make multiple passes for deep cuts without additional setup.

Cons: Top-heavy; can be difficult to adjust bit heig when table-mounted; plu depth mechanism can be difficult for beginners to learn and use.

What to look for: Ability to use guide bushings and other accessories; easy-to-use locking mechanism; precise, adjustable depth

Router jigs and tables

Routers can do wonders on their own; with a little help they can do miracles. One big help is the router table. With the router attached upside down underneath the table and the bit poking through the surface, the router becomes a mini-shaper, terrific at cutting profiles on edges. With the addition of a fence, the router can cut grooves cleaner than anything your tablesaw can turn out.

Router tables can be as simple as a piece of plywood with a router screwed to it. (Make sure it's firmly attached, put in a straight bit, and raise the bit through the table with the router running.) They can also be commercial units with fancy fences, dust-collection hoods, and lift mechanisms that raise and lower the router with a special crank. Most woodworkers opt for something in between.

Router jigs make even more possible. A simple jig (below) lets you cut out circles with your router. Dovetail jigs rout dovetails and box joints, and hinge-mortising jigs help hang doors. Sign-routing jigs guide your router as it makes custom signs. Like router tables jigs can be shop-made or commercially made. Most woodworkers have some of each type. (See Resources, page 236.)

MUST-HAVE BITS

A professional shop might have 50 or 100 router bits sitting on a shelf. But in reality only a handful of them see regular use. The same is true in the home shop. Regardless of your skill level, there is always a core group of bits you should keep on hand. The six bits here are old standards that will serve the needs of many projects. Get them first, as you are starting out, and add others as the need arises.

Whatever bits you buy choose high quality. Bits should have carbide cutters. The pilot bearing on bits that guide along a workpiece edge should have a ball bearing and spin freely. The bits shown here meet the criteria, but look around before you buy.

Avoid low-priced sets with bits made of high-speed steel (HSS) and pilots that are simply an extension of the shaft. High-speed steel dulls quickly and pilots without bearings can mar the wood.

If your router accepts bits with ½-inch shanks, buy them. They cost only a little more than the same bits with ¼-inch shanks and are less prone to deflection under heavy use.

45-DEGREE CHAMFER Simple chamfering (cutting a bevel on the edge of a workpiece) makes a good decorative-edge treatment for classic furniture styles, such as Shaker and Arts and Crafts. You can make virtually any size chamfer—from just breaking an edge to beveling nearly the entire face—with one bit by simply changing the cutting depth.

Carbide cutter

Shank

¼-INCH ROUND-OVER Versatility makes this bit a star performer. It cuts a bullnose (in two passes) in ¾-inch stock and works well for shaping trim moldings, which are normally ½ inch thick. Properly set up in a router table, a ¼-inch round-over bit can make ½-inch dowels in any species or bead the edge of a tabletop. You can use this bit to cut ¼-inch round-overs on the handholds of shop-built jigs and fixtures too, making them more comfortable to grip.

½-INCH STRAIGHT BIT WITH 1-INCH CUTTING LENGTH Use this bit in a handheld router for cutting dadoes and slots or with an offset outfeed fence on your router table to edge-joint boards. The ½-inch diameter is handy for cutting dadoes when building cases, and two overlapping passes with a ½-inch bit will form a dado that fits ¾-inch plywood—actually $^{23}/_{32}$ inch thick—better than a ¾-inch bit. And if you rout box joints, ½-inch-wide fingers look good in ¾-inch stock. The 1-inch cutter length lets you cut as deep as you'll likely ever need yet still retracts deep enough into your router base to make shallow dadoes.

⅛-INCH ROUND-OVER This is the bit to use for softening the sharp edges of solid-wood workpieces. The slight round-over softens the edges more uniformly than knocking them down with a sandpaper-wrapped block.

This is a case where a ¼-inch shank is acceptable because the bit removes so little material that there's hardly any strain.

½-INCH FLUSH-TRIMMING BIT WITH 1-INCH CUTTING LENGTH This is the perfect bit for copying odd-shaped pieces: Rough-cut the new piece on the bandsaw, leaving it slightly oversize, then clamp it to the original. Guide the bearing along the original to cut the new one to exactly the same shape. It's also the bit you use to trim shelf edge banding. Cut the banding a little wider than the shelf is thick, glue it in place, then rout it flush for a perfect match between banding and shelf.

Pilot bearing

RABBETING BIT WITH CHANGEABLE BEARINGS
Use this bit wherever you need a groove along the edge of a workpiece, such as the one that houses the back of a bookcase. A rabbeting bit also can create the tongue of a tongue-and-groove joint.

Rabbeting bit sets come with various-size guide bearings for cutting different widths of rabbets. These bearings fit on other bearing-guided bits to expand their versatility as well. For example installing a smaller bearing on a ¼-inch round-over bit makes it a beading bit.

BISCUIT JOINERS
THIS CLEVER TOOL LETS YOU MAKE SMOOTH JOINTS QUICKLY AND EASILY.

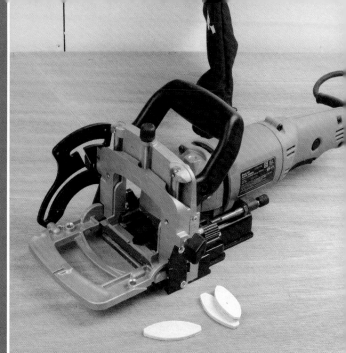

The biscuit joiner, also known as a plate joiner, does two things, and it does them in a hurry. It helps you align parts as you glue them together, and it adds strength to the joint.

Here's how it works: A 4-inch circular blade cuts a half-oval slot when you push the tool body forward into your workpiece. Cut an identical slot on a mating piece, and the slots create a football-shaped opening that holds a similarly shaped biscuit made of compressed beech.

Perhaps the simplest job a biscuit joiner can do is edge-join boards to make a wider workpiece. Start by placing the two boards together and then draw lines across the seam to mark where you'll cut biscuit slots. The lines don't have to be evenly spaced or drawn with any great precision—this is a relaxed approach to joinery. (The only caution: Keep the biscuits back from the ends if you plan to trim the glued-up piece or put an edge profile on it so the biscuits won't show on the completed project.)

Once you've made the marks, separate the boards and turn on the biscuit joiner. Depending on the make of your machine, there will be some sort of mark on its front fence. Align the mark with the pencil marks and push the machine forward. As you do, the blade, normally retracted inside the body, comes out to cut a groove in the wood. Make a cut at each mark in each board.

Glue-up consists of putting glue on the edge of the boards and in the slots, slipping the biscuits in place, and clamping the boards together. You'll discover that at this point there's a bit of horizontal and vertical play in the joint. The horizontal play comes from a slot that is slightly long—good insurance should you

accidentally cut a slot slightly off the mark. The vertical play comes from the compressed biscuit, which is slightly narrower than the slot. It quickly swells to fill the joint because of the water in the glue, but in the meantime the play lets you align things perfectly.

You can use biscuit joiners to put together cabinets or tabletops or to quickly and easily make a mortise-and-tenon. If you're building with plywood, biscuits are a fast, quick, and reliable way to glue-up a material that otherwise forms a pretty weak joint.

The fence is usually adjustable and determines where the slot will go. With the fence legs at a right angle, you can set one leg on the top of the board and adjust the biscuit joiner up or down to place the slot where you want it. Reset the fence and you can guide the cut by resting the joiner on the surface of the workbench. If you're working on mitered corners, you can set the fence to match the angle as shown in the photo.

The blade is adjustable too, allowing you to make short cuts and use short biscuits when working with narrow pieces of wood and longer cuts and biscuits in bigger pieces.

You can use a biscuit joiner on almost any joint. To reinforce a miter set the fence at a 45-degree angle and roll the machine up on the face of the miter. When cutting use a push pad from a jointer to help hold the fence against the surface.

AIR TOOLS

BREATHE POWER INTO YOUR PROJECTS AND FINISH FASTER.

You can probably go a long time without needing a power nailer. But the day you get one, you'll wonder how you got along without it.

The problem with nails is that they move things around as much as they hold them down. Long before the nail grabs, every hit of the hammer bounces the piece it's supposed to hold further out of alignment. Nailers eliminate the bounce. Hold the piece in place with one hand, pull the trigger, and the nail goes in almost instantaneously, holding everything in place.

Finish carpenters rely on three types of nailers: headless pinners, brad guns, and finishing nailers. Headless pinners shoot 23-gauge fasteners that barely show because of the small entry hole. A length range of ½ to 1 inch is typical. The pinner is an excellent choice for delicate trimwork. (See the next page for information on the compressor you'll need for all these guns.)

Brad drivers shoot larger 18-gauge fasteners that range from about ½ to 2 inches. Some brad drivers do double duty and also shoot narrow staples. Beware, however; they usually leave a staple-size dent even when driving brads.

Finishing nailers (typically 15- to 16-gauge) utilize strips of finish nails (generally from 1¼" to 2½" long) for jobs such as installing window and door moldings, baseboards, and other trimwork. A nailer with an angled magazine is easier to maneuver into corners.

Staplers and framing nailers are mostly tools of the construction trade. You're not likely to need one of these bigger nailers until you decide to build a deck (the nailer) or put in a new roof (the stapler). Ask a knowledgeable salesperson before you buy: Trigger mechanisms vary, nails come in either strips or coils,

and local building codes can affect the kind of nails you use. You can often rent these tools.

Manufacturers build safety features into air tools, but you still need common sense. To avoid injury treat a nail gun as you would a firearm—never point the tool at anyone. Realize that a fastener doesn't always go where you aim it and keep your hands well back from it. A nail will always take the path of least resistance and grain can cause the nail's point to emerge from the wood in unexpected places.

Electric brad nailer

If you'll use a nail gun rarely or don't have room in the shop for a compressor, an electric brad nailer might be what you need. You can buy an inexpensive 8- to 10-amp nailer (shown below) or a more costly 15-amp nailer that is nearly twice as powerful. Portable models that run on rechargeable batteries are also available, but they cost more than the corded models.

Electric nailers are not as powerful as pneumatic nailers: Where electric models shoot 18-gauge nails up to 1¼" long, a similarly sized pneumatic nailer drives brads up to 2 inches long.

Nonetheless if you're working largely in pine, an electric brad nailer might do the job, especially if you're using it to nail a thinner piece—such as a molding—to a thicker piece.

If you don't have the need— or the budget—for a pneumatic nailer, an electric nailer/stapler is great for light work.

CHOOSING A COMPRESSOR

The compressor's job is to produce, store, and deliver enough air to run your nailer. Before you look at the more sophisticated elements of a compressor, the first question to ask is, "How much air is needed?"

The air delivered by a compressor is measured in standard cubic feet per minute (scfm). Standard, in this case, means that each compressor's output is measured at the same humidity, temperature, and barometric pressure. Manufacturers rate the scfm of a compressor when it is delivering air at 90 pounds per square inch (psi), because many air tools run effectively at that pressure. Some tools that operate at lower pressures have their airflow requirements rated at 40 psi, and some compressors also state air delivery at that rating.

The scfm needed by typical tools is listed in the Air Requirements chart (below right). As a point of reference, the compressor shown at right, known as a pancake compressor, delivers 2.6 scfm at 90 psi. In practice it will run from time to time when powering a finishing nailer. However when running a framing nailer, which requires more power, the compressor will run almost constantly. A compressor with twin scuba-size tanks delivers about 5.3 scfm at 90 psi and can run both nailers with no problem.

As you shop for compressors, you'll discover a wide variety of tank shapes: squashed cylinder pancakes; slim horizontal hot dog tanks (single, side-by-side, or twin tanks stacked on top of each other); and large-volume vertical and horizontal tanks.

The larger the volume of the tank, the less often your compressor will run. That's a good thing because compressor motors usually are designed to operate at a maximum rate of 50 percent—the motor should not run for more than 30 minutes during any hour of use. Exceeding that guideline could overheat your motor and cause it to fail prematurely.

Maximum pressure is another factor in the volume of stored air. A compressor that delivers 135 psi, for example, will store a greater volume than an identical one rated at 120 psi.

The compressor's motor is another key consideration. Oil-free compressors use Teflon-impregnated piston rings to reduce friction inside the cylinder walls. To keep cool these compressors have a fan-ventilated open crankcase.

Oil-splash compressors run more quietly and last longer between pump rebuildings. They require regular maintenance, however, including checking and changing the oil according to the manufacturer's

recommendations. Oil-splash machines must be operated on a relatively flat surface so that the oil can flow freely.

The compressor's materials also represent compromises between portability and engineering efficiency. For example cast iron is a great material for a compressor cylinder and head because it is durable and dissipates heat well, but it makes a heavy machine. Aluminum is lighter in weight but not as efficient in shedding heat or resisting wear. Some manufacturers compromise with a steel sleeve in an aluminum cylinder with an aluminum head.

If you plan to carry the compressor to worksites, check out the tool's weight and balance. Oil-splash compressors tend to be lighter than their oil-free brothers. If the compressor will be hauled in the back of your vehicle, look for sturdy roll-cage construction for protecting vital parts.

AIR REQUIREMENTS

TOOL	SCFM @ 90 PSI
Finish nailer	3
Brad nailer/stapler	3
Ratchet	4
Drill	4
Impact wrench	6
Air hammer	6
Dual-action sander	16
HVLP sprayer	5
Siphon-feed sprayer	10

SANDERS

YOU CAN'T MAKE SANDING GO AWAY, BUT YOU CAN MAKE IT A LOT EASIER.

Although necessary, sanding is tedious and time-consuming. The tools you use and how you use them are listed in the chart at right, but if you want to minimize the sanding you do, here are a few pointers:

• **Smooth surfaces mean less sanding.** Replace worn saw blades with long-wearing carbide ones. Sharpen or replace dull or nicked jointer knives and upgrade your most frequently used router bits.

• **Cut curves as precisely as possible.** Bandsaw a curve to within 1/32" of your pattern line, and you'll waste less time using your sander as a shaping tool.

• **Scrape away globs of glue.** Remove squeeze-outs while they're still pliable. If you sand them off, bits of dried glue stick to your sandpaper and mar the surface of your work.

• **Use a random-orbit sander.** For sanding flat surfaces a random-orbit sander works best because it leaves behind small irregularly spaced swirls that sand out easily with the next-finer grit.

• **Try a combination belt and disk sander.** This tool can be a real workhorse. Use the belt for flattening and smoothing surfaces and the disk for outside curves. For inside curves you need a drum sander or oscillating spindle sander.

• **Use aluminum oxide paper.** Buy it in bulk to save money.

SANDER TYPES AND THEIR USES

TYPE	USES	LIMITATIONS
Belt	Rapid stock removal; shaping wood	Hard to control for precise sanding; gouging is a risk if not carefully controlled
Detail	Reaches into corners and tight spots; some models have attachments for sanding contours	Not suited for large areas
Finish	Fine sanding; reaches into corners of flat surfaces	Less aggressive than random-orbit sanders; more apparent swirl marks than with a random-orbit sander
Random-orbit	Flat surfaces and large panels; random action helps lessen swirl marks on stained surfaces	Doesn't sand curved surfaces, inside corners, and profiled or narrow edges
Rotary tool	Tight curves and hard-to-reach areas; valuable where light weight and portability are important	Few grit options; loads with debris quickly; can gouge wood; less precise than a spindle sander; not for flat surfaces
Disc	Flat surfaces and outside curves; preserves 90° angles or miters; fast and precise stock removal; can be used to bevel	Can't reach inside curves; burns hardwoods easily; limited to workpieces half the diameter of the sanding disc
Drum	Sands edges at 90° angle; handles inside curves; less prone to burning hardwoods; multiple spindle diameters	Limited to flat surfaces up to twice the width of the drum (on open-ended models); high prices
Oscillating spindle	Sands edges at 90° angle; handles inside curves; less prone to burning hardwoods; multiple spindle diameters	Only suitable for sanding edges, not flat surfaces

BENCHTOP AND STATIONARY POWER TOOLS

IF THERE IS A LOT OF FINISH CARPENTRY IN YOUR FUTURE, CONSIDER THESE HEAVY HITTERS.

Benchtop saws are the smallest of the 10-inch tablesaws—with tops that are typically 30×20 inches or smaller. Because they are small and lightweight, carpenters take them to the jobsite to do jobs their circular saws can't handle.

The small cast-aluminum tabletops often don't have extension wings, and their small size limits what you can do in the shop. The widest possible rip is usually about 16 inches to the right of the blade and 10 or 12 inches to the left, depending on the manufacturer. The rip fence is far shorter than on other saws, giving you less support when you rip long pieces. Because the saw is lightweight, you should bolt it to a solid work surface so that heavy pieces don't cause it to tip.

Benchtop saws are direct-drive—the motor is connected directly to the saw arbor. Power comes from a universal motor, so called because it will run on both AC and DC (although on a benchtop saw it runs entirely on AC). It's the same type of motor that runs a router and is used in the saw because a universal motor is physically smaller and significantly lighter than an induction motor. In practice there's little difference between the power generated by universal motors and that generated by the induction motor found on contractor saws. A 1-hp universal motor delivers as much power as a 1-hp induction motor, although the universal motor runs somewhat hotter and is a lot noisier.

Universal motors typically don't last as long as induction motors. Replacements aren't as readily available, and they can be expensive. Burning out the motor on a low-end portable saw could make replacement of the entire saw more economical.

When you buy a benchtop saw, make sure that the miter gauge and rip fence are sturdy, easy to adjust, and will meet your needs. Unlike contractor saws and cabinet saws, there are few aftermarket upgrades available on a benchtop saw, and any that you find might cost as much as the saw.

Benchtop saws weigh 40 to 100 pounds and can be mounted on lightweight leg stands.

Cabinet saws

At the other end of the spectrum from the benchtop saw is the cabinet saw. This is an industrial-grade machine that's capable of producing exceptional results with little fuss.

A cabinet saw also carries an industrial-size price tag, starting at about $1,500 and quickly running to twice that amount and more. The key feature of a cabinet saw: Everything is rock-solid. The motor mounts on the cabinet, not the underside of the table, simplifying alignment. Massive amounts of cast iron dampen vibration. If you choose you can opt for larger motors.

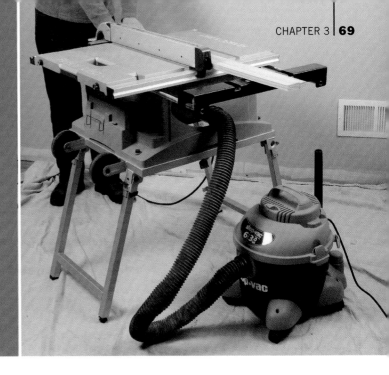

JOBSITE SAWS
THEY'RE THE BIG BROTHER TO THE BENCHTOP SAW, AND THEY PACK A WALLOP.

Jobsite saws fill the gap between benchtop and contractor saws, and they fill it well. These are saws that have the power to do the jobs you set out to do, along with the size and heft to be reliable. If you're wavering between spending $350 for a benchtop and $550 for a contractor saw, you'll find the price of a jobsite saw falls in the middle. The versatility, however, falls far closer to that of a contractor saw.

The idea of a jobsite saw is that you can fold up its legs, throw it in the back of your van, and take it wherever it needs to go. And you really can. A unique leg system provides solid support while you're working but folds like an elaborate card table for

With wheels and collapsible table legs, a jobsite saw lets you take the tool to where the action is, giving you shoplike precision wherever you need it.

storage. Wheels built into the legs make it easy to move the saw around the jobsite or shop.

Although they are still portable, jobsite saws have additional weight over benchtop saws for added stability. The table size has grown too, and with it comes more stability and a longer, more reliable fence.

The top of a jobsite tablesaw is cast aluminum and roughly 30×40 inches. Instead of the usual extension wings, some saws have telescoping rails that slide out to the right. A small section of tabletop remains attached to the end of the rails, providing support for crosscutting long boards. Because the rip fence slides along the rails, the saw can rip up to 25 inches when the rails are extended. The fences are the reliable T-square type, which automatically stay parallel to the blade. The miter gauge has a metal head, unlike the plastic one on a benchtop saw, and is approximately the size of one on a contractor saw. The area in front of the blade allows for crosscuts of up to 8½ to 11 inches as opposed to 5 to 8 inches for a benchtop saw and 13 inches for a contractor saw. In addition to the telescoping rail support for ripping wide boards, some saws have an extension that supports ripping long boards too. At least one manufacturer makes an extension wing for the left side of the saw.

The power train on a jobsite saw is similar to the one on a benchtop saw: A universal motor is connected directly to the saw arbor. The motor keeps the weight down between 100 and 140 pounds. Most jobsite saws have a built-in dust port that you can connect to your shop vacuum.

CONTRACTOR SAW

GREATER CAPACITY, LESS VIBRATION. A TABLESAW FOR A PERMANENT SHOP.

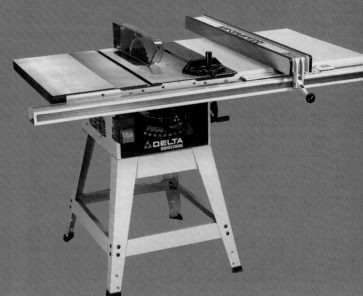

Next to cabinet saws (page 68), contractor saws are the largest and heaviest of the home shop tablesaws. Portability is not as much of an issue for woodworkers in a home shop as for carpenters, so large and heavy can be good things. A larger machine can handle larger boards, and a heavier machine is less prone to vibration.

Contractor-style saws typically have a cast-iron main table that is ground flat and true at the factory. In fact many woodworkers use the table as a reliable reference to check parts as they make them and to test the accuracy of assemblies. Extension wings—the side tables—are usually stamped steel, with cast iron available as an extra-cost upgrade. Some manufacturers offer cast-iron wings with a web pattern that reduces weight and cost, but it's easy to accidentally pinch a finger in the wing's openings.

Contractor saws weigh 200 to 400 pounds and come with a stable leg stand. There is no built-in mobility on most models. Table size is in the neighborhood of 40×27 inches. The extension wings can double the size, and rip capacity is often 30 to 36 inches. The fence is long and is typically a front-locking T-square type that automatically remains parallel to the blade.

Contractor saws are driven by an induction motor, the same type of motor that runs much larger stationary machines. Induction motors run slower than the universal motors used on some other home-shop saws, so a belt-and-pulleys drivetrain increases blade speed. The system dampens some of the vibration from the motor.

Induction motors typically have a long lifespan. If the motor gives out, it is easy to replace.

When you shop for a contractor saw, look for a fence that is sturdy, rigid when locked in place, easy to adjust, and parallel to the blade, or adjustable so that it can be. Although you can buy an aftermarket fence, it's cheaper to get a good one to begin with. Aftermarket miter gauges, on the other hand, are often an improvement over the original equipment, with stops, hold-downs, and accurate miter settings. Look for a reliable miter gauge that locks firmly as part of your saw's original equipment, then you can upgrade to an aftermarket gauge when you can afford one.

Tune up your saw

Make the following critical adjustments:
• Make sure the blade and miter gauge slot are parallel.
• Make sure the rip fence is parallel to the blade.
• Adjust the stops so the blade is at the correct angle when it bumps up against them.

Aligning the blade and miter slot involves lying under the saw and tapping the trunnions into place. Look into aftermarket add-ons like the Precision Alignment and Locking System (PALS) from In-Line Industries to make the job easier.

SAWING AIDS

SOME BOARDS ALWAYS SEEM TO WANT TO WANDER. HERE'S HOW TO KEEP THEM IN LINE.

Shop-made wooden featherboards that hold pieces against the fence or flat on the table have been around forever. They've held both simple and difficult pieces in place and prevented countless problems, many of them dangerous.

Factory-made hold-downs save you the labor of making a featherboard (which is more time-consuming than you'd think); they also have reliable mounting systems. The plastic fingers exert more consistent pressure and are less likely to break than wood fingers. With these advantages and the practical mounting systems, factory-made sawing aids can help you achieve precise results and prevent dangerous kickback.

READY-MADE FEATHERBOARD

A good featherboard holds your work down and tight against the fence, greatly reducing the risk of a mishap while sawing. The first finger on the infeed side of these boards is 1/8 inch shorter than the rest, so you can set the correct pressure by resting that finger on your workpiece. Lock it in place, and the other feathers automatically hold with the ideal pressure. The featherboard shown at top attaches to the saw table miter slot. A T-track is available to attach one to the fence. The featherboards also work on router tables, bandsaws, and shapers.

PLASTIC FINGERS

The high-density plastic fingers shown center right set at a 4-degree angle away from the work. The fingers compress as you feed stock between them and the fence, creating just the right amount of holding pressure. To set the tension press the fingers against

your workpiece until they are parallel to the board edge and then tighten the knobs. The jigs mount on the table and top of the fence. They work on a router table or tablesaw.

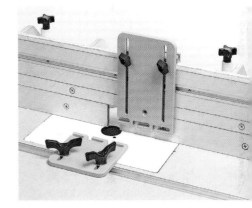

HOLD-DOWNS

Another type of hold-down attaches onto a steel or cast-iron saw table and fence with powerful magnets. Canted abrasive wheels and tough plastic fins hold the work solidly down on the table or against the fence. When it comes time to move the hold-downs, flipping a cam lever separates the unit from the metal surface.

In shop tests the magnets held no matter how much wood was pushed through the tablesaw. The canted wheels kept the wood from shifting toward the fence and eliminated burn marks, even at slower feed rates.

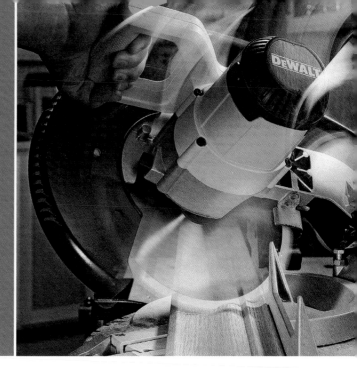

10-INCH COMPOUND MITERSAWS

THEY MAKE SQUARE CUTS, COMPOUND MITERS, AND MORE. FOR FINISH WORK, YOU CAN'T BEAT THIS SAW.

Of all the styles of mitersaw you can get, 10-inch compound mitersaws strike the best balance between cost and capability. They cut both simple miters (left to right) and compound miters (angled up and down, as well as left to right). You'll find that most saws snap automatically into place at 0, 22.5, and 45 degrees, left and right, to simplify setting up the most common miters you're likely to use. (If you plan to cut compound bevels for crown molding, look for a stop at 31.6 degrees combined with a 33.9-degree bevel angle. See pages 138–150 for more on cutting crown molding.) If you can swing the miter scale at the store, check whether the stops (called detents) click solidly in place. If the detents seem sloppy, the miters will be too. Look at another saw.

BEVEL-CUTTING ACCURACY

A bevel is the cut angling from top to bottom. Most mitersaws offer bevel stops at 0 and 45 degrees, but some also add a crown-molding stop at 33.9 degrees. Most go slightly above and below the 0- to 45-degree range, but only a few saws allow you to do so without resetting the stops.

QUALITY OF CUT

Check carefully to see what blade comes with the saw. A 24-tooth carbide blade might be adequate for decking but probably will disappoint you when slicing crown molding. For the smoothest cuts buy a quality blade with 60 or more carbide teeth.

Table inserts contribute to cut quality as well. Zero-clearance inserts have narrow slots the width of the blade. Besides helping reduce tear-out, they also prevent small offcuts from dropping into the saw, which can inhibit turntable movement.

Finally for the best possible cuts, such as when making picture frames, you'll need a stock hold-down to prevent the workpiece from shifting during the cut. Check whether the saw you're considering includes it as standard equipment.

LASER LINES

Many 10-inch mitersaws, even some inexpensive models, feature laser indicators that show exactly where the saw blade will cut. Not all of them live up to that promise of accuracy however. Blade-mounted lasers are situated in the arbor-washer at the center of the blade. With this setup the blade must be spinning to activate the laser's centrifugal switch, and the laser line can shift to the right as you lower the cutting head. Most saw-mounted lasers show where either the left or right side of the blade will cut and are adjustable for different blades. Dual-line lasers, found on only a few mitersaws, mark both sides of the kerf.

HANDLE COMFORT

You will probably find a horizontal D handle more comfortable to use. Vertical Ds and straight-handled mitersaws put your wrist in an awkward position when the blade is at full height.

A hairline cursor with a high-contrast background makes a miter scale easy to read. Small marks, ½ degree to either side of the cursor, help you make minor adjustments.

MID-PRICED BANDSAWS

A BANDSAW CAN BE TOO SMALL TO BE USEFUL, OR TOO BIG TO GET IN THE SHOP. HERE'S HOW TO STRIKE A BALANCE.

A home-shop bandsaw should have a ¾- to 2-hp motor, a 13- to 16-inch throat, and a 6- to 12-inch depth of cut. In selecting a bandsaw you should also consider the guides that keep the blade from twisting and the ease with which the table can be set to bevel. Together these five points are key to buying the right bandsaw.

1 **POWER** A 2-hp motor is generally more powerful than a ¾-hp motor, but keep your eyes on tool reviews. Heavier wheels and heftier motor construction can sometimes result in a small-horsepower machine outperforming a larger one.

2 **DEPTH OF CUT** Also known as resawing capacity, depth of cut is the distance between the table and the fully raised blade guides. It is important because you might want to resaw a board—cut it into several thinner ones. (Bookmatching grains and making bent laminations are two reasons to resaw.) The greater the depth of cut, the wider the board you can resaw, though your ability to do so also depends on the machine's power.

3 **BLADE-GUIDE SYSTEM** Guide blocks keep the blade from twisting and deflecting left or right, and a thrust bearing backs up the blade to keep it from bending back while you cut. All must be set precisely for optimal performance. Look for micro-adjustment knobs, which simplify the process. Some guides are spaced a hair's breadth away from the blade. Ceramic guides are so small that they can run against the blade without overheating it. Graphite-impregnated guide blocks actually touch the blade when properly set but self-lubricate the blade to keep it cool and prevent wear.

4 **BLADE-CHANGING EASE** It's tough to know about the ease of changing blades unless you do business with a shop that will actually let you give it a try. Keep your eyes on tool reviews for up-to-date information.

5 **TABLE ADJUSTMENTS** From time to time you'll want to tilt the table to make an angled cut. The table should pivot smoothly on a pair of sturdy trunnions and tilt 45 degrees to the right and at least 10 degrees to the left (a must-have if you want to cut bandsawn dovetails).

Bandsaw performance

Getting the most out of your saw requires setting it up properly and taking care of it. Here are the basics. Check your owner's manual for more detail.

• Clean the wheels. Brush or vacuum accumulated dust from inside the wheel housings.

• Tension the blade. Pluck it (really) until the sound turns from a dull buzz into a clear tone. That's the sound of a blade at the right tension.

• Use a folded dollar bill as a spacer to set the distance between the rear (thrust) bearing and the blade. Unfold the bill to set the space between the blade and the guide blocks.

• Slide the guide blocks back so the leading edge is just a whisker behind the gullets in the blade.

• Check to make sure the wheels are aligned by placing a straightedge across them. Adjust as directed in your owner's manual.

OTHER POWER TOOLS, SMALL AND LARGE

THE TABLESAW GETS ALL THE ATTENTION—AT FIRST. BUT SOONER OR LATER, YOU'RE GOING TO BE THINKING ABOUT THESE TOOLS.

Aside from the grinder, which you'll want almost immediately for sharpening, you can wait until you need these tools before you buy them. The scroll saw cuts intricate curves (and dovetails) with ease. The drill press lets you drill holes that really are perpendicular to the surface—or at any angle to the surface for that matter. The jointer and planer work together to give you flat surfaces or to mill rough-sawn lumber into workable boards.

SCROLL SAW

A scroll saw moves a straight, fine-tooth blade up and down quickly—making as many as 1,800 strokes per minute on some saws. The combination of speed and narrow blade result in a fine cut and allow, when necessary, tight turns. Scroll saws were originally used by cabinetmakers who did inlay and marquetry. The availability of reasonably priced scroll saws has made them popular in the home shop and has resulted in an explosion
of books with intricate patterns for clocks, puzzles, shelves, and other ornately cut projects.

When you buy a saw, the first thing you should consider is how easy it is to install the blade. That's

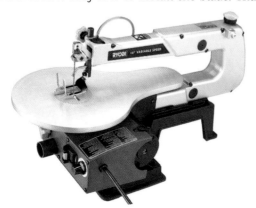

because interior cutouts are made by first drilling a hole in the wood, feeding the blade through the hole, and then clamping the blade in the saw. It's something you'll do countless times in the course of some projects. The table should be large enough to support your work and tilt easily for work that has a beveled edge. A blower tube that blows sawdust out of the way is a convenience that you might not want to live without.

GRINDERS

A high-speed grinder will remove the most metal in a hurry, but the friction it generates also can ruin a cutting edge quickly. An overheated blade can lose its temper, softening the metal so the steel can't hold a good working edge. Although it's possible to retemper the tool, it is usually so much trouble that replacement is a better option.

A low-speed grinder is less likely to draw the temper out of a tool, but a dual-range, high/low-speed grinder lets you choose between caution and aggression. Even better is a variable-speed grinder, which lets you match the speed to the job.

A grinder with an 8-inch abrasive wheel is a good size for the home workshop. If the shaft can

drive two wheels, make one a coarse 36-grit wheel and the other a fine 60-grit wheel.

DRILL PRESS

A drill press assures that the holes you drill will be at the angle you want, but there's no reason it needs to be nearly as tall as you are. Downsizing an industrial model to a benchtop tool imposes no serious practical penalties. The distance from the support column to the center of the chuck varies only ¾ inch between the largest benchtop model and a typical full-size model.

To be sure, the power of the motor and the depth you can drill a hole are smaller on a benchtop model, but the size and power are usually enough to meet most woodworkers' needs. Some benchtop models have five speeds, compared to the usual 12 on a big model, but most drill press users will admit that they routinely use only two or three speeds anyway.

JOINTER

The jointer's job is to create dead-flat faces and perpendicular, straight edges so that you can run a board through other machines and get the best results. This is the machine you should go to first when smoothing lumber. It's especially important that you joint the face of a board before you run it through the planer. A planer doesn't flatten a board—it simply creates two smooth, parallel faces. If you

put a cupped board in a planner, it will give back a cupped board with parallel faces. Put in a board with a flat, jointed face, and out comes a board that is flat on both sides.

If you're having trouble getting a flat face or a perpendicular edge with your jointer, put a straightedge across it to make sure the tables are straight and coplaner (parallel). For the best results, after 8 to 10 inches of your workpiece has passed the cutterhead, shift your downward pressure to the outfeed side.

Six-inch wide jointers match the budget and needs of most woodworkers. An 8-inch jointer costs three times as much. Unless you need to face-joint boards up to 8 inches wide or 12 feet long, it's probably not worth the extra expense. (For more information, see Resources, page 236.)

PLANER

Planers come in two varieties—large, stationary machines 15 or 20 inches wide and costing $800 or more, and planers capable of machining stock up to 13 inches wide and selling for $200 to $500.

Either kind has two or three knives mounted on a rotating cutterhead, and both do quality work. The rotary cutting action results in a problem that all jointers share, however. Planing the board leaves a series of shallow scallops, which have to be sanded away. Scalloping is reflected in cuts per inch (cpi) and is usually listed in a planer's specifications.

Planer manufacturers increase cpi and minimize scalloping by speeding up the cutterhead, adding a knife, slowing the board feed rate, or some combination of those.

A second problem common to planers is snipe: the tendency of planers to take a too-deep bite a few inches from each end of a board. Snipe happens when only one drive roller engages the workpiece, allowing it to rock the head or lift up slightly into the cutterhead. Snipe less than 0.002 inch deep hand-sands away easily; between 0.002 and 0.003 inch requires power-sanding to smooth, and anything deeper will need to be cut off. You can usually minimize snipe by adjusting the roller. Check your tool's owner's manual for details. (For more information, see Resources, page 236.)

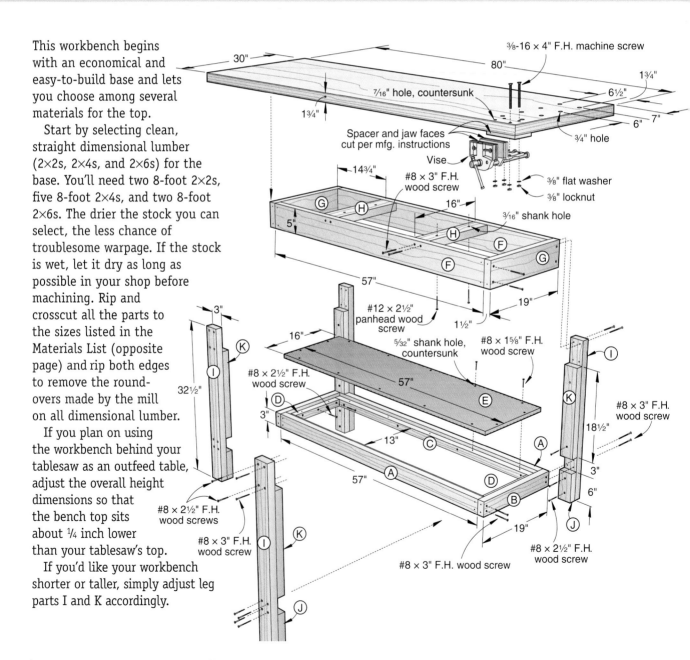

ROCK-SOLID WORKBENCH

IT'S YOUR MOST IMPORTANT TOOL—BUT YOU DON'T NEED TO SPEND A FORTUNE ON IT.

This workbench begins with an economical and easy-to-build base and lets you choose among several materials for the top.

Start by selecting clean, straight dimensional lumber (2×2s, 2×4s, and 2×6s) for the base. You'll need two 8-foot 2×2s, five 8-foot 2×4s, and two 8-foot 2×6s. The drier the stock you can select, the less chance of troublesome warpage. If the stock is wet, let it dry as long as possible in your shop before machining. Rip and crosscut all the parts to the sizes listed in the Materials List (opposite page) and rip both edges to remove the round-overs made by the mill on all dimensional lumber.

If you plan on using the workbench behind your tablesaw as an outfeed table, adjust the overall height dimensions so that the bench top sits about ¼ inch lower than your tablesaw's top.

If you'd like your workbench shorter or taller, simply adjust leg parts I and K accordingly.

Using the drawing for reference, glue and screw the base together. Cut the lower shelf (E) to fit in the opening, drill the mounting holes, and screw the shelf in place.

Choose one of the materials in the chart below for your bench top. The top shown in the photo is a solid-core door. Slightly damaged doors can often be purchased at a substantial discount from home centers and other outlets. Drill shank holes in the cleats (H), then secure the top to the base.

When choosing a top consider your personal preferences in addition to how well a surface takes abuse. Ask yourself:
• How important are aesthetics? A maple butcher-block surface looks better than a sheet of tempered hardboard, but good looks come at a price.
• Do you cover work surfaces when assembling, finishing, or painting? If not get a surface that you can clean or replace easily.
• Do you prefer a heavy surface? Many woodworkers like a dense material that adds stabilizing pounds to a bench that will remain in one place.
• Do you need the flattest possible surface? If you assemble a lot of projects on your bench, this should rank high on your list of work surface requirements.

MATERIALS LIST

Part		T	W	L	Matl.	Qty.
		FINISHED SIZE				
A	lower rails	1½"	3"	57"	C	2
B	lower end rails	1½"	3"	19"	C	2
C	lower shelf long cleats	1½"	1½"	57"	C	2
D	lower shelf short cleats	1½"	1½"	13"	C	2
E	lower shelf	¾"	16"	57"	SG	1
F	upper rails	1½"	5"	57"	C	2
G	upper end rails	1½"	5"	19"	C	2
H	cross cleats	1½"	3"	16"	C	2
I	legs	1½"	3"	32½"	C	4
J	lower dividers	1½"	3"	6"	C	4
K	upper dividers	1½"	3"	18½"	C	4

Material key: C–choice of spruce, pine, or fir; SG–choice of sheet goods (we used MDF).

Supplies: #8×1⅝" flathead wood screws, #8×2½" flathead wood screws, #8×3" flathead wood screws, #12×2½" pan-head wood screws, ⅜–16×4" flathead machine screws, ⅜" flat washers, ⅜" lock nuts.

Buying Guide

Hardware: G9851 Shop Fox Quick-Release Vise, 9" jaw. Call Grizzly Industrial, 800/523-4777, or go to grizzly.com.

GUIDE TO BENCH TOPS

MATERIAL	PROS	CONS	USE
Hardboard	Readily available; easy to cut; relatively stable; takes paint well	Can't sand faces; needs substrate support; edges damage easily; holds fasteners poorly	Tempered-grade sheets are excellent for replaceable benchtops.
Softwood plywood	Readily available; easy to cut; face veneers can have a nice appearance; stainable and paintable	Surface scratches easily; interior plies might have voids; face veneers often patched	Good for shop cabinets and countertops
Particleboard	PBU grade readily available and inexpensive; particleboard cuts easily and is fairly stable	Heavy; holds fasteners poorly; not moisture-resistant	Good as substrate (underneath a harder material, such as plastic laminate) for countertops
Medium-density fiberboard (MDF)	Flat; no face or core voids; consistent thickness; glues well; cuts and machines easily; stable; paints well	Heavy (100 lbs. per ¾" sheet for standard MDF); holds screws poorly; scratches and gouges difficult to repair	Excellent for shop cabinets and as a substrate for plastic laminates and hardboards
Plastic laminate over particleboard	Cleans easily; inexpensive; readily available; many colors and patterns available	Scratches easily; hard to repair; needs fine-tooth blades when cutting to prevent chipping	Good for light-duty benches
Solid-core door	Readily available; nice appearance; stainable or paintable; flat surface	Holds screws poorly; scratches easily; can be expensive	Good for workbenches and assembly tables
Laminate maple	Nice appearance; stable; flat; scratches can be repaired; adds mass to bench	Expensive; heavy; scratches easily	Excellent surface for workbenches and assembly tables
2× construction lumber	Readily available; inexpensive; easily repaired; cuts and fastens well	Dents and scratches easily; not attractive; has tendency to twist and warp	Good for inexpensive worktables

CLAMPS

GLUE-UP COMPRISES THE 20 WORST MINUTES OF WOODWORKING. THE RIGHT CLAMPS AND THE RIGHT APPROACH EASE THE PAIN.

Headstock

Tailstock

Pipe clamps have long been a woodworking favorite because they deliver exceptional clamping strength and durability at an affordable price. Clamp fixtures are reasonably priced and are sized to fit either ½- or ¾-inch pipe, but not both. The pipe is not included. Longer lengths of pipe can bow under clamping pressure, so the fixtures for the more rigid ¾-inch pipe are a better buy.

You can use pipes of any length you want, as long as one end of the pipe is threaded to mount the headstock. The fixtures can be removed easily and put on other lengths of pipe, saving you money because pipe is cheap. Buy four to eight sets of fixtures and keep on hand a variety of pipe lengths. If you have both ends threaded, you can make longer clamps by connecting two pipes with a coupler.

Threaded pipe is available from any home center or plumbing supply store. Choices include black or galvanized, with each having advantages and disadvantages. Fixtures slide better on black pipe, which costs about one-third less than galvanized pipe. Galvanized pipe's chief advantage, rust protection, applies only to the pipe surface, not its threads. However black pipe will leave dark stains on your workpiece if it comes into contact with glue during a glue-up.

Maintain your clamps just as you do your tools. Clean the jaws, pads, and bars after a glue-up because hard, dried glue can dent workpieces and interfere with the jaw movement. And once glue builds up, it is difficult to remove. To prevent this put waxed paper between the clamp and the workpiece. Or apply a light coat of paste wax or paraffin to the clamps so the glue won't stick. Put wax on the clamp screws for

smoother turning.

Do not use silicone- or oil-base lubricants, which can stain your workpiece and interfere with your finish.

Clamping is more than just putting pressure on pieces of wood to hold them together while the glue dries. If the pressure isn't applied evenly or is overapplied, clamps can knock an assembly out of square or open up gaps between parts. Here are some tips to help prevent problems:

• Put rubber or softwood pads between the clamp heads and the wood to keep from marring the surface.
• To create even clamping pressure across a wide joint, put a 2- to 3-inch wide board, known as a caul, along the length of the joint. Clamp the ends as shown in the photo above. Put waxed paper between the board and the joint to keep the caul from being glued.
• When you can't get a clamp where you need one, such as at the middle of a case, tape a thin wedge at the point that needs pressure. Put a caul over the length of the joint, including the wedge, and tighten the clamps.
• To square up a cabinet, measure the diagonals and angle a clamp in the direction of the long diagonal. Tighten until the diagonals are equal, and the assembly will be square.

WOODWORKING VISES

GET A GRIP ON THINGS WITH A QUALITY VISE. THE PAYOFF WILL BE IMPROVED QUALITY IN YOUR CUTTING AND SHAPING.

You can spend a few dozen dollars or several hundred on a vise, but they're all designed to do the same thing: hold a workpiece solidly without marring it. Vises come in many sizes and types, but the most popular vise for carpentry and woodworking is a bench vise, shown above. As you compare vises be sure to check out these three must-have features:

1 QUICK-RELEASE JAW To spare you the annoyance of tediously turning (and turning) the vise's handle for large adjustments, a quick-release mechanism allows you to instantly position the jaw anywhere along its range. A lever release disengages the threads from the screw when you actuate the lever, then reengages them when released. More convenient is a gravity release, which disengages with a mere counterclockwise half-turn of the screw; turning it clockwise reengages the threads. You'll especially like this style of quick release if you have limited hand strength.

2 POP-UP DOG You'll find this feature on all but the most basic vises. When used with bench dogs, this device will help hold a bench top workpiece in place for sanding or scraping.

A thumbscrew locks most vise dogs in place. A precious few, such as those made by Jorgensen, are spring-loaded and stay in the up or down position without having to be locked. The Wilton vise adds an interesting twist to the pop-up dog: The entire jaw rises to provide holding power while minimizing workpiece damage.

3 TOED-IN JAWS The jaws of a good bench vise come together at the top before they touch at the bottom. This arrangement, called *toe-in*, helps equalize clamping pressure across the jaws. Without toe-in the jaws apply more pressure at the bottom than at the top.

MOUNTING TIPS

If you're right-handed mount the vise near the left end of your bench; left-handed woodworkers should install it on the right. This keeps your "power arm" over the workpiece for hand-tool tasks, such as planing. Mounting the vise near the end of the bench lets you hold an assembly that goes around the corner, such as a portion of a frame.

The tops of the wooden jaws should be flush with or slightly lower than your bench top. You might need to shim between the vise and the bottom of the benchtop before installing it.

Pop-up dog

Applying pressure to the quick-release lever lets you remove your work without cranking on the vise handle.

SAFETY EQUIPMENT
ALWAYS KEEP PROTECTION IN MIND. HERE IS A ROUNDUP OF THE ESSENTIALS.

Shop safety involves more than leaving the guard in place on your tablesaw. You also need to think about protecting your eyes, ears, and lungs. Purchase the right protective gear and make a habit of using it.

EYE PROTECTION

When it comes to your eyes, you can choose from safety glasses, goggles, and face shields. (All will fit over glasses or contacts. You can also have prescription safety glasses made.)

Make sure you're really getting eye protection. All safety eyewear, including face masks, is officially approved by the American National Standards Institute (ANSI), which sets industry standards. Approved

Safety glasses

eyewear will have the applicable standard—ANSI Z87.1—stamped on the frame. Lenses will bear the manufacturer's initials somewhere out of the line of sight. Any protective eyewear you buy should bear both marks.

Frames and lenses work together. Safety glasses have lenses that withstand nearly 4 times the impact of regular impact-resistant lenses. Compliant frames have inner retention lips that keep unshattered lenses from being driven into your eyes under the force of heavy impact. They also meet standards for pressure and impact that regular frames do not.

Face mask

For complete protection all safety glasses should also have side shields. To prevent the lenses from fogging when wearing a dust mask or respirator, get an anti-fog spray or liquid, available at drugstores or sporting goods stores.

CAN YOU HEAR ME?

Hearing loss is cumulative and permanent. Hearing protection can't restore what you've already lost, but it can halt further deterioration. If you value your hearing, wear ear protection when you're exposed to any noise over 85 decibels (dB)—a noise level that even most sanders exceed. For very loud noise, such as that made by a tablesaw, you'll need added protection, such as earplugs under earmuffs.

Manufacturers of hearing protectors assign each of their products a laboratory-based Noise Reduction Rating (NRR). By law it must be shown on the label of each hearing protector sold.

The NRR indicates the blocked noise level in decibels. For example an NRR of 20 would reduce a 100-dB noise to 80 dB— a significant amount since the volume of noise halves with each 3-dB drop. In the real world of your shop, however, the actual NRR might prove to be somewhat less. To be on the safe side, always select hearing protection with an NRR of at least 25.

Earmuffs

Earmuffs or earplugs? That's still a matter for debate. According to a 1997 study by the National Institute for Occupational Safety and Health (NIOSH), earmuffs provide the highest real-world noise reduction. The Occupational Safety & Health Administration (OSHA), on the other hand, says that properly fitted foam or flexible plastic earplugs offer the greatest protection. NIOSH, speaking more generally, has hit on about the only thing that matters—the best hearing protector is the one that the worker will actually wear.

Researchers at 3M, which manufactures several styles of hearing protectors, have studied why hearing

Band plugs

protection frequently fails in the industrial workplace. Reasons for failure include the following:

• **Improper sizing and insertion.** The wearer tends to fit plugs too loosely, even though they're available in various sizes. If fit too tightly they cause discomfort and the wearer removes them. Also a person can have two different sizes of ear canals, so each must be sized separately.

• **Incompatibility with other protective equipment.** Earmuffs often don't seal properly over safety glasses. Long hair also interferes.

• **Communication problems.** Hearing protection tends to block high pitches, typical of voices. Wearers loosen, alter, or remove protectors to hear others.

• **Wear and tear.** Seals wear down on muffs. Foam plugs become less flexible and unable to properly mold to the ear canal. Premolded plugs shrink. Ear wax and perspiration also build up on them. Earplugs should be checked frequently and pushed in. Even the act of chewing gum can shift earplugs out of position.

Finally here's a test to see if earplugs fit properly: After inserting the plugs cup your hands over your ears, then take them away. If you hear a difference, the earplugs are not being worn correctly; remove them, refit, then try again. And don't forget to wash them in mild soap and water after a few wearings.

DUST TAKES YOUR BREATH AWAY

For many years craftspeople considered dust a mere nuisance. But exposure to dust of all kinds has recently been identified as a cause of cancer. Not surprisingly even amateur woodworkers are buying dust-collection systems to keep the problem under control. Big chips and large pieces of dust— down to about 5 microns—are relatively easy to capture, and grabbing them makes a huge difference in the appearance of the shop. The irony however is that these large pieces aren't

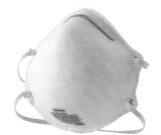
Dust mask

the problem. The culprits that do the real damage are less than 5 microns in size. So if you're in the market for a dust collector, look for one that grabs pieces as small as 1 micron or upgrade a stock collector with an aftermarket high-efficiency bag or filter.

Controlling dust should be a three-pronged attack. Of primary importance is a dust-collection system that captures dust at the source. The second prong

is an air-filtration system that pulls out airborne particles. And the third is the use of personal dust protection. Most woodworkers wear either a dust mask or a respirator in the shop—and the two are not the same thing.

A dust mask is cloth, has one supporting strap, and is not approved by NIOSH or OSHA. Dust masks are intended for nuisance dust at low levels— such as when sweeping the attic.

A particulate respirator is also cloth but usually has two straps. It's rated N95 by NIOSH, meaning that it successfully filters sanding dust and other particles from the air. Look for an N95 rating on the container.

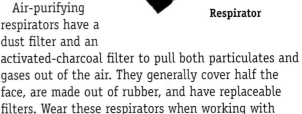
Respirator

Air-purifying respirators have a dust filter and an activated-charcoal filter to pull both particulates and gases out of the air. They generally cover half the face, are made out of rubber, and have replaceable filters. Wear these respirators when working with paint stripper, lacquer, and other chemicals.

FIRE EXTINGUISHER

A fire extinguisher is an important addition to your shop because of the ever-present danger of fire. A 10-pound extinguisher with an ABC rating is your best bet. The A designation means that the extinguisher fights fires consisting of trash, wood, and paper; B is for liquids; and C is for electrical equipment.

The units that you'll find in home centers typically cannot be recharged, so you should discard and replace them if the needle on the pressure gauge reads above or below the recommended range. An extinguisher purchased from a local safety specialty shop might be a better value in the long run because it can be recharged. It's a good idea to take it back to the shop once a year for a checkup.

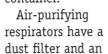

Rechargeable fire extinguisher

WOODWORKING BASICS

THIS ROUNDUP OF ESSENTIAL SKILLS WILL EQUIP YOU TO handle most trimwork and built-in projects. Many of these basics have been around for millennia. All, with a little practice and patience, are skills you can have at

MEASURING AND MARKING TECHNIQUES

Improve your speed and accuracy with these essential skills. **84**

PREPARING STOCK

How to cut, join, and shape the components of your project. . . . **86**

MAKING PROJECT PARTS

How to finetune your project's parts before final assembly. **111**

FASTENING

Learn how to put it all together in this section about screws, nails, and glue. **116**

FINISHING

A good job deserves a great finish. Here are your options. **120**

your disposal. In addition to the basics, you'll find valuable advanced tips for increasing your expertise when cutting, shaping, joining, fastening, and finishing your carpentry project.

MEASURING AND MARKING TECHNIQUES

ACCURATE MEASURING AND MARKING ARE ESSENTIAL FOR ANY WOODWORKING OR CARPENTRY PROJECT. HERE ARE FUNDAMENTAL PROCEDURES TO HELP YOU MAKE THINGS FIT.

Success in woodworking usually boils down to measuring correctly and marking precisely before cutting anything. The following tips should help you avoid common measuring and marking errors.

FINDING THAT TRUE CENTER

It's easy to miscalculate while trying to find the center of a workpiece. Eliminate the chance for math errors by using a measuring tape with a half-scale along the bottom. This board is 29³/₈ inches long [PHOTO A]. The bottom row on the tape shows 14¹¹/₁₆ inches is half that. To mark the midpoint go back to the top row, find 14¹¹/₁₆ inches, and make your mark [PHOTO B].

BURNED BY THE FIRST INCH

Ever measured from the 1-inch mark (called "burning" the first inch), then forgotten to add the inch when marking? Try using a steel rule or folding rule with a square end for greater accuracy. If you do burn that first inch, make your mark [PHOTO C], then

double-check by hooking the tape at the end and measuring again [PHOTO D]. This example shows how burning an inch increases accuracy; the bottom measurement is ¹/₆₄ inch shorter.

GO MECHANICAL

Use a pencil for most marking jobs, but make sure it has a sharp point. Flat carpenter's pencils or standard writing pencils can lead to inaccuracy because their lines get wider as the point wears down. For precise projects try a thin-lead mechanical pencil instead. For an even finer line, use a marking knife. However remember that the knife cut can pose a problem if it's visible in your finished project.

STEEL AWAY

Finally equip your shop with steel rules and squares that have engraved measurement lines. They'll be more accurate than tools with painted-on lines. The increments on your various marking tools should match one another exactly so you can switch tools without losing accuracy. Compare them to make sure.

TRY A LEFT/RIGHT TAPE

When you hold the tape in your left hand so you can mark with your right hand, the numbers on most tapes read upside down. That can lead to confusion, especially for unmarked fractions. Rather than trying to figure out which mark is ⅜ and which is ⅝ for example, buy a left-reading measuring tape or one that reads from both sides, as shown above.

Check and check again

• Double-check measurements before cutting.
• Use the same measuring tape throughout your project, when possible, because minor variations from tape to tape can add up to major headaches. Sometimes, however, you might need specialty tapes, such as for center-finding or left-right reading. You can find these tapes at many woodworking specialty stores or on the Internet.
• Before you make any cut, check and adjust machines and accessories to make sure they are square and set properly.
• Dry-fit your project before glue-up. That way you'll get a chance to find and correct assembly problems without being pressured by drying glue.

MARKING OPTIONS

To mark around a piece, use a knife and square to score along your cutline. Next place the blade in the score at one edge. Slide your square to it and score the second face. Repeat the process from the other end of the first cut, then connect the scores on the bottom of the piece.

Make your mark with an arrow point like the one shown here. When you take the rule away, the tip of the point will mark your measurement. The longer leg denotes the waste side of the cut to be made at this point.

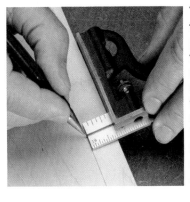

To mark a line parallel to an edge, put the pencil at the spot, then slide the blade of your combination square over to it. Put the grooved side up, so the pencil won't slip into the notch. Hold the pencil against the square as you slide it along the edge.

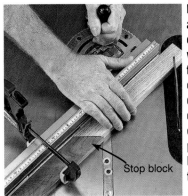

Individually measuring and cutting each one of multiple, matching workpieces (picture-frame sides, for example) leaves slight discrepancies in actual dimensions. Instead of cutting each piece to a pencil mark, use a stop block clamped to a fence or miter gauge.

Stop block

To draw a line after measuring, hold the pencil point on the tip of the arrow, then slide your square or rule until it contacts the pencil. This method ensures that your line will match the point. Now pull the pencil along the square.

Use a knife that's flat on one side and beveled on the other to define a recessed area, such as a hinge mortise. The line will guide your chisel.

Doweled butt joint

Half-lap joint

PREPARING STOCK

HERE ARE YOUR OPTIONS FOR JOINING, SHAPING, AND CUTTING YOUR CHOSEN MATERIAL. IF YOU PREPARE THE STOCK RIGHT, ASSEMBLY AND FINISHING ARE A BREEZE.

A butt joint, where one piece is cut square and joined to another piece, is the simplest joint to make. It eliminates the need for angle-cuts and adds strength for heavy-duty framing jobs. (For how to make its cousin, the half-lap joint, see page 100.) Adding dowels to a butt joint, as shown here, adds strength and a design element.

Start by cutting the stiles and rails to their finished dimensions. Label the parts, lettering each joint on both pieces. With the end of the stile flush with the rail edge, mark lines across the joint where you want each dowel [PHOTO A].

Secure a stile in a vise. Position the doweling jig to center a dowel hole on one of your marks and drill a hole just longer than half the depth of the dowel pin's length [PHOTO B]. Repeat for other dowel locations.

To extend dowels through the stiles and expose the dowel ends for decoration, remove the jig and use the holes as guides to drill through each stile. Back with a scrap block to prevent tear-out [PHOTO C]. Cut dowels about ½ inch longer than the combined depth of the hole in the rail and the width of the stile.

Allow air and excess glue to escape as you tap in the dowel by using a saw to cut a glue-relief groove to within 1 inch of one end [PHOTO D]. Drip enough glue into the holes to cover the sides by spreading it with a nail or screw and apply glue to the ends to be joined. Then immediately tap the dowels into place through the stile and into the rail, grooved end first [PHOTO E]. After two hours saw the dowels flush with the edges. Cut the dowels with a flush-cutting saw so you won't mar the edges of the stiles.

A

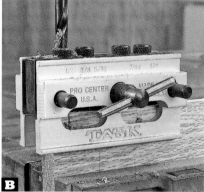

B

Backer block

C

D

E

TOOLS AND TECHNIQUES FOR TIGHT MITER JOINTS

When you make a picture frame or place solid-wood edging around a plywood panel, you want perfect, gap-free miters. Anything less detracts from the whole project. There are several ways to cut 45-degree angles and achieve right-angle miter joints that practically disappear. No single approach satisfies everyone's needs. Because some woodworkers don't have a tablesaw, some workpieces are too long to cut comfortably on a tablesaw, and some jobs call for mitering away from the workshop, there is a wide range of tools to serve every mitering purpose. You can get respectable results from all of them, but occasionally you'll need to do some finetuning by shaving or sanding.

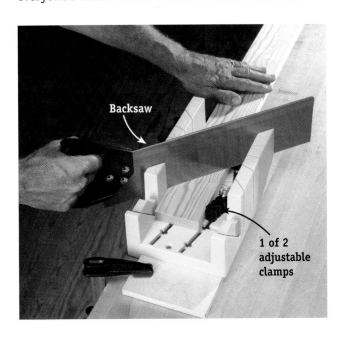

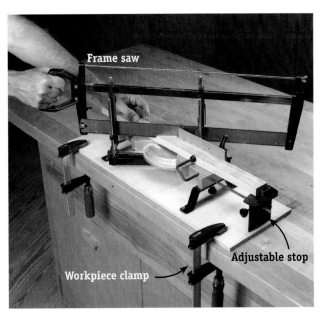

PLASTIC MITER BOX

For about $10 you can buy a plastic miter box and a backsaw. Many of them give acceptable results on narrow molding. However, with the provided saw, which has 11 tpi, cutting a larger workpiece might prove to be slow going. A slight amount of slop in the molded slots can cause miter accuracy to vary from cut to cut. The cut surfaces are usually slightly rough.

PROS:
• Good to poor miter quality.
• Super safe—no chance of injury or kickback.
• Very inexpensive.
• Very portable.
• You can substitute a higher-quality backsaw.

CONS:
• Stock width limited by size of miter box.
• No provision for finetuning the 45-degree settings.
• Clamping workpiece is awkward.
• No provision for workpiece support or stops.
• You're restricted to short saw strokes; the blade easily can slip out of the guide slot.
• Time-consuming.

ADJUSTABLE MITER BOX

You can buy several models of mitersaw boxes that allow the saw to pivot from one 45-degree detent setting to the other. They come with backsaws or frame saws. A frame saw like the one above is priced at about $85. It's easier to use than the plastic miter box, and the saw (24 tpi) cuts slightly smoother. However it provides no way to lock the saw at nondetent settings or to finetune the detent settings. If you decide to buy a similar miter box, consider these points.

PROS:
• Good to fair miter quality.
• Safe to use.
• Reasonably priced.
• Portable.
• Detents at both 45-degree settings.
• Clamp and stop included, but both have limited range.

CONS:
• No provision for finetuning the 45-degree settings.
• Blade can flex enough to affect cut quality.
• Time-consuming.

PREPARING STOCK (CONTINUED)

SHOP-MADE MITER SLED WORKS WITH A TABLESAW

This miter-cutting sled offers a dual-rail guidance system that rides in the miter-gauge slots of your tablesaw and smooth-acting stops that ride in tracks. It also features a safety channel down the middle to keep your hands away from the tablesaw blade.

To build the jig see the drawing for the dimensions. We used Baltic birch for the base and hard maple for the other parts. Refer to the photos below for building tips that guarantee an exact fit on your saw and a pair of perfectly aligned miter fences. Use an 80-tooth crosscut blade for smooth, ready-to-glue surfaces.

To make two workpieces of equal length,

start by measuring and marking your first workpiece. Miter one end of the workpiece as marked, using the appropriate fence, and then transfer the workpiece to the opposite fence. Line up the mark with the blade, slide the stop against the already mitered end, tighten it, and make the second cut. Leave the stop in place and miter the second workpiece in the same sequence. To avoid weakening the sled base, remember to stop your cut when the blade's highest point passes through the fence.

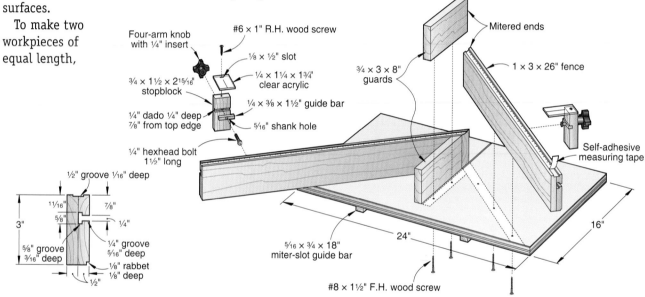

Four-arm knob with 1/4" insert
#6 × 1" R.H. wood screw
1/8 × 1/2" slot
1/4 × 1 1/4 × 1 3/4" clear acrylic
3/4 × 1 1/2 × 2 15/16" stopblock
1/4 × 3/8 × 1 1/2" guide bar
1/4" dado 1/4" deep 7/8" from top edge
5/16" shank hole
1/4" hexhead bolt 1 1/2" long

Mitered ends
3/4 × 3 × 8" guards
1 × 3 × 26" fence
Self-adhesive measuring tape

1/2" groove 1/16" deep
11/16"
3"
5/8"
5/8" groove 3/16" deep
7/8"
1/4"
1/4" groove 5/16" deep
1/8" rabbet 1/8" deep
1/2"

5/16 × 3/4 × 18" miter-slot guide bar
24"
16"
#8 × 1 1/2" F.H. wood screw

Place the sled on your tablesaw and cut a kerf about 6 inches long to serve as a guide for placing the fences.

Next cut a right triangle measuring 21½ inches on its long edge to fit on the miter sled base as shown. Place it flush with the back edge of the sled, centered from side to side, and clamp it to serve as a guide for installing the miter fences. Apply double-faced tape to the bottom of each fence; press them in place. Remove the clamps and triangle and make test cuts in scrap to check your sled's accuracy. When it's dead-on permanently attach the fences with screws.

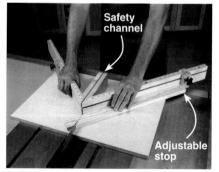

Safety channel
Adjustable stop

To fit the guide bars to your miter sled, place two stacks of two pennies in each miter-gauge slot on your tablesaw to serve as shims. Place a bar in each slot and apply double-faced tape to the top of each bar. Mark the center of the sled base and locate the rip fence to place that mark over the blade. Press the base against the bars, remove the assembly from the saw, and permanently attach the bars with screws.

Fence with rule

Adjustable stop

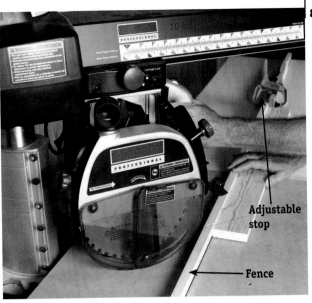

Adjustable stop

Fence

POWER MITERSAWS

Mitering long pieces is easy on a power mitersaw. Make sure the tool is aligned properly. Next make a work support flush with the saw table. Install a sharp mitersaw crosscut blade, preferably one with 60 teeth and a negative hook angle. With the workpiece held or clamped firmly in place, lower the blade through the workpiece slowly.

PROS:
• Excellent to good miters, making fast cuts, even in thick, hard materials.
• Adjustable to any angle, with 45-degree detents.
• Good for long workpieces and repeatable cuts.
• Cuts tiny amounts of material to finetune miters.

CONS:
• Hard to cut long stock without support and fence.
• Throws a lot of hard-to-collect sawdust into the air.
• More blade runout than a well-tuned tablesaw.

RADIAL-ARM SAW

A radial-arm saw requires accurate setup and adequate workpiece support. As with the power mitersaw, the radial-arm saw's main advantage over the tablesaw is its ability to handle long workpieces. Place your workpiece flat on the table and butted against the fence, with the saw head pivoted to 45 degrees.

PROS:
• Excellent to fair miters, making fast cuts, even in thick, hard materials.
• With flush worktable handles long pieces.
• Removes tiny amounts of material to finesse miters.

CONS:
• Takes up a lot of room.
• Limited capacity when cutting 45 degrees to the left because blade is located left of saw-arm center.
• Some tend to move off the 45-degree setting.

Trim for a perfect fit

It's likely that you'll need to trim one or more miters to make a perfect frame. Check each 45-degree cut as you work, as shown in the photo at right. When you fit all of the miters together, check each joint for inaccuracies like those shown in the drawings below. Problems result when one or more miters vary from 45 degrees, when a workpiece is slightly longer than its mate, or when the cut isn't square to the workpiece face.

TO FIX THESE GAPS

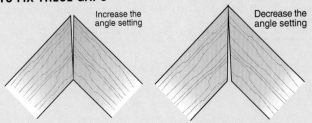

Increase the angle setting

Decrease the angle setting

A combination square such as this one quickly shows you whether your miters are a true 45 degrees. You still might have to trim those cuts slightly to produce a frame with four tight miter joints. That's because the workpiece might vary slightly in length, or your miter cuts might not be 90 degrees to the workpiece face.

PREPARING STOCK *(CONTINUED)*

FACE-KEYED MITER

To make key stock that works with the 2-inch-wide frame parts shown, resaw a piece of ¾-inch stock that's 4½ inches wide by about 8 inches long to make two 2-inch-wide pieces of key stock. The blank can be a single piece of wood or an edge-glued combination of woods. Raise your tablesaw blade to 2 inches and set the fence to cut the stock at a distance from the face of the blank to leave the stock slightly thicker than your blade kerf. Flip the piece end for end and cut a second slot, as shown **[PHOTO A],** leaving a ½-inch bridge in the middle to connect the key stock to the blank. Then, by hand, cut the key stock free.

Next set your tablesaw blade height to 2 inches for corners on 2-inch-wide stock. Make test cuts in scrap miters. Secure the mitered frame in the jig (see inset, **[PHOTO B]**), and set the fence so that the blade will cut a kerf-deep rabbet into the workpiece corner. By cutting the rabbet on the frame face pressed tight against the jig, you'll minimize tear-out. For keys on both sides of the frame, rotate the workpiece and make a second cut.

Glue and clamp the key stock to the corners on the front, back, or both faces of the frame, as shown **[PHOTO B].**

Use a bandsaw or backsaw to cut the excess key stock from the edges of the frame, as shown **[PHOTO C].** Flush-sand the edges and faces of the keys with the edges and faces of the frame.

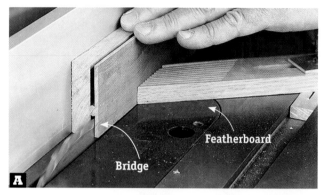

A Bridge Featherboard

B

C

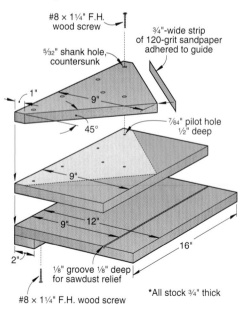

#8 × 1¼" F.H. wood screw

¾"-wide strip of 120-grit sandpaper adhered to guide

5/32" shank hole, countersunk

1"

9"

45°

7/64" pilot hole ½" deep

9"

9"   12"

16"

2"

⅛" groove ⅛" deep for sawdust relief

#8 × 1¼" F.H. wood screw

*All stock ¾" thick

Adding a decorative touch

To add plugs to your keys, first mark the locations of the plugs on the keys. The ⅜-inch plugs shown were set ½ inch from the long edge of the key, spaced 1 inch apart and equal distances from the shorter edges of the keys. The plugs extend through the key and into the frame without emerging through the face on the other side. Orient the grain of the plugs with that of the keys to allow for wood movement. Glue and seat the plugs, leaving about ⅛ inch above the surface. Remove the excess with a flush-cutting saw. Sand the plugs flush with the frame's face.

MAKING A SCARF JOINT

A scarf joint is an inconspicuous way to join two long pieces of trim end-to-end. For example when adding baseboard and base shoe to a wall longer than 16 feet (the longest molding length available), you can use a scarf joint, which will be almost invisible.

A good scarf joint depends on your ability to cut a perfectly straight miter. This is easy to do if you have a power compound mitersaw; you simply tilt the blade to 45 degrees, lay the molding flat, and make the cut. With a power mitersaw that doesn't tilt (shown), you'll have to clamp the stock against the fence to hold it exactly upright as you make the cut.

After cutting always fasten one scarf-cut piece in place before measuring for the second. Drill pilot holes before fastening with 4d and 6d finishing nails.

1. Cut the scarf
Unless you have a compound mitersaw, you'll have to cut the molding upright. Clamp it firmly, making sure that it rests on the saw table and is perfectly upright. Add a scrap behind it to avoid splintering.

2. Fasten first piece
To accurately measure for the second half of the scarf joint, fasten the first piece you cut in place, using 4d and 6d nails, one of each every 16 inches.

3. Caulk or glue
If you plan to paint the molding, add caulk before making the joint. If you plan to stain the molding (always worth doing before you install it), do not caulk or glue the joint.

4. Stagger overlapping molding
Be sure that scarf joints on overlapping moldings (in this case, base shoe) are at least 16 inches from each other.

PREPARING STOCK *(CONTINUED)*

CUTTING A COPED JOINT

Push a framing square into any corner in any room to see how true a 90-degree angle it is. Chances are good that you will see daylight on one side of the square.

Don't fault the builder. Framing members are far from perfect and even the best drywall finisher will not tape perfectly square corners. However just a slight variance from a true 90 degrees can play havoc with a miter joint. That's why coped joints were invented. And they work like magic.

Coped joints operate on the principle that if the profile of one piece of molding is severely backcut when it abuts a matching piece, the joint will be close to perfect. A little trimming is usually necessary.

Do not cut the molding to length before cutting a coped joint; leave excess in case you have to make a second (or third) attempt at the joint. Cut a square end on the first piece of the molding into the corner.

In the example shown below, a pull saw is used to cut the straight portion of the joint. This might not be necessary with lower-profile pieces of trim. Remember when sawing to cut at an inward angle so you will have only a thin edge to trim for a tight fit.

Drill pilot holes and fasten with two 4d or 6d finishing nails every 16 inches. Set the nails with a nail set and putty the holes.

1. Backcut miter in baseboard
Once you have mitered the baseboard as shown, use a pull saw (shown), a fine-tooth handsaw, or a backsaw to cut the straight portion.

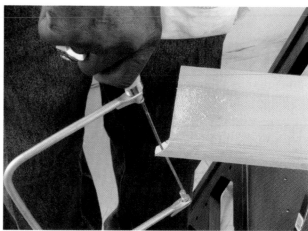

2. Cope the complex area
Firmly clamp the trim to a work surface and cut any ornate areas with a coping saw. Cut at an angle so only a thin edge will make contact at the joint.

3. Clean up cope
Use a utility knife to pare any areas too thin to saw. Test-fit the joint against a scrap. You might need to use sandpaper wound around a dowel to clean your cut.

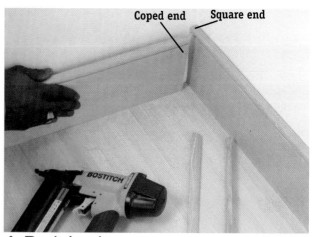

4. Push in place
Once satisfied with the joint, fasten the piece in place. Cut a longer piece to length plus ⅛ inch and bow it so it will spring tightly into place. Cut base shoe in the same manner.

USING A DOWELING JIG

Dowel pins add mechanical strength and glue surface area to almost any joint and aid in aligning parts during assembly. Dowel joinery is unforgiving though: If dowel holes don't line up or aren't perfectly perpendicular to the surface of the workpieces, the joint won't go together. A good doweling jig—coupled with a sharp brad-point bit—helps you bore precisely mating holes, minimizing both your frustration and the need to sand or plane to a seamless joint.

Each doweling jig works slightly differently (the box at right shows some variations). Look at several kinds to find one you can use easily. Practice on scrap wood, following the manufacturer's instructions, before proceeding to your project.

With any jig you must carefully mark for the dowel location before clamping the jig in place. You'll then need to drill holes for the dowels, being careful to hold the drill bit as close to perpendicular to your work as possible. (See page 86 for more on doweling.)

Take care adding glue to the drill holes. Drip enough glue into the holes to cover the sides by spreading it with a nail or screw (above) and apply glue to the ends to be joined. Then immediately tap the dowels into place through the stile and into the rail, grooved end first.

For a decorative variation on standard doweling, add a spline to the dowel tip. Cut each dowel ¼ inch longer than the holes in both pieces and add glue-relief grooves. Bandsaw a notch ½ inch deep into the top end. Next saw a spline blank of contrasting wood and sand it to fit within the notch to form a slight wedge (below). Glue the wedge in place and trim off the excess. Then glue and drive the dowels with the splines running parallel with each other and parallel or perpendicular to the grain. Allow two hours for the glue to dry, then flush-cut the splined dowels.

Doweling jig alternatives

A basic jig centers holes in ¾-inch stock, making it great for face-frame work, but for thinner and thicker (up to 1¼ inches) stock, you'll have to make shims or leave the holes off-center. The jig can also make edge-to-face or end-to-face joints in the middle of a board, as when doweling shelves into a bookcase or shadow box.

Micrometer-style dials

Indexing pin

This jig references off one face, so any difference in workpiece thickness won't show up on the good face of the joint. You can offset a workpiece up to ¼ inch by rotating the micrometer-style dials. And the brass indexing pin allows you to step-and-repeat your way down a long board.

Distance gauge

A finely built, professional-quality jig like this one is more accurate than a biscuit joiner and at least as versatile. The spacing of the five ⅜-inch drill guides and the ends of the jig are so precise you can reverse the jig and the joints still fit tightly.

PREPARING STOCK *(CONTINUED)*

BISCUIT JOINTS

The biscuit joiner, or plate joiner, does two things, and it does them in a hurry. It helps you align the parts and strengthens the joint.

With its fence in the vertical position, a biscuit joiner can cut in the middle of a large workpiece. With the fence extended at a right angle, you can set it to cut slots that match exactly from one board to the next. Or you can set the fence at other angles for mitering tasks.

A 4-inch circular blade cuts a half-oval slot when you switch on the power and push the tool body forward into your workpiece. Cut an identical slot on a mating piece, and you've created a football-shaped opening to hold a biscuit made of compressed beech. Biscuits come in several sizes; you set the tool to match the size biscuit you've selected.

The major drawback of biscuit joiners is that many of them can't use a biscuit shorter than $1\frac{7}{16}$", which means that your workpiece must be more than 2" wide. That's a problem when it comes to face frames. However you can buy full-size biscuit joiners that work with $1\frac{1}{2}$"-wide stock or smaller "detail" biscuit joiners that install biscuits as short as $\frac{5}{8}$".

A good biscuit joiner plunges smoothly into the workpiece, has plenty of power to make the cut, and blows the chips and dust into an attached cloth bag. Its blade cuts a slot that's precisely the right size for the biscuits. Its fence adjusts quickly and accurately.

FACE FRAMES

A mortise-and-tenon joint might offer more strength when it comes to face frames, but biscuits supply all the holding power you need for most projects. Unfortunately the small work surface can cause problems when you cut a slot near the end of a stile or in the end grain of a rail. Your biscuit joiner must sit flat and remain in position to cut neat slots. Clamp a block against the workpiece to hold it in place **[PHOTO A]** and clamp the joiner's fence directly onto the rail and the workbench underneath. This way the workpiece stays put and so does the tool.

EDGE JOINTS

Many woodworkers start right here with their biscuit joiners: edge-joining boards to make a wider workpiece **[PHOTO B]**. Just place the two boards together, making sure you have flat edges and a good grain match. Then draw lines across the joint to mark the locations for biscuit slots. They don't have to be

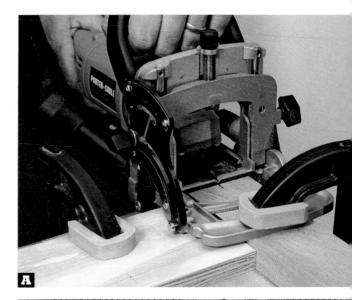

A

B

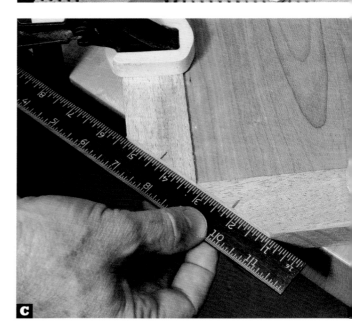

C

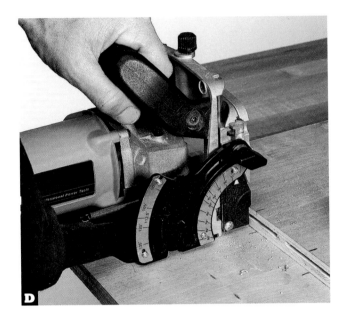

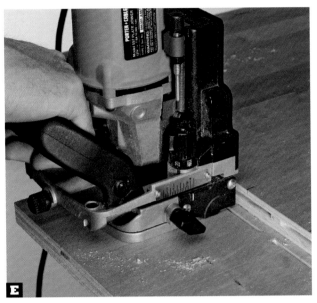

evenly spaced or drawn with great precision. Keep the biscuits back from the ends if you plan to trim the glued-up piece or put an edge profile on it.

FLAT MITERED JOINTS

For flat mitered joints arrange the two halves as shown [PHOTO C]. A thinner piece of wood or plywood, cut at 90 degrees and placed behind them, helps with alignment. Place your two workpieces against that guide with points touching, clamp them in place, and make a mark in the middle of each mitered surface.

Make sure you've chosen a slot size that will stay within the workpiece. Then go ahead and cut your slots. As you work on one piece, the adjacent piece provides support for the biscuit joiner's fence.

SHELVES AND CABINETS

Biscuits speed the assembly of shelves or plywood cabinet carcasses, especially when you use the simple layout technique shown [PHOTOS D and E]. After deciding the spacing of your shelves, hold one shelf in place and mark its position on the carcass, making your mark against the far side of the shelf. Tilt the shelf away from yourself and lay it on the carcass, keeping its edge right at the pencil mark. Align the two pieces exactly, then clamp them together and to your workbench. Mark the biscuit locations on the exposed side of the shelf. Now cut matching slots in both pieces, using your pencil marks as guides for the horizontal and vertical actions.

Biscuiting a vertical joint

First double-check your tablesaw's 45-degree setting and make sure the fence sits exactly parallel with the blade. Once you have cut the miters as accurately as possible on your saw, hold the two sides of the joint together and make your guide marks on the outside surfaces.

Many biscuit joiners are designed to hold a 45-degree angle between the solid front and the adjustable fence. If your model fits that category, clamp one side of the joint as shown. The inside surface of the joint faces down. Adjust your biscuit joiner to cut the slots near the inside of the joint, not in the middle of the workpiece as usual. Doing this eliminates the risk of cutting clear through the wood. Brace or clamp the fence as shown so it doesn't tip up and cut the slots for the biscuits.

PREPARING STOCK *(CONTINUED)*

DADOES, GROOVES, AND RABBETS

Most experienced woodworkers turn first to the tablesaw for cutting dadoes, grooves, and rabbets. Typically it takes less time to install and adjust a dado set than it does to prep a router. And the tablesaw quickly cuts channels and can handle most sizes of boards or panels.

You have two options in dado sets: stacked or adjustable. The stacked sets—which we prefer—reliably deliver a square, clean cut. Of course higher-priced sets typically produce the cleanest cuts with flat bottoms and square, no-tear-out shoulders. Most stacked dado sets, however, leave tiny, triangular "earmarks" in the bottom corners, caused by the beveled teeth of the outer blades.

Adjustable dado blades (sometimes called "wobble" blades) tempt you with low prices and quick setup. But these sets come with serious drawbacks: They create concave or ridged bottoms and unsquare corners that need considerable cleanup.

You also can make all three cuts with a good-quality 40- or 50-tooth combination blade. For dadoes and grooves cut both shoulders first, then nibble away the remaining waste. Clean up the rough bottom with a sharp chisel or a router cleanout bit.

You can cut rabbets the same way, but we prefer the following two-cut method. First make the shoulder cut; then using a tall auxiliary fence (5"–8", depending on workpiece height), adjust

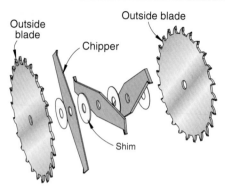

Outside blade

Outside blade

Chipper

Shim

the blade height and cut the bottom perpendicular to the shoulder. To avoid kickback be certain the waste side is not trapped between the fence and the blade.

ENSURE ACCURACY AND SQUARENESS

by making sure your tablesaw is set up correctly. The miter slots and rip fence must be perfectly parallel to the blade; the miter gauge must be set perpendicular to the blade. Even the slightest deviation will affect the fit and finish of the joint.

For dadoes and grooves cut a test scrap piece to check for fit. Adjust the fit by adding or removing shims and chippers. We like to cut dadoes and grooves slightly undersize (within a few hundredths of an inch); then sand the inserted workpiece until it fits snugly.

STACKED DADO SETS contain two outside blades, several chippers, and metal or plastic shims. (If your set does not include shims, make your own

PICKING THE RIGHT TOOL

TOOL	PERFORMANCE RESULTS		COST	OTHER USES
Stacked dado set	Pros: Cleanest cut of saw blades; can be shimmed to exacting widths.	Cons: Leaves triangular grooves in bottom corners; needs backer board to avoid tear-out across grain.	$80–$250.	Cutting tenons, box joints, half laps, shiplaps, and tongue-and-groove joints.
Adjustable dado blade	Pros: Quick and easy to adjust width; inexpensive.	Cons: Uneven bottoms; needs backer board to prevent tear-out across grain.	$50–$80.	Cutting tenons, half laps, and shiplaps, but quality suffers.
40- or 50-tooth combination blade	Pros: No need to purchase or install dado set; creates clean rabbets when machining in perpendicular cuts.	Cons: Repeated passes could create inaccurate widths; saw marks need to be cleaned up; time-consuming; needs backer board to prevent tear-out across grain.	$10–$80.	Ripping and crosscutting in regular use of tablesaw.
Straight router bit	Pros: Clean cuts with square shoulders; accurate when bit size matches channel size.	Cons: Deep cuts require time-consuming multiple passes; needs backer board to avoid tear-out across grain.	$5–$20 for a single bit; $30–$100 for a set of 6–9 bits.	Mortising, plunge cuts, template routing, and flattening rough stock.
Rabbeting router bit	Pros: Machines clean rabbets, in router table or handheld router; quicker setup than straight router bit.	Cons: Deep cuts require time-consuming multiple passes; needs backer board to avoid tear-out across grain; lifts veneer on sheet goods.	$10–$40 for a single bit; $20–$60 for multi-bearing sets.	No other uses recommended.

These ¾" dadoes were cut in red oak with a scrap board to back up the cut (left) and then without (right). The backer board eliminates tear-out.

from paper or cardstock.) Determine the width of your channel; then add the requisite number of chippers between the outer blades (see illustration, opposite) on the arbor and tighten. If the arbor washer won't fit, leave it off. It's more important to get the arbor nut tightened to full threads.

RESHARPEN A STACKED DADO SET

The carbide teeth of stacked dado sets dull over time and need resharpening. When having a set sharpened, always include each blade and chipper—even those you've never used—so that the teeth remain identical in height. If the teeth don't match exactly, some chippers will cut deeper than the rest.

DEFEAT END-GRAIN TEAR-OUT WITH BACKER BOARDS

Machining cross-grained joints on a tablesaw results in tear-out when the blade exits the wood, as shown below, unless you take some precautions. Install a wood extension to the miter gauge to back up the cut or hold a backup piece between the workpiece and miter gauge.

Use a rip fence as a stop

For dadoes and end-grain rabbets, use the rip fence and a wood extension (right) on the miter gauge in conjunction with each other. Because you're not cutting entirely through the board, it will not pinch and kick back.

Add an auxiliary fence (below) for rabbets to keep the blades from touching the rip fence. For a quick auxiliary fence, mount it to the rip fence with double-faced tape. Set up the dado stack wider than your intended rabbet. Cut an opening for the blade in the auxiliary fence. Adjust the fence to the desired width of the rabbet and cut the workpiece.

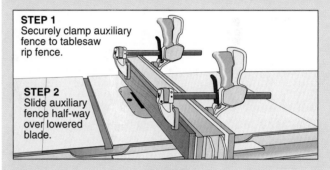

STEP 1
Securely clamp auxiliary fence to tablesaw rip fence.

STEP 2
Slide auxiliary fence half-way over lowered blade.

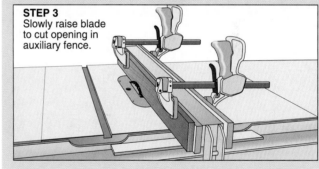

STEP 3
Slowly raise blade to cut opening in auxiliary fence.

Tape prevents chip-out

When making cuts in veneered sheet goods, chip-out always looms as a possibility. To keep a veneer face from chipping, apply painter's tape over the cutline—and at the opposite end to maintain a level surface when machining. Make a shallow scoring pass first; then with the tape still on, raise the blade and finish with a cut to final depth. Slow your feed rate accordingly when removing a large amount of material.

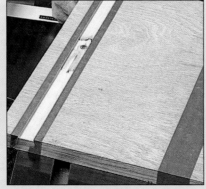

Score ¹⁄₁₆" deep to cleanly shear the veneer, then cut the channel to depth.

Gently peel off the tape to avoid lifting wood fibers. Note the flawless edge.

PREPARING STOCK *(CONTINUED)*

USE STRAIGHTEDGE GUIDES WHEN ROUTING BY HAND

For joints that will be seen on the finished project, you can't beat a router, because it cuts square, clean, flat-bottomed dadoes, grooves, and rabbets. Whether using your router by hand or in a router table, you'll get great results either way. And routers excel at machining stopped channels (those that do not exit the workpiece on one or both ends of the channel). With a router you can see the start and stop marks as well as the bit. On a tablesaw, however, the blade is hidden beneath the board, making it more challenging to start and stop precisely at a mark.

ROUT GREAT RABBETS BY HAND OR ON A ROUTER TABLE

You can use rabbeting, straight, or spiral bits to machine perfect rabbets. Purchase rabbeting bits individually or in a set with multiple bearing sizes (see box, right) to achieve different widths. When routing a rabbet by hand, move the router counterclockwise around the outside edges of a workpiece. Keep one handle over the workpiece to maintain a level cut. To avoid tear-out when approaching a corner on end grain, use a backer board or stop an inch short and rout it carefully from the corner backwards (known as climb-cutting).

RELY ON STRAIGHTEDGE GUIDES

Channels located too far from the workpiece edge for your router table fence call for handheld routing. You've got three good options at this point: Run the router base along a straightedge, use a bearing-guided

Cut varied sizes with a set
This set cuts rabbets to different widths with one bit. Smaller bearings produce wide rabbets, and larger bearings produce shallow ones.

pattern bit and straightedge, or use a router-mounted fence.

For the first option chuck a straight or upcut spiral bit into the router and set the depth. Measure the distance from the router base edge to the nearest point of the cutter. Clamp your straightedge that exact distance from the marked channel and align it. Run your router against the straightedge to machine the channel, as shown opposite, upper right.

Pattern bits—option two—save you the hassle of setting the straightedge-to-cutter distance because they have a bearing on the shaft above the cutterhead

---

How to clean the "hairs" off rabbeted veneer
When routing in sheet goods, rabbeting bits fray end-grain veneer rather than shear it cleanly. To handle this first rout the rabbet to the correct width and depth. Then using a square-edged sanding block, sand with the grain, toward the rabbet, to knock down the frayed grain.

If any fibers bend into the rabbet, simply use your sanding block to sand the vertical face of the cut. Take care to not round the edge.

Sand with the grain

---

that rides against the straightedge. This means you clamp the guide right at your cutline, as shown middle at right.

When your workpiece's dimensions prove too cumbersome for the router table, use a router-mounted fence to help you create a channel that parallels the workpiece edge—up to the maximum reach of the fence, typically 8 inches. Use straight bits or upcut spiral bits for best results.

DADO-CLEANOUT BITS REMOVE TABLESAW IMPERFECTIONS

Dado-cleanout bits shave imperfections from the bottom of a flawed cut to leave a perfectly flat, square joint. (See Resources, page 236.)

First machine your cut to width on the tablesaw, but leave the blade height about $\frac{1}{16}$" short of the final depth. Cut all your channels. Chuck the dado-cleanout bit into your handheld router and set it to machine to the finished depth. Run the router bit through the channel, with the bearing riding against one shoulder and then the other (bottom right). Don't confuse these bits with similar-looking mortising bits, which have taller cutters ($\frac{3}{8}$"–$\frac{1}{2}$" tall). This puts the bearing above the shoulders of a $\frac{3}{8}$"-deep channel, requiring a guide board or straightedge.

ALLOW FOR SHEET-GOOD VARIATION

Sheet goods, such as plywood or medium-density fiberboard (MDF), almost always come up short of their stated thickness. For example a sheet of $\frac{3}{4}$" plywood typically measures only $\frac{23}{32}$" thick. If you plan to cut dadoes, grooves, or rabbets in sheet goods, measure everything first. Thicknesses can vary even in sheets from the same stack. Make a test cut and check the fit. Use specially sized plywood router bits that come in cutting diameters such as $\frac{15}{64}$", $\frac{9}{32}$", $\frac{15}{32}$", $\frac{17}{32}$", $\frac{23}{32}$", and $\frac{25}{32}$". Or to get truly dead-on results, use straight or spiral bits narrower than the thickness of the plywood and make two cutting passes with shop-made or manufactured jigs.

If you prefer to use your tablesaw with a stacked dado set, here's a helpful trick. First label all your shims (such as A, B, C, etc.), using a permanent marker. Now set up your saw with the appropriate blades, chippers, and shims to get a precise cut. When you remove the stack, make a note indicating which chippers and shims you used. The next time you need to cut a joint for that size sheet, just put together the same combination. Still, test your cut first.

Don't spin the router
For a straight and consistent channel, maintain the same point of contact between your router base and straightedge.

Pattern bits cut to the line
Because the cutter aligns with the bearing, you clamp the guide right on the line of the joint, eliminating offset measurements.

Trimming back those ears
Dado-cleanout bits pare away the final $\frac{1}{16}$" of channel depth to bring the joint to its final, flawless state.

HALF-LAP JOINT

Half-lap joints (right) offer a powerful face-to-face glue bond that usually outlasts the surrounding wood under stress. They can be made by setting a tablesaw blade or dado blade to half the thickness of the workpiece and then making repeated passes to cut the lap, but the results can be ragged. A router table with a 1" straight bit will give you consistently clean, flat joint faces.

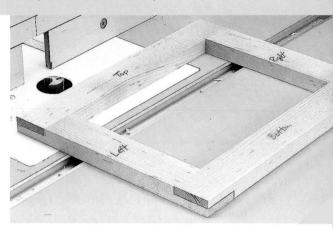

ROUT HALF-LAP JOINTS

Dimension the stiles and rails to a uniform thickness and width before cutting them to length. Save the cutoffs to test your router bit settings later. Then chuck a straight bit into your router and set its height to half the thickness of your frame pieces. Make test cuts and adjust the bit height until the faces of the two cutoffs are flush with each other **[PHOTO A]**.

Rout several shallow passes on your workpieces. To do this, repeatedly step back your router table fence until the length of the half lap comes to within ¼" of the mating workpiece width **[PHOTO B]**. Before routing the final pass, place and offset the mating workpieces along the fence to set the exact fence distance from the edge of the bit **[PHOTO C]**. Then

make your final passes on both ends of each piece **[PHOTO D]**, using a backer block to eliminate tear-out.

Dry-assemble the frame pieces on a flat surface (above) to check for a tight fit. If you plan to rabbet the back for art and glass or a mirror, start by routing rabbets no deeper than half the thickness of your workpieces along the entire length of the rails. Make at least two passes to reduce tear-out. Then dry-assemble the pieces and use the rabbets to mark the stops for rabbeting the stiles. Make the stopped rabbets and square the rounded corners using a chisel.

Next glue and clamp the pieces. Half laps help pieces square with each other, but check all four corners of your glue-up with a square to ensure 90° corners.

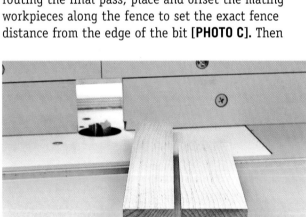

A

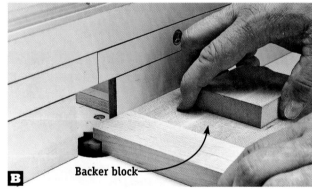

Backer block

B

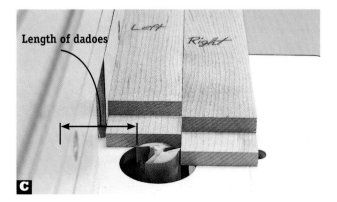

Length of dadoes

C

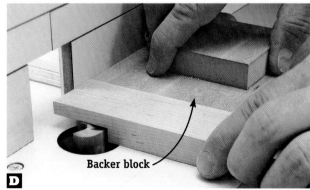

Backer block

D

MORTISE-AND-TENON

Although it takes time to master, this joint is less difficult to make than it looks. The saving grace is that you have plenty of opportunity for finetuning as you make the joint. The key is to always cut the mortise first and then size the tenon to fit snugly. It's quicker and easier to adjust the dimensions of a tenon (as we'll show later) than to change a mortise.

Establish the mortise width at one-third of the workpiece thickness. This ratio results in a joint with plenty of strength in both the tenon and the sidewalls. Most woodworking projects call for 4/4 stock, which measures approximately ¾" thick after surfacing and sanding, so a ¼"-wide mortise works well for most of your projects.

Avoid mortising less than ⅜" from the end of a workpiece. This prevents splitting as you shape the mortise and assemble the joint. For strength make the mortise depth approximately one-half to two-thirds the width of the workpiece.

CUTTING THE MORTISE

If you have a drill press and chisels, you're ready to mortise. Equip your drill press with a brad-point bit that matches the mortise width; a brad-point bit wanders less than a standard twist bit as you drill overlapping holes to form a mortise.

Now use a sharp pencil or marking knife and a combination square to lay out the mortise opening. Then set the drill-press fence to center the bit between the mortise sides and adjust the depth stop. Finally follow the two-step process shown in the photos below.

ANATOMY OF A BLIND MORTISE-AND-TENON JOINT

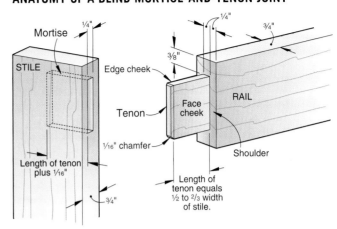

PREPARE THE TENON

After you finish the mortises, use your scrap test pieces to set up for forming tenons. The ideal tenon slides into its mating mortise with firm hand pressure. Center the tenon on the edge of the workpiece (between faces) and make it ¹⁄₁₆" shorter than the mortise depth; this hidden gap provides a place for excess glue and guarantees that the tenon won't bottom out in the mortise, spoiling the fit of the joint.

What's the best way to cut the tenons? Match your equipment to one of the following operations. If you have it all—dado set, tablesaw, and bandsaw—experiment to discover which method you prefer.

This method for cutting tenons is quick and simple, as well as reliable. To assure a square, tight-fitting tenon, align your tablesaw rip fence parallel with the

1 Adjust the fence to center your drill bit in the layout lines. Hold the workpiece against the fence and form the mortise by drilling to full depth at each end of the layout. Now drill a series of overlapping holes in between.

2 Clamp the workpiece to your workbench. Place a wide, sharp chisel on the layout line and clean up the mortise walls with hand pressure or by tapping with a mallet. Use a narrow chisel to square the ends.

PREPARING STOCK *(CONTINUED)*

dado set and make sure that your miter-gauge fence sits at right angles to the dado set.

You'll also need to install a miter-gauge auxiliary fence that extends to the rip fence. Make this fence by attaching a 2"-wide strip of straight material to the gauge with screws or double-faced tape. Now follow the step-by-step photos below.

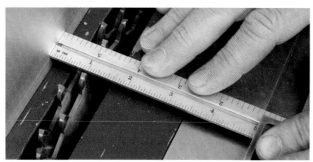

1. Install a dado and set the fence
The distance from the fence to the left side of the dado set equals the tenon length. Adjust the dado set height to establish the thickness of the tenon. For stock surfaced to ¾", set this height at ¼" and make test cuts.

2. Cut the last side of the tenon
Butt the end of the stock against the rip fence for the first pass. Follow with more passes to form the cheek. Then flip the stock over and repeat.

3. Cut the tenon edge
Adjust the dado set height if necessary and cut the tenon edge cheeks. Use the same methods you used to cut the face cheeks.

Oops. It's adjustment time.
Despite your best efforts sometimes you'll need to make a tenon thinner or thicker to achieve a good fit. Don't count on glue alone to fill gaps—that will only weaken the joint.

Fix a tenon that's too thin by gluing on oversize filler pieces as shown in the first photo below. Saw, plane, or sand the tenon to final thickness after the glue dries. For a tenon that's slightly oversize, use a sanding block to remove a modest amount of material. Sandpaper wrapped around a block is likely to ruin the straight line of the shoulder, so use self-adhesive sandpaper on the bottom of the block only for greater precision.

Finally use a sanding block to form a chamfer around the end of each completed tenon. This simple step helps you get the tenon started into its mortise with no fuss at assembly time.

When a tenon proves to be too thin, glue a wood shim on each face cheek to keep the tenon centered. Make the shims thick enough to allow remilling of the tenon.

Grab your sanding block again to shape a ⅟₁₆" chamfer around the tenon end. A chamfered tenon slides more easily into place as you put the joint together.

BOX-JOINT JIG

Sometimes mistakenly referred to as a fingerjoint, the box joint features good looks and great strength. A well-made joint has crisp, interlocking, rectangular fingers that fit snugly together. To achieve this, setup is critical. This jig provides the adjustment capability that you need, regardless of how wide or thick your workpiece. And by merely switching adjustable fences, you can use the basic sled for different size fingers. The overall dimensions of the jig can vary, depending on the length and width of your tablesaw's top or your available scrap. The drawing offers recommended sizes. The size of and the width between the runners depends on the dimensions and spacing of your saw's miter-gauge slots.

1 CUT THE BASE to size from ¼", ½", or ¾" material. Now cut two miter-gauge runners to the height and width of your slots, each at least 14" long. Test the fit in the slots, avoiding any play. Use your saw fence to square the sled base, locating the saw blade at the center of the base. Now, with the runners extending 2" beyond the front edge of the base and with the base resting flat on the saw top, attach the runners.

2 CUT TWO FENCES to size— one a fixed fence, the other an adjustable one. The fences need to be rigid, so use ¾" birch plywood or a comparable material. Drill and cut out the ¼"×1" slots

in the fixed fence where shown. Attach this fence perpendicular to the base, spacing it 2" behind the front edge.

3 ADD A BLADE GUARD to the sled for safety and fixed-fence support. Begin by cutting the parts to size and assembling it as shown **[PHOTO A]**, using glue and screws. Screw the blade guard to the base, making sure it fits snugly against the fixed fence. Then close up the back of the blade guard.

To finish the sled install your dado blade in the saw and set it to the width of the fingers that you intend to cut. Raise the top of the blade ½" above the sled base. Make a single pass to create the initial kerf

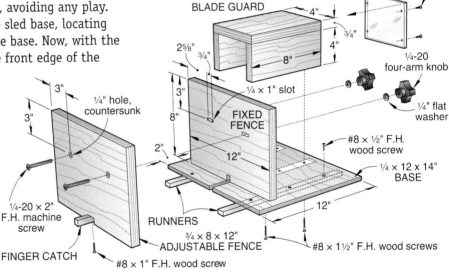

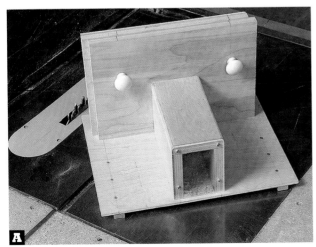

A
An acrylic back to the blade guard is a reminder not to saw through the jig. Four screws hold the piece in place.

B
While making the jig it makes sense to cut several easy-to-add front faces for different-size box-joint fingers. These attach with machine screws, washers, and knobs.

PREPARING STOCK *(CONTINUED)*

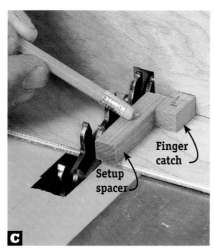

C

To establish the precise location of the finger catch and front fence, place a setup spacer between the saw blade and the catch.

D

With the edge of the piece against the finger catch, cut the first notch. Slip the notch over the catch to cut succeeding notches.

E

Use the notched first workpiece to establish the location of the beginning (open) notch to be cut in the mating workpiece.

in the fixed fence. To avoid cutting through the back of the blade guard, insert and clamp stops into the miter slots to limit sled travel.

Clamp the adjustable fence to the fixed fence, with the bottom edge and ends flush to the sled base. Now make another pass with the dado blade to create an opening equal to the desired finger width. Cut a 4"-long, ½"-thick piece of wood to the exact width of the intended fingers. Now cut it into two pieces: one 1½" long, the other 2½" long. Use the shorter piece for the finger catch on the adjustable fence. The longer piece will be your setup spacer when positioning the adjustable fence on the sled **[PHOTO C]**. Glue and screw the finger catch into the opening on the adjustable fence, flush with the back face.

To position the adjustable fence accurately, first place it against the fixed fence and slide the sled forward until the dado blade is next to the finger catch. Place the setup spacer between the blade and the finger catch. Now clamp the adjustable fence to the fixed fence and drill two ¼" holes through the adjustable fence, centering them in the fixed-fence slots. Finally insert the machine screws through the holes and slots, adding the washers and knobs. Make a cut through the adjustable fence and check it.

CUT SOME BOX-JOINT FINGERS

The length of box-joint fingers equals the thickness of the mating sides. Adjust the dado-blade height accordingly. Err on the side of making fingers too long. That way, once you glue the joint, you easily can sand the ends flush because they stand proud

of the mating sides. Cut the sides and ends of the box ¹⁄₁₆" longer than the plan calls for. Then set the blade height ¹⁄₃₂" higher than the thickness of the boards. After gluing and assembling the joint, sand away the extra finger length.

Now test-mill two scraps of wood of the exact thickness. Place the first workpiece (outside face out) on the jig, with one edge snug against the finger catch and one end resting on the sled base. Hold the workpiece firm and motionless. Make your first pass through the saw **[PHOTO D]**. Slide the sled back from the blade, reposition the workpiece by slipping the notch you just cut over the finger catch, and make the second cut. Continue cutting notches until you have cut out all the fingers.

To cut the corresponding fingers in the mating test workpiece, flip the first board around so that its front face now rests against the adjustable fence, with the first slot you cut fitted over the finger catch. Place the second test workpiece edge to edge against the first and make the first pass through the blade **[PHOTO E]**. Complete the cuts using the step-and-repeat process used earlier until you have cut all the fingers.

Finally fit the mating workpieces together. If the fingers seem tight or fail to interlock, the space between the finger catch and the dado blade is too wide. Loosen the knobs and slide the adjustable fence a hair closer to the blade. Retighten. If you have play between the fingers, move the adjustable fence a hair away from the blade. Repeat the test until you get a snug fit. Now you're ready to glue-up the joint.

DOVETAIL JOINTS

With practice and patience you can master the satisfying skill of hand-cutting dovetails. Start by gathering the essential tools, shown at right. Practice on moderately soft wood, such as poplar, and machine your pieces to equal widths and thicknesses. Temporarily label the part faces ("front inside" or "side inside") and edges ("top") to keep the pieces in order.

1 SET YOUR SIDING BEVEL. Here's a simple way to find the correct angles for the dovetails you'll make. Place a square along the straight edge of a scrap panel and mark a 90° line about 10" long down the center. Mark that line at 6" and 8" from the edge. Now place two marks on the edge, 1" from the line on both sides. Draw lines from your 1" marks to the 6" and 8" marks. Set your sliding bevel to the angle of the shorter triangle for softwoods or the longer triangle for hardwoods. Traditionally dovetail angles are 81° (a 1:6 ratio) for softwoods and 83° (a 1:8 ratio) for hardwoods.

2 MARK YOUR PIN CUTS. Pins always include the pieces closest to a part's edges and are marked at an angle on the ends, while tails have angled marks on their faces. For evenly spaced pins select the number of pins you want between the half-pins on the ends. Divide the space between the half-pins by that number and then mark the centers of the pins at even distances along the end of the board at the edge of the inside face. After deciding what width you want for the pins at their narrowest point, mark the edge of the board. Avoid making the narrow side of the pins ¼" or smaller; you'll need more working space than that between the tails to be cut later.

Using a marking gauge set to ¹⁄₆₄" greater than the thickness of your stock, score a line on both faces and edges of the ends where you'll cut your pins and,

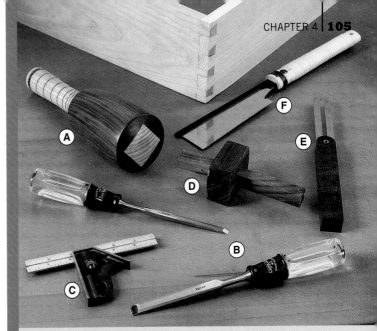

Essential tools
Tools you'll need include a mallet (A), chisels (B), a combination or try square (C), a marking gauge (D), sliding bevel (E), and fine-tooth saw (F). Not shown are a crafts knife or marking knife, a ruler, and pencils.

later, your dovetails. You'll sand both faces flush after the final assembly. With your sliding bevel set, mark your pins on the end of the board with a crafts knife **[PHOTO A]**. Using a square score lines from the edges of the pin lines down to the line you scored earlier **[PHOTO B]**. Shade the scrap areas to be removed.

3 CUT THE PINS. Use a thin-kerf saw, such as the Japanese pull saw **[PHOTO C]**, to cut along the score lines to the scored marking-gauge lines on both sides. Hold your saw at 90° to the end grain and cut slowly to prevent the grain of the wood from drawing the saw blade off course. A small square beside your saw can help you maintain a true 90° angle until experience allows you to visualize it unaided.

4 REMOVE THE WASTE. With a chisel make shallow stop cuts along the scored line

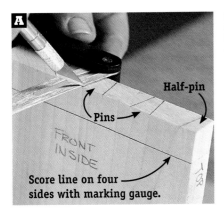

Pins → Half-pin

FRONT INSIDE

Score line on four sides with marking gauge.

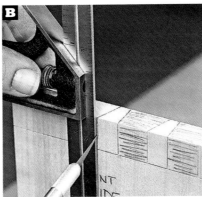

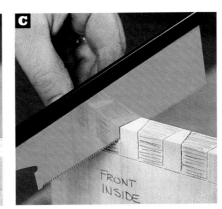

FRONT INSIDE

PREPARING STOCK *(CONTINUED)*

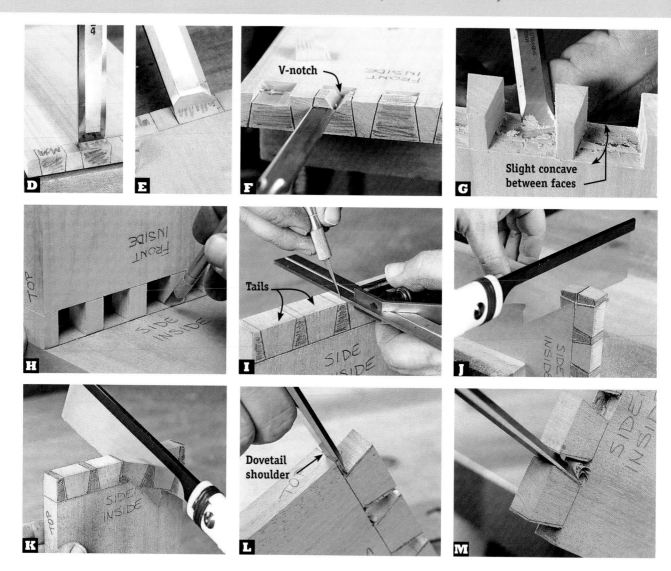

[PHOTO D]. Don't cut too deep into the wood—⅛" is deep enough for the first pass. Carefully remove the waste from the end [PHOTO E] with light taps on the chisel. Work until you're about halfway through the thickness of the board. Creating small V-notches helps the waste pop out as you cut between the wide faces of the pins [PHOTO F]. Repeat this on the other face.

5 **CLEAN BETWEEN THE PINS.** Clean the area between the pins with a chisel [PHOTO G]. To make the joint easier to assemble, create a slight concave in the end grain between the pins below the faces of the board. Your pins are ready; don't alter them after you begin cutting the dovetails.

6 **MARK FOR THE DOVETAILS.** The pins serve as your pattern for laying out the dovetails. Hold the front inside board vertical and place it on the inside face of the end of the other board [PHOTO H]. Line up the wide side of the pins on the score mark of the other board. Mark the dovetails using a knife, then use a square and a knife to mark your 90° saw lines [PHOTO I].

7 **SAW THE DOVETAILS** on the waste side to leave a margin of error for finetuning the joint [PHOTO J].

8 **TRIM SHOULDERS.** Cutting on the waste side [PHOTO K], saw away the shoulders of the dovetails. Then clean up your work with a chisel [PHOTO L], until the shoulders match the scribed line.

9 **CUT BETWEEN THE DOVETAILS.** Cut on the waste side up to your score lines to finetune the joint [PHOTO M]. You can see the danger of making your pins too narrow at their tips: Narrow pins make it hard to work a chisel between the dovetails.

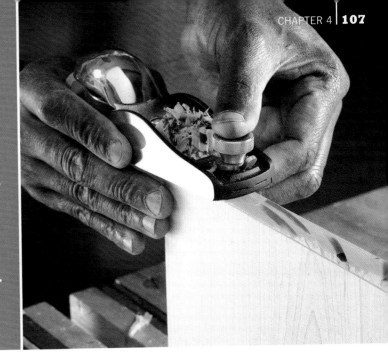

PLANING AND CHAMFERING

TOOLS WITH MOTORS CUT FASTER AND WITH LESS EFFORT THAN MANY HAND TOOLS. BUT THE QUIET AND SIMPLE BLOCK PLANE PERFORMS SOME TASKS BETTER AND FASTER—WITHOUT THE RACKET.

During the past 100 years, the block plane has remained essentially unchanged in form and function. It's a compact and rigid one-handed plane capable of producing whisper-thin wood shavings. Whether you are removing milling marks from the edge of a jointed board, trimming the end of a tenon, or softening the hard edges of a bedpost, the diminutive block plane serves even power-tool devotees well.

PLANING EDGE GRAIN

Think a jointer gives you a perfect gluing surface? Think again. Any rotating cutter, including router bits and a power planer, creates a series of closely spaced scallops, as shown below right. A few quick strokes with a block plane levels those peaks and valleys into a truly smooth surface for gluing.

Wood cuts easier with the grain than across it, so you can cut a little deeper in this situation. If your block plane has an adjustable throat opening, close it so just a sliver of light peeks between it and the blade. Without this limitation the knife tends to "dive" into the grain and then bounce back up, breaking off the shaving and leaving the wood with a rough surface.

SMOOTHING END GRAIN

You won't believe how glass-smooth your cross-grained cuts (such as dovetails, box joints, and tenons) can be until you've sliced them clean with a sharp block plane. Power-tool crosscuts in hardwoods can burn, and softwoods might fuzz. Trying to sand away those imperfections causes even more fuzzing.

To clean up end-grain cuts, secure the workpiece in a vise with the end grain up. It's easy to blow out

Don't try to remove too much wood at once when planing end grain. This translucent walnut shaving is just about perfect.

Before   After

Looking closely at the edge of this power-jointed board (left) reveals a not-so-smooth surface that can weaken a glue joint. A few shallow passes with a sharp block plane removed the scallops and left a noticeably smoother edge (right).

PLANING, CHAMFERING *(CONTINUED)*

the end of the cut as the plane exits the workpiece, so clamp on a scrap wood backing board or slightly chamfer the trailing edge before making your first cut. Cut shallow on end grain; you should be able to peel off a thin shaving like the one shown on page 107. If the plane chatters across the cut, sharpen the blade and/or back out the blade slightly.

CHAMFERING

To soften the sharp edge where two adjoining faces meet on, say, a table leg or bedpost, you might be tempted to reach for your router or a sanding block. By the time you find your chamfering bit (much less install it), you could have knocked off those hard

edges with a block plane with less effort and smoother results than using sandpaper. Not only is a block plane faster, but it also can chamfer in ways power tools cannot, such as creating a tapered or asymmetrical chamfer.

Simply breaking an edge requires no special instructions: Set the plane's cutting depth for a light cut, then make a few passes while holding the plane at about a 45-degree angle to one face of the workpiece. For wide, tapered, or asymmetrical chamfers, draw layout lines, as shown below right, then gradually plane down to the lines. The job is even easier if you are dealing with a workpiece square in cross section and can clamp it in your vise, as shown below left.

When planing end grain attach a piece of scrap wood to prevent blowing out the grain as the blade exits the workpiece. The scrap tears out instead of your project.

Draw layout lines to define the limits of the chamfer on a table leg. As you plane adjust the angle of the tool on the table leg as needed to meet the lines.

Easy planing with a handy bench hook

A bench hook makes it easy to smooth edges. The sole and side of a block plane form a right angle to ensure a square cut. In addition the bench hook holds your work firmly without the use of clamps, allowing you to flip the piece to attach the other edge.

You can quickly put together a bench hook using scrap lumber. Follow the diagram at left; adjust the dimensions according to your needs.

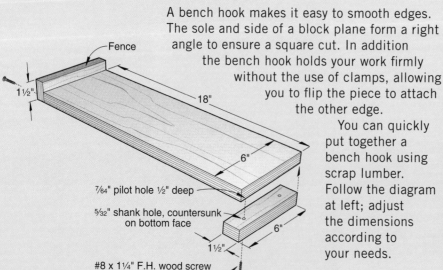

Fence

1½"

18"

6"

7/64" pilot hole ½" deep

5/32" shank hole, countersunk on bottom face

6"

1½"

#8 x 1¼" F.H. wood screw

Bench hook

Fence

RIP-CUTTING SAFELY AND ACCURATELY

ALMOST EVERY PROJECT WILL REQUIRE RIPPING A COMPONENT OR TWO. THERE IS A RIGHT WAY AND A WRONG WAY TO DO THE JOB.

CAUTION !

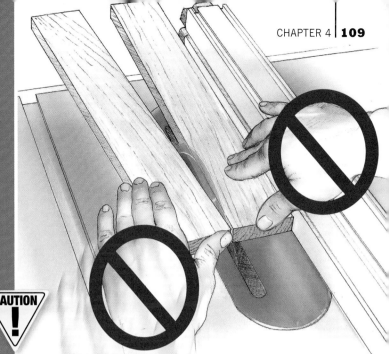

Never get too comfortable with your tablesaw. Taking a chance with a dangerous procedure isn't worth an injury. To keep hands safely away from the saw blade, follow these pointers:

• Use a blade guard. Make sure it's securely in place and working properly.

• After completing a cut shut off the saw. Let the blade stop. Then remove the cutoff.

• Avoid awkward operations and body positions where a slip could direct a hand into the blade.

• Never reach around or over the spinning blade.

• When ripping boards longer than 3', use a support stand at the rear of the saw for safe control of cutoffs.

• Depending on the rip width, use the appropriate method to safely hold and guide the workpiece, as shown on this page.

Note: In the photos the blade guard is removed for clarity only.

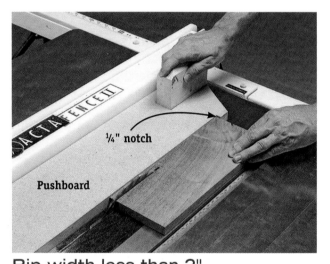

¼" notch

Pushboard

Rip width less than 2"

When the rip width is too narrow for the pushstick to clear the blade guard, use a shop-made pushboard to feed the workpiece.

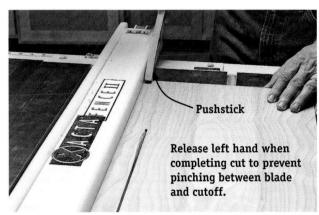

Pushstick

Release left hand when completing cut to prevent pinching between blade and cutoff.

Rip width between 2" and 6"

Feed the workpiece through the blade using a pushstick in your right hand. Use your left hand as a guide.

Rip width greater than 6"

Hold the workpiece tight against the fence and feed it through the blade with your right hand. Use your left hand to guide the piece.

CROSSCUTTING TO A MARK

YOU'LL LIKELY MAKE 100 CROSSCUTS IN THE COURSE OF A PROJECT. HERE'S HOW TO DO EACH SAFELY AND RIGHT.

The fundamentals of cutting perpendicular to the grain—crosscutting—are simple. Make a clear mark on your workpiece. Let the blade get up to speed before pushing the workpiece forward and push slowly enough that the saw maintains its speed. Cut to the waste side of the mark.

The safety issues are straightforward too. Wear eye and ear protection. In addition to their obvious functions, both reduce stress and distraction, the better to keep you on task. If it is the time of day when you usually enjoy a can of beer, wait. Alcohol and power tools don't mix. Finally always keep your hands well away from the blade.

That means using the miter gauge as your primary push tool. By gripping the workpiece and the gauge at the same time, your hands will stay away from the blade. Make a tentative cut on the waste side of your mark, pull back and then slide the workpiece toward the blade and try again until you are cutting exactly to the waste side of the mark. Turn the saw off before clearing away the cutoff.

Most woodworkers equip their tablesaw with a good combination blade that can give a reasonably clean cut whether they are crosscutting or ripping.

If you find that you have to cut several pieces to the same length, attach an extension to your fence and clamp a stop block to it (see photo above).

Tune your tablesaw for accurate crosscuts

Make sure the miter gauge is accurate at 90 degrees and 45 degrees. Rest one edge of a plastic drafting triangle on the blade body—not on the teeth. Loosen the miter gauge knob, slide the head against the triangle, and lock the knob. Do the same at 45 degrees.

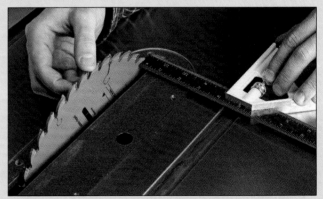

Align the blade for straight, burn-free running. Mark one blade tooth and measure, at the front of the throat opening, from the miter gauge slot. Rotate the blade and measure to the same tooth at the back of the throat opening. If the distances vary reposition either the trunnions or the saw table.

MAKING PROJECT PARTS

ONCE YOUR STOCK IS CUT TO SIZE AND GENERALLY SHAPED AND ANY JOINTS PREPARED, IT IS TIME FOR FINETUNING. HERE'S HOW TO CLEAN UP YOUR COMPONENTS.

CHISELING

Whether the job calls for cleaning up a mortise, crafting a dovetail joint, or just shaving off a dried glue glob, chisels remain the tools to use.

Chisels come in specialized sizes and designs. However unless you need short and small chisels for woodcarving or large framing chisels that are rugged enough to shape massive posts and beams, the type you'll reach for most is a bevel-sided framer chisel, like those pictured below.

BEVEL OPTIONS

You can buy most types and brands of chisels individually or in sets of different widths, usually ¼"–1" wide. For detail work, such as closely spaced dovetails, you'll also want a ⅛"-wide chisel. If you're doing large mortises, a chisel 1¼"–2" wide helps you cut clean, even sides.

Most bevel-edge chisels have 24- to 31-degree cutting bevels. Bevels are angled to suit the type of work the chisel was designed to do.

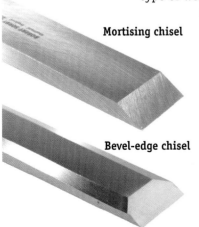

Mortising chisel

Bevel-edge chisel

The 27-degree cutting bevel of a mortising chisel is steeper than the 24-degree bevel of the bevel-edge chisel, to reinforce the cutting edge and keep it from blunting or breaking from mallet blows.

CHOOSING A CHISEL

The best chisel handle is the one you find most comfortable. Try gripping different styles and diameters of chisel handles to get a feel for what best fits your hand while using the chisel either alone or with a mallet. For most jobs there is no durability difference between plastic and wood handles.

Heavy-duty chisels made for big jobs, such as timber framing, traditionally had socket-style handles. That's where the tapered end of the wooden handle fits inside a metal socket on the blade. A metal ferrule keeps the handle from cracking. On a tang-style handle, shown at right, the shaft of the blade extends to the inside of the handle.

KEEP IT SHARP

A dull chisel isn't just frustrating, it's dangerous. So make certain that your chisels are sharp before attempting the practice exercises on the next page.

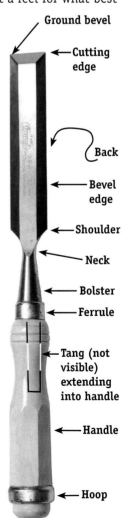

Ground bevel

Cutting edge

Back

Bevel edge

Shoulder

Neck

Bolster

Ferrule

Tang (not visible) extending into handle

Handle

Hoop

MAKING PROJECT PARTS *(CONTINUED)*

CLEAN UP A DADO

If you don't have a dado set for your tablesaw or radial-arm saw, a chisel can clean out waste between multiple saw cuts when finetuning a dado. Begin by making shallow slices with the chisel's bevel side down—this will let you determine the direction of the grain. (The chisel will want to follow the path of the grain.)

1 **CUT IN THE DIRECTION** where the grain pushes the blade upward **[PHOTO A]**. If you feel the chisel being pulled downward into the wood, you're going in the wrong direction. Use a mallet if you need extra cutting power when working with hardwoods, but switch to shallow, two-handed slicing cuts as you near the bottom of the dado. Practice making long slices until you're nearly to the bottom of the saw kerfs, as shown. Work slowly until you get a feel for how the chisel handles with and without a mallet.

2 **FLIP THE CHISEL** over and use the flat back to clean and level the cut **[PHOTO B]**, making it smooth and flush with the bottom of the saw kerfs. Work carefully around the edges to avoid tearing out the wood there.

FLUSH-CUT WOOD PLUGS

Chisels excel at this simple task, leaving a smooth surface that's ready to sand. For practice we glued a handful of plugs into a piece of oak scrap. Wait until the glue dries before you begin practicing. For this exercise use a chisel wider than your plug.

1 **WITH THE CHISEL** held bevel side down, shave a slice of the topmost part of the plug to determine its grain direction **[PHOTO C]**. Again you'll want to cut in the direction where it feels like the grain is pushing the chisel upward instead of pulling it down into the surface of the scrap. If you cut in the other direction, the plug could split off beneath the face of the wood.

2 **WITH THE PLUG SHAVED** to just above the surface, flip the chisel over with the bevel side up and press the chisel back firmly against the face of the scrap. The flat back of the chisel will keep the blade from digging into the wood as you shave away the rest of the plug flush with the surface of the wood face **[PHOTO D]**.

A

B

C

D

PREPARING FOR HINGES

Regardless of the door type or hardware that you choose, a few tools and preparations will simplify the installation job. Begin by working on a solid, dead-flat surface. An irregular work surface can cause the cabinet carcass to rack, making doors hard to fit and mount.

Minor off-square mistakes can escalate into bigger problems. A door that's off-plumb by just 1/32" needs to be planed by that much along the two stile edges, ultimately adding 1/16" to the gap. That doesn't sound like much until you recall that inset doors should have a gap of only 1/16"–3/32".

These shop-made accessories and specialty tools increase your chances for success:
• A precise try square or combination square ensures square glue-ups. Use a precision steel rule and a fine-lead pencil or crafts knife for exact marking.
• A 1⅜" or 35mm Forstner bit to drill flat-bottom holes for European-style hinges (see page 38 for hinge options).
• An assortment of spacers for consistently positioning your hinges on both the door and frame, as shown below.

If you install multiple doors, avoid confusion by marking which are right-hand or left-hand doors and which end you want at the top. In the case of flat-panel doors, also indicate the side that should face out. If you're making several cabinets, label which doors go in each cabinet.

To avoid marring a finished door, temporarily mount your hinges after the doors and cabinet have been sanded to their final thickness but not stained and finished (except for the center panel).

Door spacer (3")

Frame spacer (3 1/16")

Gap between door and frame

Rather than measure for each hinge, tailor some spacers from hardboard. You'll find spacers much faster and more accurate to use. Note that the door hinge spacer is slightly shorter than the frame spacer to allow for the gap between the door and the cabinet frame.

Getting the pilot hole dead-center

Drilling pilot holes in the exact center of a hinge hole or slot is essential for door-mounting accuracy. If you get the pilot hole even slightly off-center, the screw head will pull the hinge off center and turn a neat hinge job into a nightmare. Often the problem isn't your aim; the alternately soft and hard layers in the grain of the stile will force the bit off-kilter.

Here are two alternatives for getting centered.

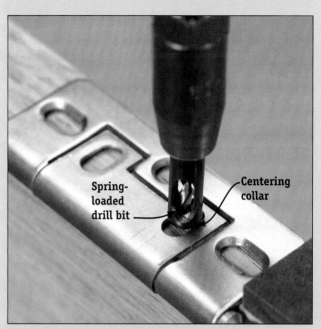

Spring-loaded drill bit

Centering collar

The spring-loaded Vix drill bit above not only finds the center of a slot, it drills a pilot hole to the depth you set.

Spring-loaded point marks pilot hole

The more economical self-centering screw-hole punch requires taping the hinge in place to free both hands for marking the pilot hole.

MAKING PROJECT PARTS *(CONTINUED)*

CUTTING CONTOURS

For cutting smooth, large curves, a bandsaw is by far the best tool to use. With its hundreds of teeth tearing through the workpiece each second, it can effortlessly cut through even hefty stock. However if you aren't lucky enough to have access to a bandsaw, a jigsaw is a handy substitute. It is affordable, portable, and versatile—just what the doctor ordered for finish carpentry.

In fact one woodworker, a surgeon by profession, settled on a jigsaw as his tool of choice to build an entire wooden speedboat. His reasoning? A jigsaw could do cutting he needed but offered the least risk of suddenly taking off a talented digit.

Not that a jigsaw is a slam dunk to use. Always follow these safety rules:
• As with any powered cutting tool, you want to let the motor come up to full speed before pushing it into the wood.
• Do not reach under the workpiece while cutting.
• Don't force the tool; let the blade do the work.
• Use a blade appropriate to the job; thinner blades make tighter curves without binding.
• Allow the blade to come to a complete stop before backing it out of the groove.

Jigsaws can handle most types of molding, but if you take on heavier stock, even 1×, be aware the pressure of rounding a curve while cutting can bend the blade outward, creating a less-than-square cut. For anything larger than 5/4 stock, see if you can find a friend with a bandsaw.

Jigsaws come with a variety of options. Variable speed is well worth the modest additional cost. Also look at how the foot is adjusted—it should be easy to adjust but hold its position once adjusted. Orbital cutting adds some "reach" to the cut as the blade works. Higher settings help cut particleboard and hardwoods.

Cutting a curve
If you are cutting a gentle curve, use a blade with as much width as you can manage—the extra width will force a smoother cut.

Bore access holes
Avoid plunge cuts. When making interior cuts like this cutout for a receptacle, bore a couple of holes big enough to allow the blade to slip in easily.

Smoothing tools
The greater the severity and complexity of the curve you are cutting, the smaller smoothing tool you'll want. A sanding block might suit gentle outside curves, while a rat-tail file might be needed for tight interior curves.

The more teeth, the finer the cut. A thin scroll blade (at left), with 12 teeth per inch, is ideal for tight curves. With a reverse-tooth blade (second from left), any tearing will be on the bottom of the work, not the top.

DRILLING

It happens to the best of us. You position the bit right on your mark, start the drill, and watch the bit dance off to one side before sinking into the wood. Or you drill what should be a nice, perpendicular pilot hole but, when putting in the screw, find that it is decidedly angled. Or perhaps you have drilled what looks to be a pretty neat hole topside, only to find the back splintered. Here's how to tighten up your drilling technique.

To get the hole started right, use an awl, or even a nail, to punch a little hole exactly where you want to drill. When attaching a hinge (where precision *really* counts), use the centering bit or punch shown on page 113. A variable-speed drill allows you to start the hole slowly and keep the bit where you want it. If you are using a large twist drill—say ½" or greater—you might find it difficult to see, much less hold your drill in position as you start to drill. In such cases drill a small pilot hole first.

For a good enough perpendicular hole, drill slowly and occasionally check the alignment of the bit from two angles as you work. With practice you'll drill passable perpendicular holes. Some drills have a level bubble on the heel of the drill that helps you plumb the drill as you work. However for the truest perpendicular hole, there is no substitute for a drill press (if you have access to one). It is also ideal for plug cutters and hole saws.

To avoid splintering always back up your workpiece with a scrap of wood, using one of the techniques described in the box below.

For holes deeper than a couple of inches, get in the habit of backing out the bit to rid the hole of waste and reduce friction. You'll be doing your bits and drill a favor, and you'll wind up with neater bores.

Next to the elimination of the power cord, quick-change drill and screwdriver bits represent the greatest time- and aggravation-saving innovation in drill technology. The downside: With time some quick-change holders tend to give up their grab.

A hole saw is a great way to cut a large, neat round hole, but it can bind unexpectedly. Grip tightly or, better yet, attach an extra handle to your drill as shown.

Preventing tear-outs

If backed by a scrap, your workpiece won't tear out as the drill bit pierces it. Clamp a backup scrap in place or set your workpiece on top of a scrap as you drill down through it.

To drill workpieces with curved surfaces, use scrap created when the piece was cut to shape. The underside of the arch shown was sanded after cutting, but it fits closely enough to prevent tear-out as the bit exits.

Scrap clamped to the inside of this drawer front prevents tear-out on the back surface.

This curved scrap is the perfect shape for backing up a hole being drilled through this curved workpiece.

FASTENING WITH NAILS, BRADS, AND SCREWS

A FINISH CARPENTER HAS MORE OPTIONS THAN EVER FOR PUTTING COMPONENTS TOGETHER.

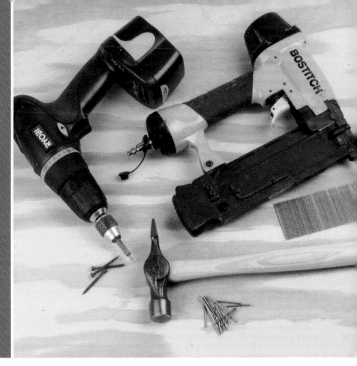

The hammer will always be with us, but the role of the nail as a convenient fastener is more limited than ever. For framing screws make more sense than nails: You can easily remove them if you made a mistake, and when you get things right, you can be sure that the screws will hold like crazy (see opposite page). For molding and other finish work, finish nails involve a tedious three-step process—drilling a pilot hole, pounding, and setting (see photo at right). A pneumatic nailer does it better.

Still, for small jobs, for "persuading" pieces into position, for demolition, and for framing, the hammer will hold a place of honor on our tool belt. Smaller (10- to 16-ounce) finishing hammers are designed for precision. Framing or rip hammers (20 to 28 ounces) will pound home 16d sinkers with ease—especially if you have practiced swinging from the shoulder, not the elbow. To avoid a split drill a pilot hole roughly three-fourths the diameter of the nail shank. And it is always wise to "start" your nails on a flat surface before positioning the workpiece and driving the nails home.

USING A PNEUMATIC NAILER

Ever felt the need for a third hand—one to hold the workpiece, one to hold the nail, and the third to hammer? A pneumatic nailer is just as good; hold the work in place with one hand and shoot the brad (set nicely just beneath the surface) with the nailer. If you've set the nailer up right, the brads will go right in and set themselves. Even if you are only trimming out one room, it is well worth your while to rent a compressor and nailer. Not only will the job go faster and with less stress, the results will be better.

Setting a finish nail
Drive the nail until the head is just above the surface. Use a nail set to drive the nail just beneath the surface. To avoid dings place the tip of the set on the nail and then keep your eye on the head of the set as you pound.

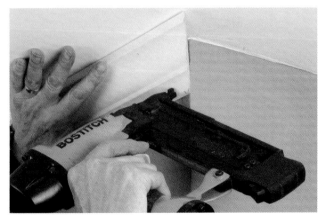

Pneumatic makes it easy
One hand to hold the workpiece, one hand to shoot the pneumatic nailer. With a little practice even a beginner can install trim flawlessly.

(You might even want to buy a compressor and a couple of nailers—they often come in sets. You'll find handy uses for the compressor, from spray painting to topping up your tire pressure. And should you tackle a serious remodeling project, the compressor can be used with framing and roofing nailers as well.)

For finish carpentry you can choose between brads (up to about 1¼" long) and finish nails (up to 2½" long).

The major downside of pneumatic nailers is that the compressor really roars and can surprise you when it kicks on to top up its pressure. Also be aware that brads are rectangular in cross section and can split thin pieces if not oriented right. Make sure the thin side of the brad is parallel to the grain.

FASTENING WITH SCREWS

The beauty of fastening with screws is that if you screw up, so to speak, you can simply back the screw out and try again. If you get it right, rest assured that the screw will hold on tight. Screws are ideal for framing and for any joints in cabinetwork that won't be seen.

Driving screws
Most drills have a setting for driving and a faster setting for drilling. Use your variable speed to drive a screw, starting slowly and speeding up when the bit is engaged in the screw head.

Determine a screw's pilot-hole size by holding a drill bit against it. The appropriate bit will cover the shank but not the threads.

Drill correct-size shank- and pilot holes for screws, according to the chart on page 54, or make a good guess by eyeballing, as shown at left. This proves especially critical near the ends and edges of a workpiece, which split easier than the field. With some softwoods you can get by without drilling holes by using self-tapping screws (which bore their own pilot holes), shown in the box below. But these screws will split many hardwoods, medium-density fiberboard (MDF), and even some softwoods such as cedar and redwood. When in doubt play it safe: You can't go wrong with pilot holes.

The right screw, the right driver

Check the screw's box to determine the right driver bit to use. Most screws require a #2 phillips screwdriver. Other phillips drivers will work for a while but, if too small, will strip the head, or if too large, will hop off the fastener. Some screws need a square-drive bit; still others, a phillips–square drive combo.

All self-tapping screws feature a groove at the tip that bores its own pilot holes.

All square-drive trim screws have a ³⁄₁₆" head—a way to achieve good holding power without a large, unsightly head.

Exterior screws, aka "deck screws," are coated to eliminate rust. They are very strong and ideal for interior and exterior framing.

General-purpose screws are for jigs and for framing interior projects.

GLUING

HERE IS HOW TO NAVIGATE YOUR WAY THROUGH THE OFTEN BAFFLING OPTIONS IN GLUES AND ADHESIVES—AND HOW TO CORRECTLY APPLY THEM.

Glue that's used properly produces joints that are stronger than the wood itself. As a result you'll have great-looking projects that will be sturdy for generations. (To sort through the many glue choices, check the chart on pages 40–41.)

Prevention is a better strategy than repair. Before you reach for the glue, dry-fit each joint first. Apply the glue with care. Otherwise you can have the worst of two worlds: hidden weaknesses that can make

joints fail prematurely plus highly visible surface defects. As you'll see in the following tips, a thin bead of glue squeeze-out along the joint line is good. It indicates that the joint contains sufficient glue and that you've applied even, adequate clamping pressure. How much clamping pressure is enough? Stop as soon as you see squeeze-out along the entire joint line. If you have to bear down on the clamp screws to see squeeze-out, the joint might need to be recut.

Four common gluing mistakes to avoid

1 **Gluing pieces not acclimated to the room temperature and moisture level.** Glues won't set up properly if the boards are at different temperatures. And you'll notice a dimension change (stepped joints) if boards aren't at the same moisture level. So before machining and gluing, allow at least 3 days for all workpieces to adjust.

2 **Overlooking the importance of glue shelf life.**
A manufacturing or expiration date should be printed on the glue container. Contact the manufacturer's customer service department if you can't decipher the code. For Titebond products (see example at right), the first number represents the final digit of the year in which the glue was produced; it's followed by a letter designating the month. ("A" represents January, "B" February, and so forth, skipping "I.") Ignore the rest of the code, which relates to the particular batch of glue.

3 **Poor procedures in removing glue squeeze-out.**
If you don't completely remove glue left on surfaces next to joint lines, your finish will have a splotchy appearance. To avoid problems allow glue to skin over before removing excess. After glue loses its wet look, remove the squeeze-out with a sharp chisel or scraper. Then soak a clean rag in tap water, squeeze out the excess, and wipe down the joint. Follow with a dry rag.

4 **Not waiting for the glue to cure before machining.**
Glue temporarily swells the wood along a glue line
[DRAWING A]. If you joint, plane, or sand too quickly and remove the swelled wood, the joint will look good for only a short time
[DRAWING B]. When completely dry your hastily machined joint will have a valley **[DRAWING C].** To avoid problems let the glue completely cure. (Effect exaggerated for clarity.)

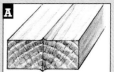
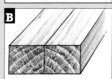

For a strong joint brush a thin, even coat of woodworker's glue onto both mating surfaces. (Polyurethane glue requires only one surface coated with glue and the other dampened with water.) Don't go overboard on clamping pressure—you'll "starve" the joint by driving out most of the glue.

Seal off adjoining joint surfaces from squeeze-out with masking tape. Apply the tape during the dry-fitting, taking care that the tape doesn't get pinched into the joint, ruining its fit. After gluing-up the joint, scoop up any squeeze-out, then peel up the tape to complete the cleanup.

After the glue congeals use a flexible putty knife to scoop it up without smearing it. (You might want to grind the corners round to prevent the tool from digging into the surface.) Then lightly wipe the surface with a damp cloth until no visible glue remains.

When not to glue

Allow for wood movement. Wood shrinks and swells as it adjusts to seasonal changes in humidity, so design and assemble projects with this in mind. Fasten wide tops to cases with hardware, such as that shown below, designed to hold securely but still allow wood movement. Screwing or gluing tops tight to a case likely will result in a split top when the wood moves.

Tabletop fasteners hold the top tightly but still can slide in the saw-kerf groove to allow for wood expansion across the grain.

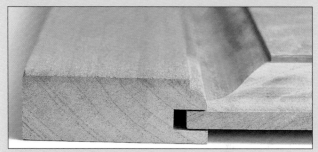

Frame-and-panel assemblies need room for swelling and shrinking. Leave about a ⅛" gap in each groove for unglued panels to expand.

Before staining wipe your project with a cloth dampened with naphtha to reveal any areas where glue still resides. Sand any problem surfaces and repeat the naphtha test. To avoid this problem altogether, try staining adjoining surfaces before gluing them.

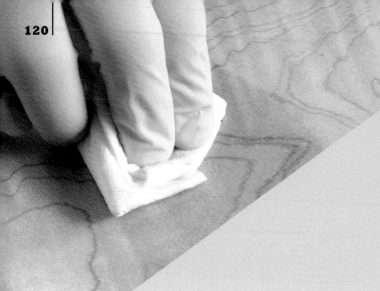

FINISHING

THE HEAVY LIFTING IS DONE. NOW IT IS TIME TO DO YOUR PROJECT JUSTICE WITH A GOOD FINISH.

It's a sad but true tale. The project is done. It has been painstakingly planned and built, attention lavished on every detail. And then finishing is rushed and the project is all but ruined.

Prep, good tools and materials, and a methodical approach will yield a finish that does justice to your project. Here's how to get it done.

SAND IT SMOOTH

Buy good-quality sandpaper, because the inexpensive kind will dull quickly and can load rapidly with sanding dust. Start with 100-grit in most cases, use 150 next, and stop at 220. Sometimes you might want to use even finer paper on end grain, but remember that higher grits can create a burnished surface that won't accept stain properly.

Make simple sanding blocks to smooth flat surfaces. You can sand concave and convex areas, such as molded edges, without a block. However a backing material that matches the desired shape makes the job neater and easier. Dowels, profiles made of rubber, and countless other shapes will work just fine.

Sanding dust must be removed as you sand and between grits. The cleaner you keep your surface, the more effective your sanding will be. Grit and dust that remain on the surface tend to ball up and clog your paper and scratch the surface.

If your electric sander includes a dust-collection bag or vacuum attachment outlet, be sure to use it.

SPOT PROBLEMS EARLY

What you see when you wipe on paint thinner is what you will see with a finish. Here's how to handle three typical defects:

1. Vacuum away the dust
A vacuum with a hose and a brush attachment does a good job of cleaning dust from your project.

2. Paint thinner reveals all
Next with a clean cloth, wipe on paint thinner to reveal any flaws that will be highlighted by the final finish.

1 SCRATCHES. If you see scratches or machine marks from sanding, you might not have sanded adequately with your last grit of paper. Resand. If you still find prominent scratches, go to the next finer grit and sand the wood thoroughly once again.

2 BLOTCHES. Woods that have fine pores, including pine, cherry, birch, and maple, tend to blotch when stained. This uneven coloration is a result of variations in the density of the wood. Anything put on the surface tends to absorb more in the softer areas than in the harder areas of the wood. To avoid blotching apply a commercial conditioner. It will leave a slight amber cast, often unnoticeable if a stain will be applied. For a colorless conditioner or one that will be coated with a water-base finish, use a thin coat of clear shellac. The premixed, canned shellac found at most home centers and hardware stores is too thick for a conditioner, so mix 1 part shellac with 4 to 5 parts denatured alcohol to make the amount you need for your project.

3 GLUE SPOTS. Dried glue will produce an unsightly spot in the finish. Let the glue start to set, then scrape it off with a sharp blade and wipe the wood with a damp rag. If the spots show up after you have applied stain or a top coat, you'll have to scrape or sand to remove them.

CURING GAP PROBLEMS

Despite our best efforts we often have to deal with gaps at joint lines, cracks in the wood, nail holes, and

Make your own filler paste
Mix sanding dust with hide glue, linseed oil, or a bit of your final finish into a thick paste. Force it into the gap with a putty knife. Sand it to aid in drying and to level the surface.

other surface flaws. With the proper techniques you can make those shortcomings disappear.

Whenever possible fill wide gaps and cracks with slivers of the same kind of wood used in your project, as shown below left. Cut and glue in place a matching sliver. After the glue dries use the flat face of a chisel to trim the protruding filler piece flush with the surface of your project. Follow that with light sanding.

Pastelike wood filler will disguise smaller gaps, but it won't take stain like wood. Use a mix of your final finish and sawdust for smaller gaps, as shown above.

Don't use putties and sticks until you've stained and applied a coat of finish and can see exactly what color to match.

PACK THOSE PORES

No matter how thoroughly you sand wood, small pores remain, preventing you from attaining a perfectly smooth base for your finish, especially if you're working with a coarse-grained species, such as oak, walnut, or mahogany. After filling it's much easier to produce a glass-smooth surface.

You can fill the grain with repeated applications of a finish. Sand after each coat has dried. After two or three applications, you should have a smooth surface as a base for a hard, film-forming finish.

Another option is to apply oil- or water-base paste filler to the wood with a small squeegee. Work across the grain and leave just enough to cover the surface. Remove streaks by rubbing across the grain with a rag. Wait two or three days until the filler has dried completely (water-base filler dries more quickly), then sand the surface lightly.

Fill gaps with matching wood
Use a chisel to take a sliver from another piece of matching wood, making it deeper than the gap. Rub the sides of the sliver on sandpaper until it fits the width of the gap perfectly. Force glue into the opening with a knife or a piece of paper, then slip the filler into place.

FINISHING *(CONTINUED)*

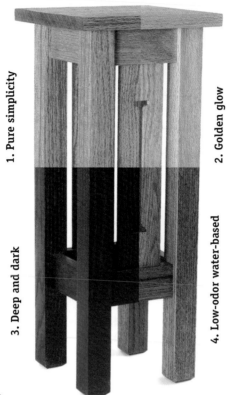

1. Pure simplicity

3. Deep and dark

2. Golden glow

4. Low-odor water-based

STAINS

Attractive finishes don't always have to be difficult. Sometimes you can get the look you want in a couple of simple steps. Here are four easy finishes, each shown on red oak (above). Except where noted these basic finishing rules should be followed:

• Sand all parts to 120 grit before finishing, then vacuum and wipe them free of dust.

• Wait 2 hours between coats of water-base finishes and wait overnight for oil-base finishes before recoating.

• Dyes and water-base stains should dry for 4 hours, and oil-base stains should dry overnight before you apply any top coats.

• Between each top coat, scuff-sand with 320-grit sandpaper.

1. PURE SIMPLICITY

A combination of boiled linseed oil followed by wipe-on polyurethane gives wood pores subtle emphasis and the surface a natural look that protects the wood against moisture and abrasion. Here's how to apply these no-fuss, inexpensive finishes.

• First flood the surface with generous amounts of boiled linseed oil. Reapply oil anywhere it's absorbed by the wood, then wipe the surfaces dry. As oil dries it might bleed from the wood pores and harden on the surface. Wipe away these deposits every hour

until you no longer notice them. Allow the project to sit four to seven days while the oil dries.

• For the top coat mix 2 parts polyurethane with 1 part low-odor mineral spirits and stir. With experience you can alter the mixture ratio to 3 parts polyurethane to 1 part mineral spirits for thicker coats with each application. Use a clean cloth to wipe on this finish. Remove any excess before it runs or puddles. Apply at least three coats.

Compared with brushing on straight or lightly thinned poly, this technique avoids a host of problems with dust nibs and brushstrokes. Take your time. If you rush the first coat of poly before the boiled linseed oil dries, the added mineral spirits will reactivate the oil and cloud the finish.

This finish builds slowly, partly because you'll scuff-sand (and wipe clean) the already-thin coats between applications. Consider applying two additional coats where needed to protect any surfaces likely to be marred or scratched.

With boiled linseed oil lay oil-soaked rags flat on a non-flammable surface to dry before discarding.

2. GOLDEN GLOW

Here's a novel look for accent furnishings, small projects, or part of a larger project. Pearlessence (see Resources, pages 236–237), a translucent finish, adds a subtle gold sheen that also reduces the contrast between oak's pores and the surrounding wood (see photo below).

• Begin by sanding bare wood to 180 grit for a smooth surface. Wipe the surface with mineral spirits to check for flaws that will later be exposed by stains or reflected on a Pearlessence surface. (Although none was applied in this example, any shade of stain or dye can be used.)

• Add the top coat by brushing or spraying both the Pearlessence and any optional clear top coats. As for the number of top coats: Use one coat of Pearlessence for color and shimmer. An optional two coats of semigloss water-base finish adds wear protection.

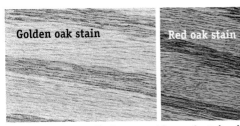

Golden oak stain   Red oak stain

Pearlessence applied over golden oak stain yields a slightly greenish tint; red oak stain turns a coral shade.

Although Pearlessence dries as quickly as other water-base film finishes, it leaves few brush marks.

Stain colors beneath this finish make a big impact on the final color and amount of surface shimmer. Golden oak stain plays up the metallic sheen, while red oak stain mutes it (see photos above). Stir the coating well before and during application for a consistent sheen.

Ebony dye lays the groundwork for a dark finish, but it doesn't fill oak's deep pores. For that you need a stain with pigment particles.

3. DEEP AND DARK

Going just one step beyond a basic stain and top coat produces an elegant ebony finish. The secret? Start with an application of water-soluble ebony dye, followed by a dark oil-base stain. Unlike black paint this finish still reveals red oak's grain lines as a matte color that contrasts against the smooth surrounding wood.

Because missed spots stand out against a dark finish, dye, stain, and finish parts before assembly.

First sand to 150 grit, then raise the grain with a damp towel and lightly scuff-sand to remove raised nibs. Tape off joint areas before finishing each part for a solid glue bond.

Mix ebony dye (see Resources, pages 236–237) at 2 tablespoons of black dye to 6 ounces of water. Generously apply dye using a cloth or sponge brush. Allow the dye to dry, then remove surface dye residue with a clean, dry cloth. With a new cloth apply a dark

walnut stain in a circular motion to fill the pores. Wipe away excess stain with the grain.

For the top coat brush on semigloss water-base poly to seal the wood, followed by two top coats. Vary the dye concentration and choice of stain to customize the color from all black to a medium chocolate hue. The dye and stain should be roughly the same degree of darkness for best results.

The color might seem bland after applying stain over dye. But the film finish will bring it to life and give it depth.

4. LOW-ODOR WATER-BASE

Water-base stains and film finishes offer an alternative that won't spread fumes throughout your house. Water-base stain can be a challenge to apply. Leave it on a few seconds too long, even under ideal conditions, and it quickly dries. And dry air only exacerbates the problem. Sanding up to 220 grit reduces blotching, but the smooth surface traps fewer stain pigment particles for a lighter color.

Work quickly in small areas but keep overlaps to a minimum to avoid lap marks. To slightly darken light spots, remoisten the towel used to apply the stain and gently wipe the light section until it matches the surrounding area.

To remove dried excess stain, make a couple of passes with a moistened coarse cloth, such as burlap, until the color evens out.

Take care when staining projects that mix veneer plywood and solid oak. The plywood might require additional stain applications because it absorbs less stain, producing a lighter color. Should the stain raise the grain slightly, make three light passes over the stained areas, using 320-grit abrasive. Do not sand through the stain. As a final step add a top coat of water-base satin finish.

Apply stain with a circular motion to work pigments into the pores. Then wipe with the grain and remove any surplus. A moistened, coarse cloth can be used to remove dried deposits of water-base stain.

FINISHING (CONTINUED)

FILM-FORMING FINISHES

Once your project is prepped and perhaps stained, it is time to give a final protective, grain-enhancing finish. Polyurethane, varnish, and shellac, are three of your options. Here is how to handle them.

PERVASIVE POLYURETHANE

Aggressively marketed and widely available, polyurethane isn't just the favored finish of many woodworkers; it's their only finish. True, there's a lot to like about poly. The long drying time makes brushing a breeze and once dry, the tough finish resists moisture and abrasion.

Oil-base poly isn't perfect though. That long drying time allows plenty of dust nibs to collect on the tacky surface, and bubbles left by brushing will flaw the finish. Once dry, gloss poly can look too shiny, like the tabletop shown at right. (Even satin poly finishes can call attention to surface flaws unless you rub them out.) You'll also need to carefully scuff-sand each coat to ensure proper adhesion. If polyurethane remains your first choice, master these strategies for working around its shortcomings.

GETTING READY

You can't fix problems you can't see, so shine a bright light on the work surface at an angle that emphasizes drips, surface debris, and bubbles. Other accessories you'll need include a natural-bristle or fine synthetic bristle brush (see "Pick a brush that gets your finish off to a smooth start," opposite), an angled (or sash) brush of the same type for working finish into inside corners, a separate container for holding finish, and a supply of shop rags.

Prepare the wood by sanding to 120 grit for unstained wood or 180 grit for surfaces to be stained. Any added smoothness from sanding to higher grit at this stage disappears after you apply the finish. Hand-sand at the final grit with a flat, lightly padded block. Vacuum the wood surface thoroughly, then wipe it clean using a rag soaked in mineral spirits.

For fewer dust flaws in the finish start with a clean work area. Vacuum the dust from overhead lights and surfaces within your finishing area. Then vacuum and damp-mop the floor to avoid kicking up dust while you finish. After any airborne dust settles, run your hand across the wood just before applying a finish. The oils on your skin will pick up the last bits of dust on the surface.

If you don't rub out a gloss poly finish, glare highlights dust nibs and drips, and the surface feels rough.

An angled light source helps you check the consistency of your sanding as you level the last coat of finish.

Slurry of rottenstone and oil

Mix mineral oil or paraffin oil into the pumice or rottenstone directly on the wood surface.

START WITH A SEALER COAT

Avoid the frustration of digging a stray brush bristle out of a dried coat of polyurethane. First slap the bristles against your palm to detect any strays. Just before you apply the finish, completely dip the bristles into mineral spirits and blot or shake away the excess. Check again for loose bristles.

If you apply finish directly from the original can, you risk contaminating the polyurethane with debris picked up by your brush. Instead pour enough finish for the project into a separate container. If you're using a previously opened can, strain the polyurethane through a paper paint filter to remove debris and globs of partially dried finish.

Whether you thin the first coat of finish or apply it at full strength might depend on whether or not you're covering a stained surface. A thicker, full-strength sealer coat provides added protection against accidentally sanding through polyurethane and stain to bare wood. If you're finishing unstained wood, polyurethane that's thinned 50 percent with mineral spirits creates a thin but fast-drying sealer coat.

Apply finish to horizontal surfaces whenever possible, even if that means tilting your project

Polyurethane's slow drying time can cause sags. An angled light source reveals excess finish you'll need to brush off.

on edge. Where the work surface must remain vertical, use the angled light source to check for drips, as shown above. Do this as you work and after coating the surface but before the finish skins over.

Grip the brush by the metal ferrule between your thumb and fingers and dip the bristles about a

Pick a brush that gets your finish off to a smooth start

Just about any brush will transport poly onto your project. The right brush, however, will lay down a finish that's smooth and level. The benefit: less sanding time and a better-looking result.

Natural China bristle brushes have long been popular for applying polyurethane and for good reason: They're fine enough to flex as you brush on a finish without producing grooves, as stiffer nylon bristles might do. Some synthetic bristles, such as Purdy's Syntox, rival natural bristles for their size and flexibility. Regardless of the bristle type you choose, look for these positive traits.

Flagging Think of these as split ends on the hairs of your brush. Each flagged tip provides an even finer applicator than the body of the finest bristle.

The result: Finish flows from the brush to the surface of the wood without leaving ridges.

Chiseled tip Don't confuse this term with the sharply defined point of a foam brush. "Chiseled" describes how some of the bristles stop short of reaching the end, forming a slight wedge shape that lays down a smooth finish as you draw the brush along at an angle.

Tapered bristles Picture how a fishing rod flexes more at the tip than at its base. The slight taper of individual bristles from the ferrule to the flagged tip can be hard to see, but it allows the brush to hold a firm shape while remaining flexible at its tip for a smooth finish.

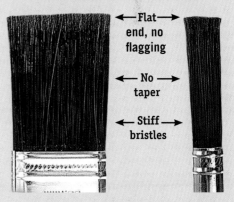

NYLON BRISTLES: TOO COARSE

← Flat → end, no flagging

← No → taper

← Stiff → bristles

NATURAL BRISTLES: JUST RIGHT

← Flagged → tips

Chiseled end

← Thin, → flexible bristles

FINISHING *(CONTINUED)*

third of their length into the finish. Gently drag the bristles against the container's edge to remove excess.

Begin brushing with the grain from the center of the project surface to the ends, reloading your brush as needed. Apply a complete strip of finish from end to end before starting the next strip at the wet edge of the previous one. Work as quickly as your brush can release each load of finish.

You can't avoid leaving at least a few air bubbles in the finish, and polyurethane's slow drying time can produce unexpected sags. Reduce the number of bubbles and drips by "tipping off" each strip of finish. To do this hold the brush perpendicular to the work surface and lightly pull the brush tip along the length of the strip. To drain the brush of excess finish that it picked up while tipping off, wipe the brush against an empty container.

Once the sealer coat dries, use 220-grit abrasive and a flat sanding block to knock down dust nibs and surface flaws. You might need to sand more after the sealer coat than you will between top coats but avoid cutting through to the wood below. Sand molding details using your fingers and a gentle touch. You're most likely to sand through the finish at crisp edges. Afterward carefully vacuum the surface and wipe away sanding dust with a soft cloth.

Polyurethane doesn't bond well with other surfaces, especially itself. You'll need to lightly scuff-sand the surface between coats with 220-grit abrasive to create tiny grooves where the next coat can grip the previous one. Wipe away all sanding dust.

Avoid the temptation to apply too thick a coat, which can allow drips or sags to form. Polyurethane hardens by reacting with oxygen, so even a surface that's dry to the touch might still be hardening.

When should you thin top coats? Some polyurethane formulas do a better job than others of leveling off brush marks. If you've done everything possible to brush on a smooth finish and you still get brush marks or unpopped bubbles, sand that layer and thin your finish about 10 percent before applying the next coat.

VARNISH: THE KING OF DURABILITY

Varnish reigns as the most resistant and durable film finish among those that are generally available to the home woodworker. Manufacturers combine oil and resin, cook the mixture, and produce a finishing material that's very tolerant of heat and water. However all varnish finishes are difficult to repair.

Depending on the type of oil and the resin, varnish varies in color from clear to a deep amber. Most varnishes combine an alkyd resin with oil—either linseed oil or one of the less expensive oils, such as soya oil. The amount of oil in the varnish determines its hardness.

You can buy varnish in many forms. The only difference between a polyurethane and any other kind of varnish is the addition of a bit of polyurethane resin. This resin makes the varnish slightly more scratch-resistant.

Choose the resin that best matches your needs

"Polyurethane" might be a synonym for varnish to some woodworkers, but the word really only describes one of three varnish resins: phenolic, alkyd, and uralkyd. Varnish makers mix one or a combination of the following resins with oil under heat. The types of resins in the mix partly determine a finish's abrasion resistance, clarity, and cost.

Phenolic resins grew out of the early 20th-century's plastics industry. Phenol extracted from coal tar was mixed with formaldehyde and combined with oil such as tung oil. Though a durable replacement for shellac at the time, its ingredients tended to yellow more than later varnish resins. Phenolic resins still find their way into high-

end marine varnishes, such as McCloskey Boat Koat Spar Varnish and Pettit Paint's Bak-V-Spar Varnish.

Alkyd resins made by mixing alcohol and acid proved less costly than phenolic resins while producing less yellowing. That cost savings continues to make them a main ingredient in many varnishes labeled as polyurethane. Alkyds can be purchased unblended in varnishes, such as Pratt & Lambert 38 and McCloskey Heirloom.

Uralkyd resin best describes the type of polyurethane that most woodworkers use. These combine alkyd and urethane resins to gain the strengths of both: alcohol resistance from alkyds, for example, and scuff resistance from urethanes.

Brushing is the most common method of applying varnish, but it takes practice to do a top-flight job. You'll encounter two major problems—brush marks and bubbles. Most brush marks result from going back over the surface too often. Most varnish starts to skin over soon after it hits the surface, and further brushing creates flaws. Bubbles come from a variety of sources, including a poor-quality brush and careless brushing habits. Also don't create bubbles by shaking the can; stir its contents gently. After brushing gently scrape the surface between coats to remove any bumps. Take a utility knife blade, hold it nearly vertical between your forefinger and thumb, and keep the pressure light. Buff down the surface with gray Scotch-Brite, 0000 steel wool, or 320-grit sandpaper before applying your final coat.

It's a pleasure to apply varnish by wiping it on, but this works best when you add thinner to the varnish. You can buy a wiping varnish or make your own by mixing equal parts of varnish and thinner. Naphtha makes a good thinner because it dries faster and clearer than mineral spirits. A few companies make a gel varnish, a thick product designed to be wiped on. It is strictly a surface film and offers little penetration. Gel varnishes are susceptible to chipping and difficult to repair.

SHELLAC: SAFE AND TOUGH

Shellac ranks as the most environmentally friendly of the finishing products. Manufacturers use the resin to coat candies, glossy pills, and even fruit. It reigned as the finish of choice before the development of lacquer. If you find a film finish on furniture made before about 1920, it's probably shellac. The survival of such furniture, with the original finish still intact, proves the durability of shellac. However shellac offers relatively poor resistance to water, alcohol, heat, and cleaners that contain alkali.

Once mixed shellac starts to deteriorate and finally reaches a point where it won't dry. You can't predict when that will happen. Some premixes claim a three-year lifespan, which starts on the day the shellac is mixed by the manufacturer. Check the date on the bottom of the can for either the manufacturing date or the three-year expiration date.

For the most dependable results, buy shellac in flake form, mix the flakes with denatured alcohol to make the amount you need, and dispose of any that's left over when you're done finishing your project. This might seem wasteful, but the most expensive finish is one that has to be removed from your project because it is old and will not dry.

OILS

Oil-base finishes are widely available and by far the easiest to apply. Simply wipe on a generous coat, let it soak in for several minutes, wipe off the excess, and let it dry.

Unfortunately no true oil finish offers much in the way of water or heat resistance. However oil finishes do a terrific job of bringing out the color and grain of the wood. Add protection with a film top coat (pages 124–127) and you have the best of both worlds.

Boiled linseed, tung, and soya are the most common oils used in finishing. Boiled linseed and tung serve as straight oil finishes, and soya appears as an ingredient in other finishes.

Blend oil, varnish, and thinner, and you have a "Danish oil," "tung oil finish," "antique oil finish," or almost anything else that's labeled as an oil finish. A side-by-side comparison of these products reveals few, if any, differences among them.

Some commercial oil/varnish mixes contain an added color. Or you can tint any of the clear oil/varnish mixes by adding oil-base stain or a compatible dye. Be aware that if you add a stain to either a commercial product or your own recipe, you're adding oil too. Adjust your ratio accordingly.

Oil/varnish mixes do not provide a high degree of protection and can't give you a glossy finish, but they're easy to apply and repair. A couple of coats of an oil/varnish mix followed by a paste-wax coat will produce a wonderful, hand-rubbed, satin appearance. Apply an oil/varnish mix like a true oil finish. Flood it on, let it soak in, and then make sure to wipe off any excess. On some woods, especially large-pored species such as oak, this finish tends to "bleed back" and pool on the surface. Keep wiping to remove these spots until the finish has dried. Oil/varnish mixes dry slowly, especially in high humidity. Don't build them up beyond two coats.

FINISHING *(CONTINUED)*

PAINT

For woods such as pine, poplar, and aspen, a little cover-up can do wonders. Painted finishes give you a rainbow of options to complement your home's decor. Easy to maintain and repair, they stand up to direct sunlight far better than clear finishes. However you'll need to paint with more finesse than what's required for walls, ceilings, or siding. Here's how.

PRIMED FOR PAINTING

Primer fills sanding scratches. After you sand the flat surfaces, use 150-grit abrasive to lightly round over the sharp edges. (Paint won't stick to sharp edges, leading to premature wear.) Fill defects with vinyl putty, sand them smooth when dry, and then remove all surface dust using a vacuum or tack rag.

Match your choice of primer to the surface you'll paint (see chart below). With a synthetic- or natural-bristle brush, apply one coat on the surfaces and edges. Apply two coats, spaced 5–10 minutes apart, on the end grain. To save time while painting the doors, use a board with exposed nail points, as shown above right, to support the wet side while applying primer to the opposite side and edges.

After the primer dries overnight, sand the large, flat faces using 220-grit abrasive on a random-orbit sander or a hand block. Use a sanding sponge or profile block on routed profiles. Use a light to spot any flaws in the primed surface. If you sand through the primer to bare wood, just reprime, let it dry, sand

A nail board can support a freshly primed component, allowing both sides and all four edges to be finished at once. With their fine points drywall nails provide even support with only imperceptible marring.

until smooth, and wipe it clean with a tack cloth.

Apply one more coat of primer and sand it with 220-grit abrasive. Sanding the primer and putty creates a lot of dust, so vacuum the surface before wiping it with a damp rag (for latex paint) or a tack cloth (for oil-base paint).

PAINTING LIKE A PRO

Objects stick to latex painted surfaces, such as shelves, because the paint remains soft even after it dries. To avoid this problem use acrylic latex trim enamel. For a smooth finish and easier brushing, include an additive such as Floetrol to slow drying time and allow brush marks to level off.

	PRIMER	BEST USE	COMMENTS	DRY TIME
WATER-BASED ACRYLIC		Use on all new wood, except for pine and other knotty or resinous woods. Use under water-base acrylic paints.	Advantages include low odor, fast drying, and easy sanding with less clogging of abrasives. However water raises grain more than the two other types do.	Dries to touch within 1 hour; a top coat can be applied after 4 hours.
OIL-BASED (ALKYD)		Suitable for new wood, oil-base primer penetrates deeper than latex primer to seal lightly weathered wood. Spot-priming seals knots.	Use beneath oil-base paint. Check the label to see if it seals in smoke damage or surface marks that might bleed through an unprimed painted finish. Apply using a natural-bristle or all-purpose brush.	Dries to touch in 45 minutes; top coat after 8 hours (longer in cool weather).
PIGMENTED SHELLAC		Seals knotty or resinous woods that might bleed through latex and some oil-base primers.	Shellac's alcohol base dries within minutes, and the odor can be less objectionable than oil-base primers. Can be used beneath oil- and water-base paints. Apply using a natural-bristle or all-purpose brush.	Dries to touch in 15 minutes; recoat after 45 minutes.

Be strategic in your painting. For example by waiting until after a cupboard is finished but before attaching the back, you'll have more convenient access to the inside.

Latex paint requires two types of synthetic-bristle brushes: a 2½" square chisel brush for flat areas and a 1½" angled sash brush for the details. Practice your brushstroke to get a feel for how paint flows out of the bristles. First condition the bristles by dunking them in tap water and wringing out the brush. This helps smooth the finish and makes the brush easier to clean afterwards. Next dip the brush halfway up the bristle length and tap it against the side of the cup if necessary to remove excess paint.

Hold the brush at a 75-degree angle to flow the paint onto the surface. Before it can dry lightly brush back and forth to further spread the paint and reduce brush marks.

Sand with 320- or 400-grit sandpaper between the first and second coats. Then remove the dust using your vacuum and a wet rag. Let the second coat dry overnight.

Six success tips for handling a paintbrush

1 Never start the newly loaded brush in a corner, or paint will pool there. When working on a flat surface, start 3" from an edge and pull the brush toward the edge to avoid drips. Then come back to where you started and complete the stroke.

2 If paint pools in corners or crevices, use a brush emptied of paint to collect the surplus.

3 Brush in long, even strokes. Then lightly drag the tip of your brush over the still-wet surface to level it out.

4 Limit your work to manageable sections where you can maintain a wet edge on your finish before the latex dries enough to form a skin.

5 Keep your work surface horizontal, even if that means tipping the piece on its sides to apply finish.

6 Two thin coats are better than a single heavy coat, which can run or sag.

Add glaze for instant age in three easy steps

To give a project a rustic appearance, add a water-base glaze on your newly painted surface. Start by lightly smoothing the dried paint with 600-grit sandpaper on the flat surfaces and a gray synthetic abrasive pad on the contours to remove minor blemishes.

Apply the glaze at room temperature and avoid excess ventilation that might dry it too quickly.

If you've never used glaze before, practice spreading it on scrap. Start on the back and inside of the project to get a feel for how much time it takes to apply and remove the glaze. If you make a mistake or the glaze starts to dry, reactivate it with a mist of water or remove it with a damp cloth.

Once applied give the glaze 24–48 hours to dry. Then finish it with a clear water-base acrylic.

1 Apply the glaze with a sash brush. Work the glaze into all the crevices and grooves, then cover the flat area.

2 Wipe off the excess glaze. Even it up by wiping lightly with a clean, soft cloth. Avoid removing it completely.

3 Work the glaze into the contours by lightly whisking a dry brush over the surface.

MOLDINGS

IT'S ALL ABOUT COVERING GAPS AND ADDING DIMENSION
and doing so in the neatest possible manner. This chapter
will equip you with techniques for installing most common
types of molding—and a few unusual approaches as well. If

TRIMMING WINDOWS AND DOORS

Whether you are trimming a new window or upgrading an old one, here's how to do it right.. . . . . **132**

INSTALLING CROWN MOLDING

Beauty doesn't come easily. Discover how to tackle crown. . **138**

CROWN MOLDING FOR BOOKCASES AND CABINETS

Learn how to give your built-in a crowning touch. **147**

BASEBOARDS

Here's how to cope with the inevitable imperfections in walls and floors. **151**

WALL FRAMES

This simple approach will give your walls depth and dimension . . . **156**

WAINSCOTING

Try some new twists on this tried-and-true trim approach **158**

you haven't already chosen the molding profiles you want, check pages 30–33. For some beautiful project ideas, see our molding gallery on pages 14–17.

TRIMMING WINDOWS AND DOORS

HERE'S HOW TO DO A CRISP TRIMOUT—EVEN IN LESS-THAN-PERFECT CIRCUMSTANCES.

Trimming a window or door is straightforward if you start with a new jamb, but if you are upgrading the trim on an old jamb, you'll first have to sand smooth any paint buildup and mark for the reveal. In addition you might have to cope with a jamb that is warped or out of square.

Even a new window or door can pose challenges. For example a new vinyl window or patio door might require a jamb insert.

Fortunately you have several approaches to choose from, at least one of which should offer the style you want and work with the type of window you have.

TRADITIONAL SILL AND APRON

Common in older homes where double-hung windows prevail, this trim approach including a sill (in molding terms often referred to as a stool) and an apron is the most complex way to trim a window (see illustration at right). After allowing for the width of the trim, the sill must be notched at both ends to fit onto the frame. It is sometimes rabbeted to match the incline of the exterior sill. The apron is attached beneath it. Variations in the wall surface material often make applying sills and aprons tricky. Casing corners can be mitered, butt-jointed, or joined with rosette blocks (see page 137).

TRIMMING WITHOUT A SILL AND APRON

Too often a good miter goes bad once the casing is applied to the window jamb. Using the picture-frame casing method avoids this problem because you can finetune and fasten your miters on a flat surface and later apply the resulting frame to your window.

PREFABBING THE EXTENDER AND TRIM

Many newer homes have vinyl windows that are flange-mounted from the outside, leaving a considerable gap on the interior between the window frame and the finished wall surface. Trimming

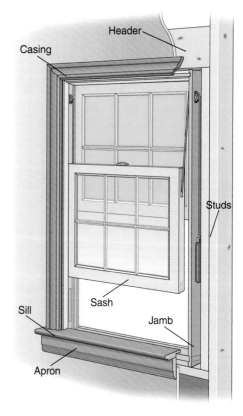

This cutaway of a double-hung window (including sash weights) includes a sill and apron. Note the framing. When trimming make sure you are nailing into the jamb and the framing—not just the wall.

The sill should be notched so it fits against the window sash and extends beyond the casing a distance equal to the thickness of the casing.

For a finished edge to the apron, mark and miter-cut both ends. Glue a piece of miter to the thickness of the apron stock.

them out requires a pretty deep jamb extender. Rather than adding the jamb and trim in place, save yourself a lot of aggravation by prefabbing the unit. You'll end up with a perfectly square installation that installs quickly (see box below). If you have a very complex situation, you might want to draw it out on a piece of particleboard and then fabricate it right on the drawing. A drywall T-square helps the process.

WHY A REVEAL?

Almost every window has a ¼" gap between the inside jamb edge and the edge of the casing. This is not only for looks (another one of those nice shadows that molding makes) but to disguise any warps in the jamb as well. It also spares you having to line up the casing exactly with the jamb—something that is more difficult than it might seem. Some trim carpenters have a steady enough hand to set a compass at ¼" and scribe around the jamb to mark the reveal. However a more accurate approach is to use a combination square.

FASTENING TECHNIQUES

Nowhere does a pneumatic nailer prove its worth quite as well as when you trim out a window. It is accurate, it lets you hold the trim in place with one

Prefabbing jambs and trim

Mark for sill notches and side jamb. Begin by ripping your jamb stock to size. In this situation the sill stock has to be notched for the framing between the windows.

Prefab the jamb, muntin, and casing. Fabrication on a flat surface greatly improves your chances of tight, accurate joints. Assemble the jamb and fasten the muntin in place. Square up the frame with a framing square.

Shim and set the unit in place. Apply casing to the finished frame. Set and level the shim on the sill. Tip the finished jamb into the opening and fasten to the framing through the casing and jamb.

TRIMMING WINDOWS AND DOORS
(CONTINUED)

hand while you shoot in the brad with the other, and it eliminates the need for setting nails. (See pages 116–117 for more on automatic fasteners.) Especially if you are doing a lot of trimming out, renting a unit is well worth the cost and trouble.

If you choose to nail by hand, drill two pilot holes and tack the trim in place. Check the fit before drilling the rest of the pilot holes and pounding the nails in. Use 4d nails for the jamb and 6d nails when attaching to framing. Avoid dents by pounding the nail only within ⅛" of the surface. Use a nail set no larger than the head of the finishing nail to set the nail slightly beneath the trim surface.

Whichever method you use be sure you are attaching the trim to more than just wallboard or plaster. Nails should go into the jamb or framing members.

THOSE PESKY GAPS

Too often door or window trim overlaps slightly uneven wall surfaces. This can wreak havoc with not only miter joints, but even butt joints. Often they just won't line up, and a slight gap results. One tried-and-true method for smoothing things out is to slip a shim behind the joint. The shim will force the two pieces of trim onto the same plane while it is fastened. In some cases you can then remove the shim, but it is best to score it with a utility knife, crack it off, and cover any gap with a bit of caulk.

Cut one miter, mark other in place

Whenever possible instead of measuring, hold the workpiece in place and mark before cutting. Always mark the most complicated cut first. For example if you are cutting window casing that will rest on the sill, cut the miter first, leaving the piece a couple of inches longer. Then hold the piece in place, mark, and make the straight cut where the casing meets the sill.

Give your project individuality by combining trim types

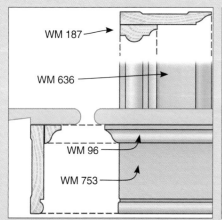

Layering
Baseboard (WM 636) is the foundational casing layer, with panel molding (WM 187) on top. For the apron WM 753 baseboard turned upside down is combined with small cove (WM 96).

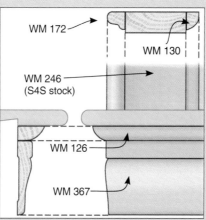

Stacking
Colonial casing (WM 367) topped off with base shoe comprises this stacked apron arrangement. S4S sandwiched between base shoe and base cap makes up the casing.

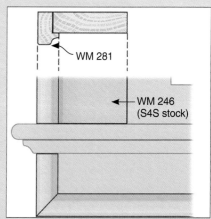

Backbanding
For a framed effect add a backband to S4S stock and carry the same approach through to the apron.

ADDING A FALSE TRANSOM

GIVE AN ORDINARY WINDOW AN EXTRAORDINARY NEW LOOK WITH NEW TRIM AND THE ELEGANT ILLUSION OF A TRANSOM WINDOW.

Opalescent-glass transoms give the illusion that a window is taller, without enlarging the existing opening. Here's how to work this magic on a window in your house.

1 **CUT THE SILL.** After the new window is in place, cut a ¾"-thick blank for the sill (A). To determine its width measure from the window's frame to the inside surface of the wall (the width of part C shown in **DRAWING 1A** on page 136) and add 1¹¹⁄₁₆". To determine its length measure the overall width of the window and add 6³⁄₈". Notch the sill's ends, as shown on **DRAWING 1A.** Cut the 1"-wide apron (B) 1½" shorter than the sill. Finish-sand the sill and apron to 220 grit and nail them in place, where shown on **DRAWING 1.** Center the apron under the sill.

2 **EXTEND THE JAMBS.** Add side and top jamb extensions (C, D) to bring the window frame flush with the surrounding wall. (In this case cherry was used to match the new window casing.) Drill pilot and countersunk shank holes and screw the extensions to the window frame.

3 **CUT THE CASING.** To find the length of the side casings (E), measure from the sill to the top jamb extension and add ³⁄₁₆" for the top jamb extension reveal, 3" for the width of the transom casing (F), and the desired height of your false transom. (You can adjust this dimension to suit the proportions of your window and the distance from the top of the window to the ceiling. In our example this dimension is 7⁷⁄₁₆".) Cut the side casings to size. For the length of the transom casing (F), measure between the side jamb extensions and add

³⁄₈" to allow for ³⁄₁₆" side extension reveals on each side. Cut the transom casing to size. For the length of the top casing (G), add 6" to the length of the transom casing. Cut the top casing to size.

4 **MARK FOR THE MULLIONS.** Temporarily clamp together the transom and top casings, edge-to-edge with their backs up, centering the transom casing on the top casing. Mark the locations of the mullions (H) on the transom casing, then transfer the marks to the top casing, as shown on **DRAWING 2.** To determine your spacing subtract the total width of all the mullions (shown are two ¾"-wide mullions, for a total of 1½") from the length

MATERIALS LIST

Part		T	W	L	Qty.
		FINISHED SIZE			
A	sill	¾"	*	*	1
B	apron	¾"	1"	*	1
C	side jamb extensions	¾"	**	**	2
D	top jamb extension	¾"	**	**	1
E	side casings	¾"	3"	***	2
F	transom casing	¾"	3"	***	1
G	top casing	¾"	3"	***	1
H	mullion	⅝"	¾"	†	††
I	vertical stop	³⁄₁₆"	⅜"	†††	††
J	horizontal stop	³⁄₁₆"	⅜"	††	††

*	See Step 1 of the instructions.
**	See Step 2 of the instructions.
***	See Step 3 of the instructions.
†	See Step 6 of the instructions.
††	Depends on the number of lights in the transom. See Steps 4 and 7.
†††	See Step 7 of the instructions.

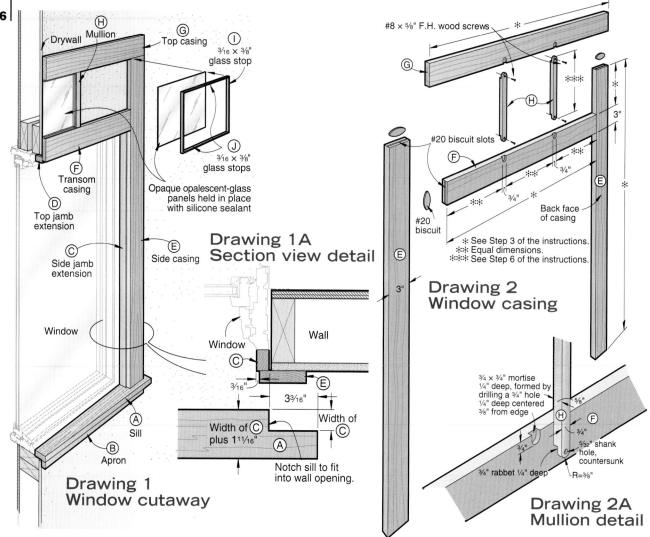

Drawing 1A
Section view detail

Drawing 1
Window cutaway

Drawing 2
Window casing

* See Step 3 of the instructions.
** Equal dimensions.
*** See Step 6 of the instructions.

Drawing 2A
Mullion detail

of the transom casing (F), then divide this dimension by the number of lights you want in your transom. (This transom has three lights.)

5 **SEPARATE THE CASINGS.** Form mortises by drilling the casings with a Forstner bit, where shown on **DRAWING 2A,** and then squaring the sides with a chisel. Dry-assemble the frame face up on your bench and mark the biscuit locations. Plunge the biscuit slots and glue and clamp the frame together.

6 **ATTACH THE MULLIONS.** Measure the distance between the transom casing (F) and the top casing (G) and add 1½". Cut the mullions (H) to this length. Form rabbets in the ends so the mullions fit snugly between the casings and round their ends to fit the mortises. With the mullions in place, drill pilot and countersunk shank holes. Remove the mullions, apply glue to the mortises, and screw the mullions in place.

7 **PREPARE THE STOPS.** Resaw and plane stock for the vertical glass stops (I) and horizontal glass stops (J). Fit the vertical stops first,

then cut the horizontal stops to fit between the vertical ones. Glue and clamp the stops in place, setting them ³⁄₁₆" from the back faces of the casings and mullions.

8 **FINISH-SAND THE FRAME ASSEMBLY TO 220 GRIT.** Select an opalescent glass and have panes cut to fit the transom openings. (For opalescent glass look in your local Yellow Pages under Glass—Stained, Leaded; or check crafts supply stores.) Insert the panes from the rear and secure them with a few dabs of silicone sealant.

9 **ASSEMBLE THE COMPONENTS.** With the silicone cured stand the frame on the sill, check that the side jamb extension reveals are equal, and nail the frame in place. Nail to both the jamb extensions and the wall framing. Fill the nail holes in the sill, apron, and frame. When the filler dries sand it smooth.

10 **APPLY THE FINISH.** Mask the window, the surrounding wall, and the opalescent-glass panes. Apply two coats of clear finish (see pages 124–127).

TRIMMING A DOOR WITH PLINTHS AND CORNER ROSETTES

TRY THIS CLASSIC LOOK THAT DOESN'T CUT CORNERS.

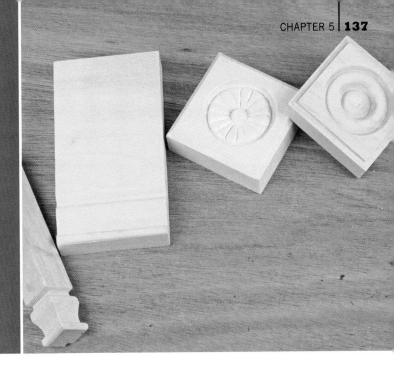

Doors trimmed with plinths (a vertical block joining baseboard to door casing) and rosettes (blocks set at the casing corners) evoke a style of trim common in homes built near the beginning of the 20th century. While often used in combination, as in this project, each element can also be used by itself. Rosettes can be used to trim windows; plinths are necessary to make the transition to casing when you choose a high baseboard.

You won't have to finesse miter joints when using plinths and rosettes, but that doesn't mean they are easy. They actually introduce more joints and therefore more opportunity for gaps. That means you'll have to be careful to square them up as you apply them.

Drill pilot holes and tap in the nails on a flat surface before installing. Use 4d finish nails when attaching these components to the jamb and 6d or 8d nails (depending on the thickness of the components and wall surfacing) when attaching through to the framing.

Hold the casing in place to mark for the cuts. Drill pilot holes and attach it to the jamb with 3d finish nails; use 6d nails for attaching to the framing.

Set the rosettes

Mark a ¼" reveal on the door jamb. Predrill two holes in the rosette and start two 4d finish nails. Using a combination square position the rosette and partially drive one nail to hold the rosette in place. Check for square again before pounding the second nail home.

Set the plinths

Line the plinth along the reveal line. Check that the floor is level. If it is not you might want to scribe along the bottom of the plinth and trim it. Drill pilot holes and apply construction adhesive before installing. Hold the casing in place to mark it for cutting.

INSTALLING CROWN MOLDING

TURN AN ORDINARY ROOM INTO SOMETHING SPECIAL BY USING THESE TECHNIQUES FOR A REMODELING CORONATION.

Crown molding isn't the pinnacle of finish carpentry—stair building is harder, and hanging a door is no picnic. But crown molding elevates a room from the ordinary, recalling elaborate Victorian cornices and simple New England elegance.

Before you start installing crown molding (and it won't take long to learn), stop for a minute to think about moldings in general. Molding profiles have been standardized by the Wood Moulding & Millwork Producers Association. The ones you think of as crowns come in 13 sizes, from 1½" wide up to 4⅝" wide. They have a flattened S-shape (called an ogee) at the top, a flat toward the middle, and a cove at the bottom. They're actually far thinner than they look when in place, usually somewhere between ½" and ¾" thick.

They slope from wall to ceiling, which is what creates both the illusion of thickness and the challenge that you face during installation.

Traditional crowns are not the only moldings that go around the top of the room however. Coves are often used and like crowns they slope (technically they are "sprung") from wall to ceiling. Beds, which look like small crowns, can either be sprung in place or laid flat against the wall.

There is more than one way to install crown—some simple, some not so simple; all of them are described in the following pages. No matter which method you choose, the secret is simple: Take your time. Practice on some scrap. Be confident. Measure carefully. You might need a good ladder and a helper with an equally good ladder. The folks who do this every day might have more experience, but you have more time. What's your hurry?

THE BEAUTY OF BACKER STRIPS

Here's the way it's *supposed* to work. The ceiling is flat and at a 90-degree angle to the wall, which is also

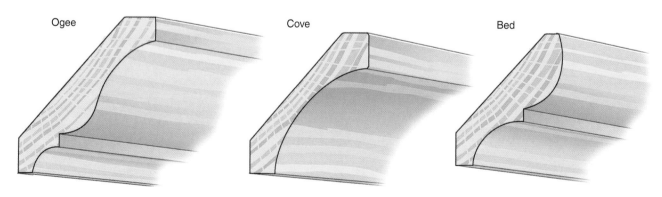

Ogee is the molding most associated with crowns. It ranges from ¹¹⁄₁₆" × 3⅝" to ¹¹⁄₁₆" × 4⅝".

The profile of a **cove** molding is a simple curve. They range from ⁹⁄₁₆" × 2" to ⁹⁄₁₆" × 3¼".

Beds are the smallest of the crown moldings, as small as ⁹⁄₁₆" × 1½".

flat. You put the top of the crown molding against the ceiling and the flat at the back against the wall. Presto. A perfect crown molding, sloping from wall to ceiling at exactly 38 degrees.

Here's the way it really works. Despite appearances the wall isn't truly flat. Neither is the ceiling, although the two do occasionally meet at a true 90-degree angle. The piece of molding is long and is hard to handle. The face of the molding that rests against the wall is small. The face that rests against the ceiling is even smaller. And once you start nailing, everything moves.

What you need is a backer strip—a board with a 38-degree bevel on it that supports the crown molding. To make one you first need to know how big it should be. Put a piece of scrap crown in the framing square as shown below and measure the height and width of the space behind the molding. In this case it's 1⅝"×2", close enough to rip out of a 2×4, so that's what you'll use to make the backer.

Cut a 38-degree angle on a piece of scrap with your mitersaw and use it as a gauge to set your tablesaw blade to 38 degrees. (Ignore the angle markings on the tablesaw. They're often woefully inaccurate.) Set the inside distance between the rip fence and the blade to the height of the space you measured against the framing square—2" in this case.

Before you rip all the 2×4s to size, it's a good idea to rip a short sample backer and to cut a piece of sample molding. Test-fit them against the wall and ceiling and make any necessary adjustments.

Rip the stock you'll need to make all the nailers. Mark the location of the studs on the wall and fasten

Rip a bevel on the backer. Set the blade to cut a 38-degree bevel—the angle of the back of the molding when in place.

Drill pilot holes and use screws to fasten the backer to the studs in the wall.

Use a scrap and a framing square to measure the height and width of the space behind the molding.

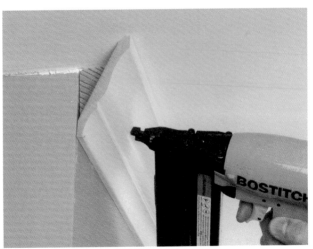

Beveled to the right angle, a backer strip assures that the crown molding will be at a consistent angle, guaranteeing tight joints.

INSTALLING CROWN MOLDING
(CONTINUED)

the backers to the studs with screws. Fastening is a lot easier if you predrill holes for the screws first.

COPED CORNERS

Home building is the art of illusion. The walls and ceiling only *look* flat, and more importantly for crown molding, the corners only *look* square. Cutting a miter in a piece that slopes from wall to ceiling is hard enough. Cutting one when the walls are at a random angle and the corner is partially filled with joint compound is infinitely more complicated.

Carpenters don't even try. Instead of a miter they use a different joint, called a cope joint, in which one piece of molding is cut to nest against the other. A cope is less likely to show gaps initially, and because the nesting partially locks the pieces together, a cope is less likely to show gaps over time.

Here's how it works. The first piece of molding runs from wall to wall and is square on both ends [PHOTO A]. The molding on the next wall is cut to nestle against the molding on the first wall.

And here's why it's called a cope joint. You reveal the profile of the molding by cutting it on the mitersaw, and then you cut along it with a coping saw.

Begin by laying out the cut that reveals the profile. Hold the molding roughly in place and draw a line

A
Nail the first piece in place. Cut a piece long enough to fit snugly between the walls and nail it to the backing strips.

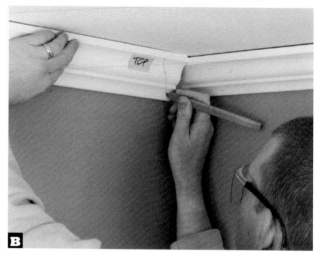

B
Lay out the slope. Put the molding in place and draw a line angling up from the bottom corner. The exact angle doesn't matter. Label the top of the molding as shown.

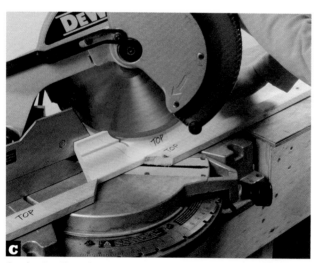

C
Cut in the direction of the line. Put the part of the molding labeled "top" on the saw bed, as shown. Set the saw to cut 45 degrees in the direction of the line you drew. Make the cut.

D
Double-check. Once you have cut the miter in preparation for coping out the joint, hold the piece in place to confirm that you cut at the correct angle.

on it that starts at the bottom and angles away from the corner [**PHOTO B**]. Don't worry about the angle—just sketch in the slope.

Put the crown molding on the mitersaw with the top against the bed and the bottom against the fence. Set the saw to 45 degrees, sloping it in the same general direction as the line you drew on the molding. Cut the end off the molding [**PHOTO C**]. Hold it in position to confirm you got the cut right [**PHOTO D**].

The cut exposes the profile of the molding—it's obvious on the primed molding shown here. On an unprimed piece it helps to trace the profile in pencil.

Put the finest blade you can find in your coping saw—they come as fine as 32 teeth per inch. Most stores only stock a medium blade, but it's worth your time to mail order a fine blade if you have to. Don't force the saw or try to push it forward when you cut [**PHOTO E**]. Let the saw do the work.

Once you've made the cut, test-fit it. It's seldom perfect on the first try, but you can finetune the fit with a half-round mill bastard file and a rat-tail file [**PHOTO F**].

Cut the molding to final length once you're happy with the fit of the joint. Start by measuring the length of the wall and then cut the molding to length with a square cut. Cope the piece on the third wall to fit against the square end of the second wall. The molding on the fourth wall gets coped on two ends, but you can cut them on separate pieces and splice them together.

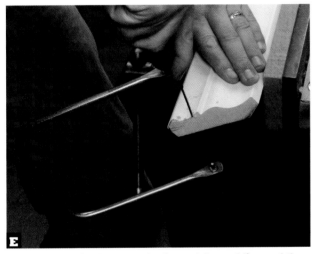

E

Cut along the line between the face of the molding and the newly exposed surface, angling the coping saw to create a sharp edge.

F

Finetune the joint. File away high spots that are causing gaps. Measure the length of the molding and cut it to length with a 90-degree cut. Put the molding in place and nail it to the backer.

Gapitis cure

Gaps in a molding that will be painted are easy to fix. Before you paint caulk them to close the gaps and wipe off the excess with your finger. Run caulk along the seam at the ceiling and along the seam at the wall too. Fill nail holes with glazier's putty.

Molding that will be stained and varnished is another story. You can fill the gaps and nail holes with stainable wood putty, but they will never be invisible.

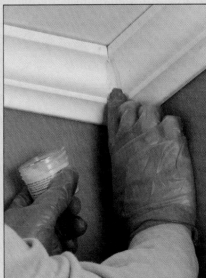

INSTALLING CROWN MOLDING
(CONTINUED)

A

To cut the scarf joint, lay out the slope of the scarf on the wall, set the saw to 45 degrees in the direction of the slope, and make the cut.

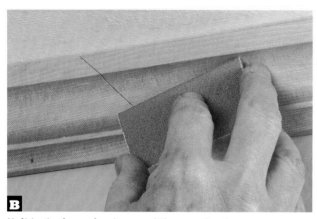

B

Nail both pieces in place and then sand out any irregularities.

SCARF JOINTS

Sometimes you cut a piece short. Sometimes the molding isn't long enough in the first place. Or maybe you want to save a little by using a few good-size cutoffs. That's when it's time to splice two pieces together using a scarf joint.

Once you've cut the ends to shape, put the first piece in place. Draw a line for a splice that is longer at the bottom than at the top; the exact angle doesn't matter. Put the molding on the saw, with the top on the bed and the bottom against the fence. Set the saw at a 45-degree angle that slopes in the direction of the line. Make the cut [PHOTO A] and nail the piece in place.

To get the length of the second piece of molding, measure from the corner of the room to the long tip of the molding and add the width of the molding. Mark the length on the top of the molding. Cut with the saw at the same angle as before but with the molding coming in from the opposite side of the saw. Apply glue to both miters, nail the piece in place, and sand it smooth [PHOTO B].

CUTTING COMPOUND MITER CORNERS

If you're cutting compound miters, the angles need to be accurate to .01 of a degree, so make sure your saw has stops for crown moldings. As you make initial cuts following the directions below, check the fit by cutting test pieces in scraps [PHOTO C] and trying them in place.

Butt joint scarfs

The butt joint has never been popular in crown molding because of the difficulty of keeping the pieces aligned. A biscuit joiner and a spline change that—as long you remove any backers that might be in the way. Start by cutting a smooth, square end on both pieces to be joined. Put one molding and the biscuit joiner flat on the bench and cut a slot. Repeat on the other molding. Before you glue the pieces together, hotmelt glue a piece of ½" plywood to the back of one molding. Then apply yellow glue to the joint and hotmelt glue to the exposed part of the ply. Assemble and hold until the hotmelt glue has dried. The next day screw the plywood to the molding and install.

Cut a biscuit joint in a square, clean end of the molding.

Glue a spline to the back to keep the scarf from breaking.

C

If you don't want to cope a joint, cut a compound miter using the stops on your saw and adjust as necessary for a tight joint.

To cut a left inside corner, put the molding flat on the saw with the top of the molding against the fence [**PHOTO D**]. Set the bevel at 33.85° and set the miter to the right at 31.62°. Use the piece to the left side of the blade.

To cut the right half of an inside corner, put the bottom of the molding against the fence. Set the bevel at 33.85° and the miter to the left at 31.62° [**PHOTO E**]. Use the piece to the left of the saw blade.

On the left half of an outside corner, set the bottom against the fence [**PHOTO F**]. Set the bevel at 33.85° and the miter to the left at 31.62°. Use the right-hand piece.

To cut the right side, put the top of the molding against the fence with the bevel set at 33.85° and the miter to the right at 31.62°. Use the right-hand piece [**PHOTO G**].

D

For an inside left corner, put the top of the molding against the fence. Set the bevel at 33.85° and the miter to the right at 31.62°. Use the piece to the left side of the blade.

E

For an inside right corner, put the bottom of the molding against the fence. Set the bevel at 33.85° and the miter to the left at 31.62°. Use the left piece.

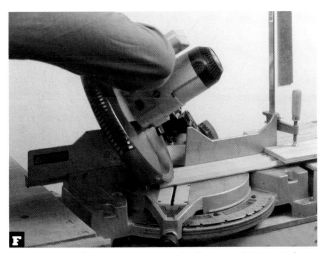

F

To cut an outside left corner, set the bottom of the molding against the fence. Set the bevel at 33.85° and the miter to the left at 31.62°. Use the right-hand piece.

G

To cut an outside right corner, put the top of the molding against the fence. Set the bevel at 33.85° and the miter to the right at 31.62°. Use the right-hand piece.

INSTALLING CROWN MOLDING
(CONTINUED)

INSTALLING OUTSIDE CORNERS

For an outside corner—a simple miter—some glue and a couple of nails do the trick. If an outside corner is square, installing crown molding requires a straightforward 45-degree miter. When you make the cut, put the top of the molding on the saw bed and the bottom against the fence.

1 **TO MITER THE RIGHT SIDE,** first straight-cut or cope the end that fits into an inside corner. Then mark for the cut and feed the molding in from the left. Set the saw 45 degrees to the right. Make a cut at the mark **[PHOTO A].**

2 **MARK FOR THE SECOND CUT.** Mark where the bottom of the molding crosses the corner **[PHOTO B].** Make a light angled mark to confirm the correct angle of the cut.

3 **TO MITER THE LEFT SIDE,** feed the molding in from the right side and set the saw to miter 45 degrees to the left. Cut at the mark **[PHOTO C].** Put glue on the end grain, nail the molding to the studs, and drive a 3d nail through the bottom and top of the corner to tie the pieces together.

Nonsquare corners

If the corner is less than 90 degrees, the miter will be less than 45 degrees. Use a framing square to check. If it is more than 90 degrees, the miter will be more than 45 degrees. Experiment with scraps to get the right setting. Write down the setting of each attempt, so you can go back to it if necessary. Make adjustments until you get a good fit.

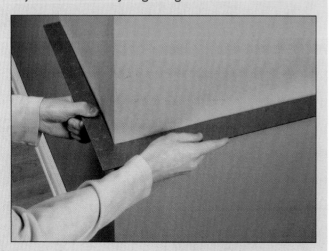

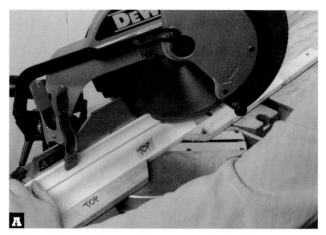

A Cut the joinery on the end that goes in the inside corner. Feed the molding from the left of the saw. Put the top of the molding on the saw bed. Set the miter to 45 degrees to the right and make a cut at the mark.

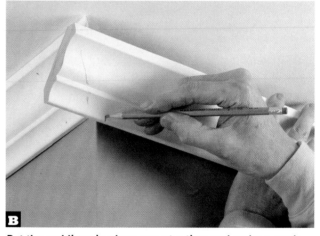

B Put the moldings in place one at a time and make a mark where the corner meets the bottom of the molding.

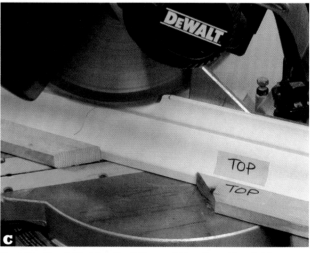

C To miter the left side, feed the molding from the right, with the top on the saw bed. Miter 45 degrees to the left.

BUILT-UP CROWN MOLDING

GET CUSTOM EFFECTS FROM STOCK MOLDINGS USING SIMPLE TECHNIQUES.

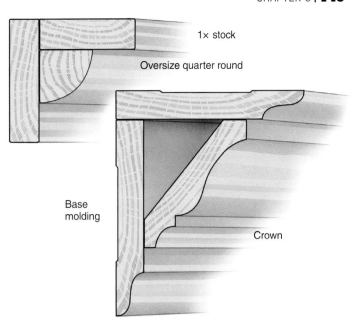

1× stock

Oversize quarter round

Base molding

Crown

The world of crown molding is far bigger than what's at the lumberyard. You can mix, match, and combine moldings to custom-make your own. The moldings sold for use as crown vary widely in size but not appearance. You can choose from two basic designs—the cove or the cove and ogee (S-curve). But you don't have to settle for the norm. Combining crown with other crown molding, or combining crown with a completely different molding, creates a whole new series of designs for you to work with.

MAKING THE COMBINATIONS

In most cases you'll build up the combinations on the wall, rather than gluing them together in advance. In part it's because it's easier to handle a smaller piece of molding. But it's also a question of what your saw can handle. A 10" saw isn't going to cut a 12" molding.

One of the simplest combinations, shown above right, is a crown molding sometimes found in country homes. Nail a piece of wood that's ¾"×2½" to the wall and nail a piece that's ¾"×1¾" to the ceiling. Butt the ends together in the corners and don't worry about gaps in the horizontal seams. Nail a 1¹⁄₁₆"×1¹⁄₆" quarter round to the boards to complete the crown and cover the gap.

Install like regular crown: Butt the first piece of quarter round against both corners and cope the second piece to fit against it and so on. You won't find an easier cope anywhere.

BUILT-UP VARIATIONS

Of course the molding doesn't have to have a quarter round. Once the two flat pieces are up there, you

could nail almost any molding between them.

If you want to dress up a typical piece of crown molding, nail a piece of baseboard to the ceiling so that the edge that would normally be the bottom is against the wall. Nail a similar piece of baseboard to the wall with the "bottom" edge against the first piece of baseboard. Nail in the backer strip and then slope the crown molding from one baseboard to the other.

Possible variations: Substitute cove or bed molding for the crown. Instead of crown substitute a piece

Install inverted baseboard
Who says the cove has to be on the bottom? Cut your joints with the cove closest to the bed, instead of the fence, and install the piece upside down.

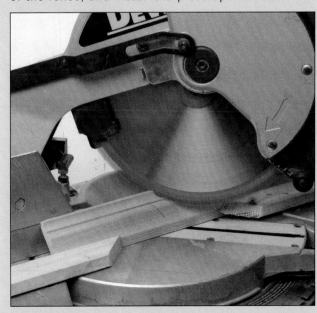

of baseboard—narrower than the first piece—and nail a still narrower piece of baseboard on top of that **[PHOTO A]**. Or use only one piece of baseboard instead of two. Check out the sample board at the lumberyard or home center for other possibilities.

CAN'T COPE WITH COPING?

Crown molding, combined with a corner block, lets you install crown in a room without having to cut a single cope joint. Instead of coping the joints, you put in a block that fills in the corner and presents

a flat face that meets the crown molding at 90 degrees. Put the corner blocks up first and then cut a butt joint in the crown molding. Snug it up against the block and you're done **[PHOTO B]**. There are separate corner blocks for inside and outside corners; outside miters are cope-free too.

Miterless crown molding is available in both wood and urethane. Wood, of course, is traditional. Urethane can be molded, however, which means it's available in a wide variety of profiles. It paints well, looks good, and costs less than wood.

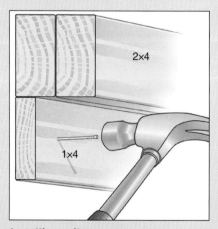

A

Dress up the molding that goes against the ceiling by combining it with a molding that goes along the floor.

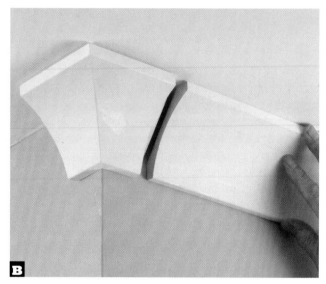

B

Although they look a bit clunky, miterless crown kits can get the job done if you want to avoid some tricky carpentry.

Create wide moldings with nailers

If you're willing to make and put in some nailers, you can create a single wide molding by stacking two pieces of crown molding, one above the other. Start by fastening two 2×4s to the wall at the ceiling and attaching a 1×4 below them. Install the molding, working from the bottom up. Install all of the cove molding first. Nail a piece of crown against the cove and the bottom of the outer 2×4 and install it all around the room. Put the second piece of crown between the ceiling and the top of the first crown to finish the job.

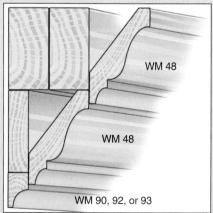

2×4

1×4

Installing nailers
Nailers create a structure that supports wide built-up moldings.

WM 48

WM 48

WM 90, 92, or 93

Installing the molding
Install one layer at a time. If the voids make you uneasy, install backer before installing the molding.

CROWN MOLDING FOR BOOKCASES AND CABINETS

HERE'S HOW TO ADD A STATELY FINISHING TOUCH TO YOUR BUILT-IN PROJECT.

Crown molding is simple to cut and install on woodworking projects, once you know the correct techniques. The necessary compound cuts at every corner combine a miter cut with a bevel cut, all of which can be machined on your mitersaw set up with an auxiliary fence, table, and stop assembly. The wider, detailed moldings further accentuate the need for precise-fitting joints, but there's a bag of simple tricks you can dig into.

The key to working with crown molding lies in an accurate mitersaw with a quality blade. Although you can cut compound angles on your tablesaw by tilting the blade and angling your miter gauge, it's much simpler to use a mitersaw. And by using our technique—cutting molding in its spring-angle position (see page 148) and upside down—you don't even need a compound mitersaw.

The accuracy of your cuts results directly from your mitersaw, but the finish and quality of those cuts fall directly on the blade you use. For best results when cutting any type of molding, apply the following guidelines: Use an 80-tooth carbide blade for 10" saws and a 90- to 100-tooth blade for 12" saws. They'll cost $80–$250 apiece, but the payback in splinter-free precision makes the investment worthwhile. The teeth should have a hook angle between 5 degrees and –5 degrees.

Next ensure that your mitersaw's bevel angle is 0 degrees—with the blade perpendicular to the table. Check this

with a square. Then with countersunk carriage bolts, attach an auxiliary fence made of ½" MDF or plywood that's as long as the saw's fence. Make the fence as tall as possible without impeding the saw's ability to cut at full depth. It provides backside support to help prevent tear-out, as well as a consistent fence height the length of the table, below.

Cutting crown works best when you have table extensions to support the molding and hold it level, a necessity for accurate cuts. Add the stop that will

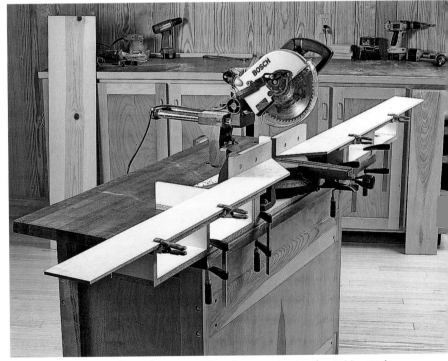

Supporting your molding using an auxiliary fence and extension table, made from plywood or MDF, eliminates tipping of long moldings and enables you to produce accurate cuts.

CROWN MOLDING FOR BOOKCASES AND CABINETS *(CONTINUED)*

hold the crown at the correct spring angle. First cut a 6-inch-long piece of your molding and rest it on the auxiliary table with the bottom edge against the fence (remember, you cut crown upside down) **[PHOTO A]**. Measure from the auxiliary fence to the edge of the molding that's farthest from the fence and then cut a spacer from MDF or plywood to match that width **[PHOTO B]**.

Screw a 2"-wide stop to the auxiliary table while sandwiching that spacer between the auxiliary fence and stop **[PHOTO C]**. Set your mitersaw at 45 degrees on each side and cut through the auxiliary fence and table. (You will need to adjust the position of the stop for different-size moldings.)

CUT MOLDINGS TO FIT SPECIFIC LOCATIONS IN A MITERED JOINT

For every mitered corner you'll need to understand the elements: There are inside and outside corners and left and right parts for each. Think in terms of a room in a house: Inside corners are the four typical corners that define a square or rectangular room, while outside corners are those on protruding closets, for example. You'll cut the mating parts of a joint on opposing sides of the mitersaw.

To cut a piece of molding, first cut one of the mitered ends as needed. In most instances you'll measure the length for the next cut along the bottom—or short—edge of the molding. This proves

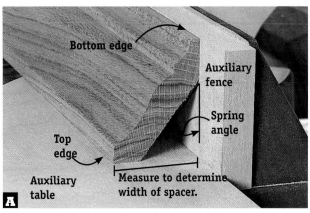

A Place a short length of crown in this position—upside down and at the spring angle—to automatically set the bevel angle.

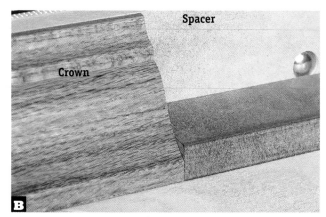

B Cut a spacer that's flush with the front of the crown's inverted top edge when the molding is positioned at the spring angle.

C Place the molding stop against the spacer and screw it to the auxiliary table with 1" brass flathead screws.

D Measure mitered crown to length by aligning the bottom of the miter with the fence end, then hook a tape onto the fence.

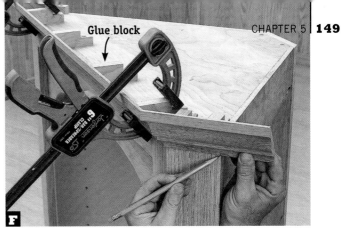

E Use a sliding bevel gauge to determine the spring angle for your crown molding, then transfer that angle to your saw.

F With the front molding dry-clamped, hold your side moldings in place and mark flush with the cabinet back.

Glue block

difficult when trying to catch a measuring tape's hook on the miter. Instead use the auxiliary fence to help with measuring **[PHOTO D]**.

ATTACH CROWN WITH SUPPORT BLOCKS

Wrapping crown molding around a woodworking project always centers around tight-fitting joints. To achieve this either assemble the mating pieces to each other directly on the project or assemble them in a glue-up jig made to ensure squareness and attach the assembly after the glue dries. Either way yields great results. (As with all woodworking assemblies, check your joints in a dry fit on the project before reaching for glue and fasteners.)

You can assemble the crown molding in place on the corner cabinet because of the glue blocks mounted to the cabinet top and hidden from view by the crown. To do this first make the glue blocks from ¾" plywood or hardwood. Hold a piece of your molding in position to obtain the spring angle for the glue blocks **[PHOTO E]**. Then machine the blocks on your mitersaw, alternately cutting

the spring angle and 90-degree cutoff from a long blank rather than cutting the spring angle onto blocks precut to length, which would place your fingers dangerously close to the blade. Attach the glue blocks to the cabinet with glue and screws.

When cutting any molding on a mitersaw, always plunge through the cut and then let the blade stop spinning before lifting. Lifting too soon could allow the blade to catch on the molding and damage it or it could forcefully eject the cutoff.

For the corner cabinet you'll need three pieces of crown: right, front, and left—with all miters cut at 22½ degrees. For the best grain match, cut the pieces in order, with as little waste as possible between the miters. Cut the right piece first, about 1' in length, with an outside right miter on the left side. Measure, mark, and cut the front piece with miters at each end, beginning with the right side. Finally cut the left piece 1' long, with an outside left miter on its right side.

Mark the left and right moldings **[PHOTO F]** and cut them to length with 90-degree cuts. Use yellow glue to attach the molding to the glue blocks, as well as to

Make all four cuts from just two positions

By setting your mitersaw at 45 degrees to the left, you can cut inside right and outside left miters.

Switch your saw to 45 degrees on the right side, and you can cut outside right and inside left miters.

Inside right

Outside left

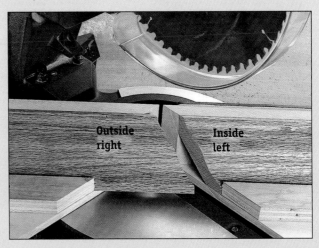

Outside right

Inside left

CROWN MOLDING FOR BOOKCASES AND CABINETS *(CONTINUED)*

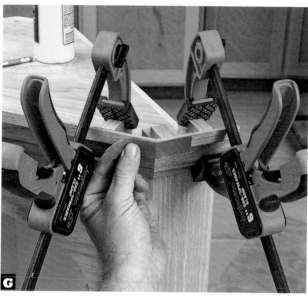

G

Use clamps to hold the crown molding to the cabinet and apply painter's tape to help draw the miters tight.

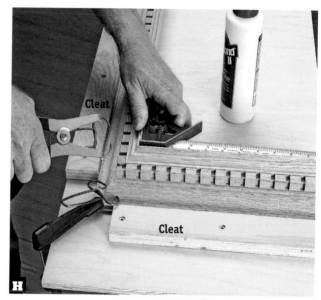

H

Assemble the moldings with PVA glue, holding the miters tight and square with spring clamps at the outside corners.

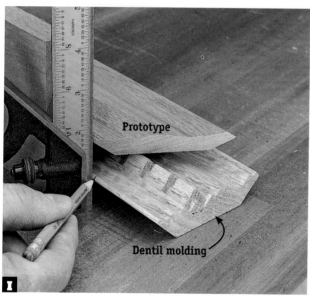

I

With the prototype piece centered on the dentil molding, use a square to transfer the bottom corner mark for cutting.

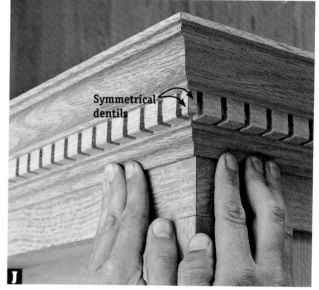

J

Hold the mating pieces of dentil crown in place on the project and cut them so their miters are symmetrical.

the back edge of the crown that contacts the project face, and clamp it to the glue blocks **[PHOTO G]**. (See Resources, pages 236-237.)

ASSEMBLE CROWN IN A JIG TO ENSURE SQUARE CORNERS

Assembling crown molding directly on a project can be difficult when you are not using hidden glue blocks or when clamping proves nearly impossible).

For these situations preassemble your molding in a jig that guarantees square results. Cut your moldings to the exact lengths needed and then build a simple jig of cleats attached to a piece of plywood **[PHOTO H]**. If your situation won't allow prefabing the corners, cut a prototype piece to check the fit. Once satisfied, use the piece as a guide to mark the dentil molding **[PHOTO I]**. Cut the facing piece so the dentils mirror each other **[PHOTO J]**.

BASEBOARDS

DECORATE AND PROTECT YOUR WALLS WITH BASEBOARDS. INSTALL THEM WITH BUTT JOINTS, COPE JOINTS, MITERS, OR A COMBINATION OF ALL THREE.

Baseboards and window or door casings are often designed and installed with each other in mind. The molding that the Wood Moulding & Millwork Producers Association calls WM 618 is commonly known as "colonial" and is often used with "colonial" casing (WM 346), shown in the illustration below. "Clamshell" (WM 709) baseboard is almost always used with clamshell casing (WM 329). WM 750 and WM 376 combine for a more Victorian look.

Like crown molding baseboard is traditionally put together with a cope joint. The reason is much the same: Walls seldom meet at a true 90-degree angle. Even when they do there is a buildup of plaster or joint compound that throws the miter out of whack.

Baseboard is available in seven basic styles, although your lumberyard or home center might not stock them all. If you want something custom, build up your own baseboard by combining other moldings. "Base cap" in particular is designed to be used to cap off a flat 1× baseboard.

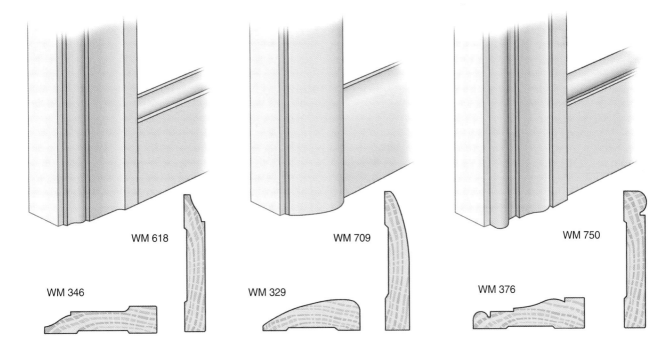

WM 618

WM 709

WM 750

WM 346

WM 329

WM 376

BASEBOARDS *(CONTINUED)*

Lay out efficiently

Speed up a job and make fewer errors by planning ahead. Start opposite the door with a molding long enough to reach from corner to corner, so people entering the room won't be distracted by a splice. If there's no molding on the wall opposite the door, butt-joint a piece against the corners of the longest wall, so that a cope doesn't accidentally make the piece too short.

Keep coped surfaces perpendicular to the line of sight so that gaps are less evident. This might mean installing more than one piece with two square ends, as shown at the bottom of the illustration.

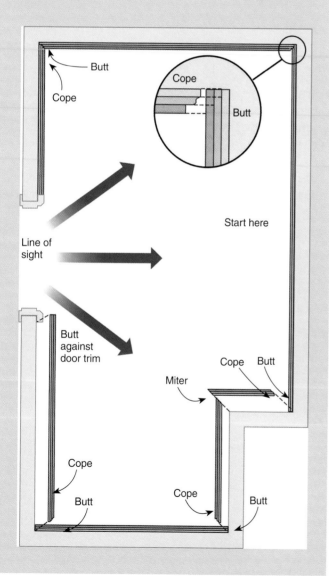

CUTTING CORNERS

Baseboard moldings that are perfectly flat in profile can be butted against each other at inside corners. They can overlap on outside corners, but the difference between end grain and face grain will call attention to the joint. It's far better, and not much more difficult, to miter the corner.

If the baseboard profile has any shape to it, however, it needs more complicated joinery. Once again because the walls are imperfect at corners, miters will fail you. Cope joints (see pages 140–141) not only work better, they hold together better as the house settles.

Outside corners *can* be mitered. Cutting a miter for an out-of-square outside corner is simple, and once the molding is installed, other imperfections are usually hidden.

INSTALLING THE MOLDING

Built-up moldings might use several joints. When you're working with built-up moldings, install all of one type of molding before you move on to the next, allowing you to use the easiest joints. The molding in the illustration opposite bottom includes baseboard, a base cap, and base shoe. Your combination might be simpler. (See other baseboard options, opposite.)

Start by installing the baseboard all the way around the room, butting inside corners and mitering outside corners. Install the base cap next, coping inside

Outside corners are rarely perfectly square. Use a framing square to check a corner.

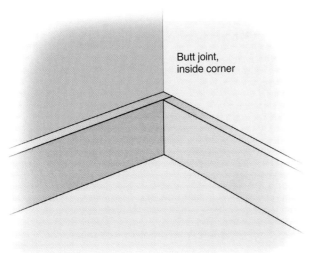

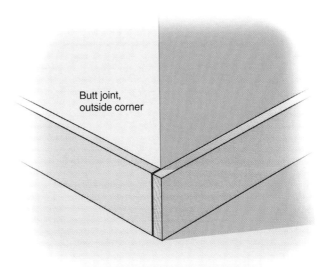

Baseboard with a flat profile

When the molding is completely flat, you can butt-join inside corners. Flat pieces can overlap on an outside corner as shown, but a miter hides the end grain and looks much more finished.

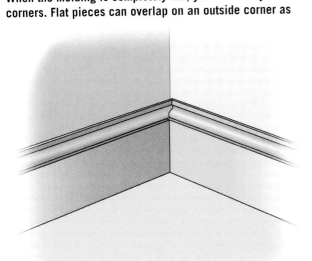

Baseboard with contoured profiles

If a molding profile has any contours to it, installation is more challenging—butt joints aren't an option. You'll need to cope the molding at all inside corners and miter all outside corners.

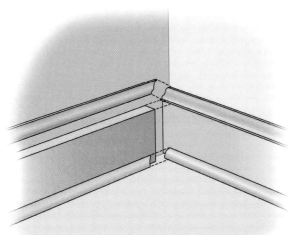

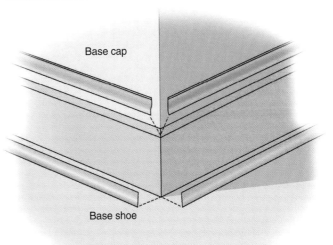

Combination joints

With this combination you can butt-join the baseboard stock in an inside corner—the joint will be covered by the base cap. However miter the baseboard (cap and base shoe as well) on all outside corners.

corners and mitering outside ones. Finish up with the quarter round, installing it like the base cap—cope inside corners and miter outside ones.

The cope joint handles any out-of-square inside corner, but outside corners are another matter. If the angle is less than 90 degrees, the miter will be somewhat less than 45 degrees. If the corner is more than 90 degrees, the miter is somewhat more than 45 degrees. But how much less or more?

Simple geometry saves you from protractors and cutting trial pieces until you happen to get it right. Trace along the edge of a board to draw a line on the floor parallel to each wall. A line connecting the corner of the wall with the corner formed by the lines is the angle of the correct miter. Simply follow the steps shown here to set a sliding T-bevel to the angle and then use the T-bevel to set the proper angle on your saw.

1. Draw layout lines.
If the corner is out of square, draw a line on the floor parallel to each wall using a scrap of wood.

2. Set the angle.
Set a T-bevel to the angle of the line running from the wall corner to the intersection of the lines you drew.

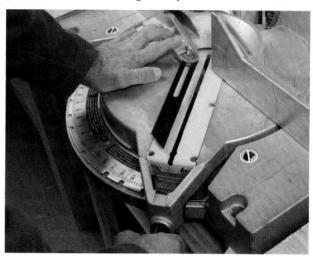

3. Set the saw angle.
Set the saw to match the angle of the bevel and miter the baseboard. Set the angle to the other side to cut the second baseboard.

Using block corners
Corner blocks, popular in Victorian trim, make it possible to install baseboard without cutting miters. Several different profiles are available in different woods from home centers and lumberyards.

Install the corner blocks first, checking to make sure they are plumb (straight up and down). Measure, cut the baseboard to length with straight cuts, and nail in place.

SCARF JOINTS

While you can simply butt two pieces of baseboard together to get a longer piece, the joint doesn't hold up over the long run. As floors settle and wood expands and contracts, the joint eventually breaks and stands out for all to see.

The better way to splice is with a miter, an approach known as a scarf joint. Because the two pieces overlap and are tied together by nails and glue, they stay together over time.

For the best joint cut the outer miter first and anchor it firmly over a stud. Tuck the other miter behind it and nail through the joint, and the front of the two pieces will automatically align.

1. Miter the first piece.
Measure so the splice is centered over a stud. Cut the miter so it will overlap the second piece.

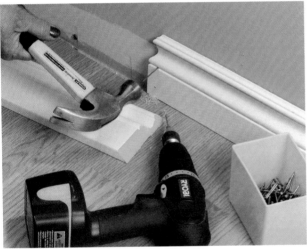

2. Nail the first piece in place.
Nail the molding in place. When fastening the mitered end, keep the nails just outside of the joint.

3. Add the second piece.
Tuck the second piece behind the first. Nail through the miter and then into studs along the rest of the wall.

Built-up base options

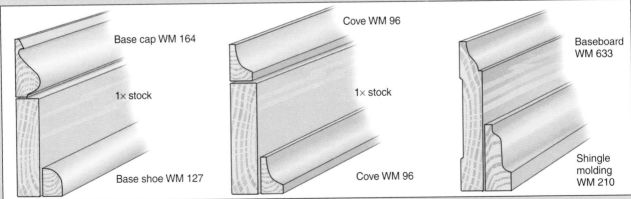

Base cap WM 164

1× stock

Base shoe WM 127

Cove WM 96

1× stock

Cove WM 96

Baseboard WM 633

Shingle molding WM 210

This combination tops 1× with base cap. Base shoe finishes off the bottom.

For a cove baseboard top a 1× with a cove and use a cove along the base.

Nail shingle molding to Colonial base for profiles that echo each other.

WALL FRAMES

THIS TREATMENT IS A BEAUTIFUL WAY TO SET APART ANY ROOM IN YOUR HOUSE. MITERS AND MOLDING MAKE THE PROCESS EASY.

Wall frames take the place of the frame-and-panel wallcoverings that you might see in the library of a British mystery movie or in the lobby of a Victorian mansion. With beveled panels housed inside mortise-and-tenon frames, frame-and-panel walls are labor-intensive and require a fair amount of skill.

A frame wall, on the other hand, mimics the panels with what are essentially a series of simple picture frames. A few 45-degree miters combined with complementary baseboard and chair rail give much the same effect as true frame-and-panel without requiring advanced degrees in both cabinetmaking and carpentry.

Before you start sketch out your plans on graph paper. Draw in the chair rail first, somewhere between 30" and 40" off the floor. Then draw in the baseboard; prefab baseboard runs between 2¾" and 5¼" wide, but you can make your own at almost any height.

At this point designing becomes a matter of simple arithmetic. Frames are traditionally 1.5 times as

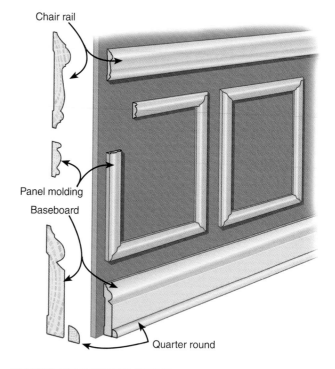

Chair rail

Panel molding

Baseboard

Quarter round

1. Miter the frames.
Fasten a stop to the saw bed so that similar pieces will be exactly the same length.

2. Make a jig.
Screw a piece of sheet goods to a larger piece of plywood. Screw in a stop and assemble the corners.

3. Prefab the frames.
Remove the stop. Glue the miters and clamp the pieces in place. Fasten the corners together to make the frame.

4. Attach the frames.
Strike a level line. Make a T-spacer to easily maintain consistent spacing. Fasten through studs where possible.

5. Adjust for obstructions.
When you run up against a window or door, adjust the size of frames, maintaining consistent spacing.

6. Fill the gaps.
Fill any gaps with paintable putty or caulk. Put on a latex glove and wipe the filler smooth with your finger.

long as they are high. The spaces above, below, and between the frames average about 3", although you can experiment. A chair rail 36" high, with a 5-inch baseboard and 3-inch spacing, would call for a frame 25" high:

36" – 5" (baseboard) – 3" (below the frame) – 3" (above the frame) = 25".

And a frame 25" high would be 25"×1.5 or 37½" long.

You can use any molding you want for the frames and can even put something like wainscoting or wallpaper behind them. The key to success is assembling the frames *before* you put them on the wall, so that you get tight joints. The simple jig shown here makes the job easier by ensuring that the corners stay square during assembly. For best results build the frames in stages. Assemble half of each frame—two pieces—first. When the glue has dried, glue the halves together. This minimizes the number of joints (and problems) that you're dealing with at any one time.

Adding a picture rail
A framed wall is often topped with picture rail. Although largely decorative the Victorians actually attached an elaborate hook and fabric rope to the molding and hung pictures from the rope. On a framed wall picture rail creates a unified look for the entire wall.

In a standard 8' room, install the rail with as little as a 1" space between it and the ceiling. In a room with 10' ceilings, the rail might be as much as a foot below the ceiling.

Lay out the molding with a laser level or by snapping a level chalkline. Make pencil marks below the line to show where the studs are. Start by butting two ends along the most visible wall and cope as you work around the room.

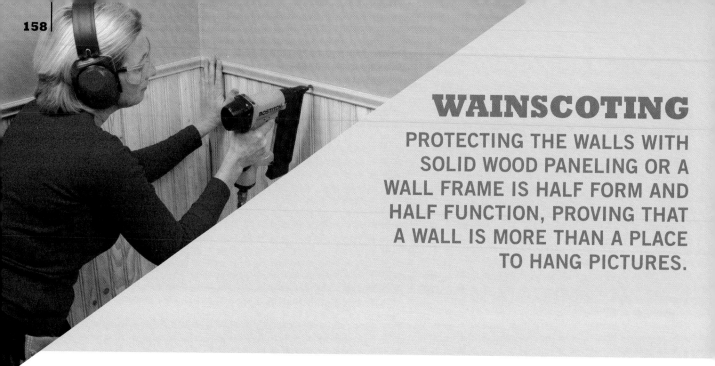

WAINSCOTING

PROTECTING THE WALLS WITH SOLID WOOD PANELING OR A WALL FRAME IS HALF FORM AND HALF FUNCTION, PROVING THAT A WALL IS MORE THAN A PLACE TO HANG PICTURES.

Wainscoting is a layer of solid wood applied over walls, in part to protect them and in part as decoration. Though it can enhance any room, it seems to be most often applied to dining rooms. That tradition likely began because the dining room was where chairs were most often pushed back, potentially damaging walls. Wainscoting takes two primary forms—beaded board and frame-and-panel.

BEADED BOARD, V-BOARD

Beaded board and V-board are made of long, narrow strips that fit together side by side with tongue-and-groove joinery. With beaded board a bead or two runs along the long edge of the board; V-board has a V-groove. Both contribute decoration and camouflage

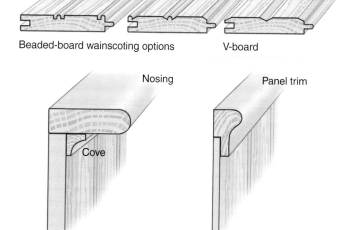

Beaded-board wainscoting options   V-board

Nosing   Panel trim

Cove

Prepping the wall

Each of the boards in board wainscoting needs to be anchored firmly to the wall. Because studs are 16" apart on center, creating some sort of anchor in between them is part of installing wainscoting.

There are two approaches. One is to cut away part of the plaster or drywall and replace it with plywood nailer for attaching the tongue-and-groove boards.

A less labor-intensive but messier method is to skip the plywood and put construction adhesive on the back of every strip. Nail the pieces to the drywall to hold them in place while the adhesive dries.

Replace a strip of drywall with plywood to create a more solid nailing surface.

Construction adhesive works as well as a nailer. Have paint thinner on hand to clean up dribbles.

1. Install nailers, scribe first piece.
Cut away part of the drywall and replace it with plywood so that each strip is nailed into something solid. Starting in a corner scribe (see box below) and test-fit the first piece.

2. Cut the pieces.
Mass-produce subsequent pieces using a fence and stop attached to the miter gauge. They make it easier to cut pieces to the same length.

3. Install the boards.
Level and temporarily install a guide strip against which you can push each board for a consistent edge. Fasten through the second piece into the wall, leaving $1/16$" between the edge of the first and the second board.

the seam. Sometimes the pieces you install are a single strip. Other times a wider strip is made to look like two narrower strips. Either type is easy to install, although the wide boards go in twice as fast. The boards are topped off with nosing, panel trim, or chair rail. Or you can put together your own arrangement by combining various moldings.

INSTALLING TONGUE-AND-GROOVE WAINSCOTING
Some things are more or less automatic when installing tongue-and-groove wainscoting. Start by drawing a level line on the wall to show where the top of the boards of the chair rail will be. To simplify installation attach a temporary guide strip along that line. Butt the boards against it as you install them.

Scribing for a tight fit
Wainscoting needs to be plumb and tight against the wall. If the wall isn't flat or plumb, trim or "scribe" the edge that goes against the wall. Start by tacking the piece to be trimmed so that it's plumb and as tight as possible against the wall. Set a compass to the width of the widest gap, or slightly wider, and trace along the wall. Remove the piece and cut along the line with a jigsaw. Reinstall it with the untrimmed edge plumb, and the trimmed edge will nest against the wall.

To simplify measuring cut a batch of boards that reach from the line to about a ½" above the floor. Don't worry about the gap that this will create: The baseboard will cover it.

Some things are not so automatic. The first board you install has to be perfectly plumb, or all the boards will go in crooked. Scribe and plumb the first board before you install it. Space the following boards ¹⁄₁₆" apart—the width of an 8d nailhead—and check every other board for plumb. With some thicker wainscoting boards, you can fasten through the tongue; the fastening head will be hidden by the groove of the next board. Some boards are too thin for this; nail into the indentation along the bead or into the V-groove instead.

4. Butt inside corners.
Continue spacing and nailing along the wall. At inside corners butt corner pieces together.

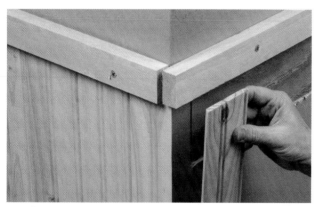

5. Overlap outside corners.
Cut the piece along the first wall to fit, removing the tongue if it's exposed. Cut the groove off a piece or rip a miter joint as shown. Nail it to the second wall so that it overlaps the installed wainscoting.

6. Add the cap.
Remove the guide strips and install the panel trim (shown) or chair rail. Nail the baseboard and shoe in place.

FRAME-AND-MOLDING PANELING

The building block of a frame-and-panel wainscoting is a frame biscuit that's joined (or if you want to get fancy, mortise-and-tenoned) together. Once upon a time a beveled panel was housed in grooves in the frame, filling the space inside the frame. Doors were once made this way and, like a door, a frame usually had several openings and several panels. Instead of using a panel, a popular variation of frame-and-panel has a molding that runs around the inside of the frame to create a beveled look.

Accurate crosscuts are vital to this project. Pieces that are supposed to be the same length must be *exactly* the same length if a frame is to be square. The ability to cut pieces to the same length without measuring speeds things up considerably.

1. Cut the pieces and test-fit.
Rip the pieces to width, then cut them to length using a stop (see inset). Test-assemble them without glue and lay out the biscuit joints.

2. Cut the biscuit joints.
Put the wood and the biscuit joiner flat on a piece of sheet goods and cut the biscuit slots.

3. Assemble the frame.
Make another test assembly with clamps, disassemble, and then glue the frame together. Allow plenty of drying time—you don't want the frame loosening as you place it on the wall.

4. Install the frame.
Locate and mark the wall studs. Set the frame in place and level it. Use shims to hold it level while you fasten it. Fasten it into the studs.

5. Install molding.
Install chair rail above the frame. Choose a molding (cove is used here), miter-cut it to length, and install it around the inside edges of the openings.

The best way to make accurate cuts or to cut without measuring is to attach a wood fence and stop to the saw. On a mitersaw clamp the fence in place. Tablesaw miter gauges usually have holes or slots through which you can run screws to make the attachment.

Make the stop from a small piece of wood with the ends cut square. Clamp it to the fence with spring clamps or small C-clamps (see inset photo, Step 1). When you put boards against the stop, do so gently; banging repeatedly into the stop can edge it away from its original position, making each board slightly longer than the one before.

Frame-and-molding paneling is best assembled in the shop or on the floor near where it will go. Doing so gives you far more control over the way the pieces go together. Your joints will be tighter, and your corners will be squarer.

Trying to assemble the frame piece by piece on the wall, on the other hand, leaves you at the mercy of a board that might be warped or slightly out of plumb. You might well find yourself cutting pieces to fit, one by one, and struggling with spacing and keeping things square.

This is definitely a job for a biscuit joiner. The biscuits allow you to successfully glue end grain to edge grain and hold the piece together.

To save wood the bottom of the frame can be several inches above the floor, as long as the distance is about an inch less than the width of the baseboard. If you use this approach, run a strip of furring across the wall at floor level and nail the baseboard into the frame and furring.

There's no need for an inset nailer or construction adhesive. The frame will span several studs that you can nail into.

PROJECTS

chapter 6

WHETHER YOU ARE PLANNING A MINOR KITCHEN UPGRADE
or a major interior redo, the projects in this chapter are at
your service. You can build a project exactly as designed
or adapt it for your particular situation. Each builds upon

WALL PANELING

FAUX CEILING BEAMS

COLUMNS AND ARCHES

SHELVES AND BOOKCASES

KITCHEN CABINETS

skills, tools, and materials covered earlier in this book and includes enough detail for you to successfully complete the project even if you are new to finish carpentry and trimwork.

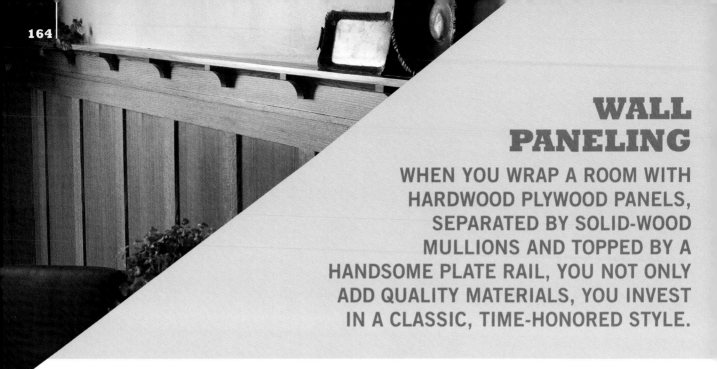

WALL PANELING

WHEN YOU WRAP A ROOM WITH HARDWOOD PLYWOOD PANELS, SEPARATED BY SOLID-WOOD MULLIONS AND TOPPED BY A HANDSOME PLATE RAIL, YOU NOT ONLY ADD QUALITY MATERIALS, YOU INVEST IN A CLASSIC, TIME-HONORED STYLE.

You'll find the woodworking for this project fairly straightforward. But the planning stage could pose a challenge. Will you need to add or move electrical outlets and switches? How will you handle the HVAC registers? If you have windows to trim around, does that dictate the mullion spacing?

Make a scale drawing of each wall involved in your project. It will focus your attention on any potential problems and help you visualize the end result. Adapt the dimensions shown in the Wall panel and plate rail assembly drawing, opposite.

Just like cabinet doors these panels need proper proportions to look good. To avoid waste you could plan to cut a 4×8' sheet of ¼" plywood lengthwise into three equal strips, each 15⅞" wide. However 17" widths were chosen in this project to center one mullion on the wall and one under each window for a nice, symmetrical look. If you need to make an end panel wider than the rest by an inch

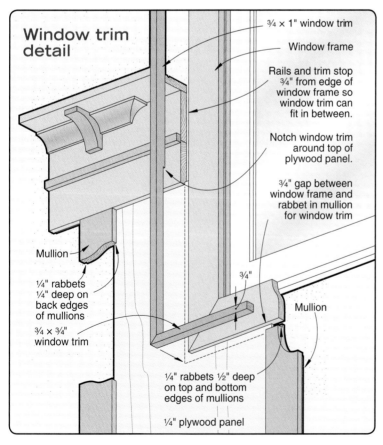

Window trim detail

- ¾ × 1" window trim
- Window frame
- Rails and trim stop ¾" from edge of window frame so window trim can fit in between.
- Notch window trim around top of plywood panel.
- ¾" gap between window frame and rabbet in mullion for window trim
- Mullion
- ¼" rabbets ¼" deep on back edges of mullions
- ¾ × ¾" window trim
- ¾"
- Mullion
- ¼" rabbets ½" deep on top and bottom edges of mullions
- ¼" plywood panel

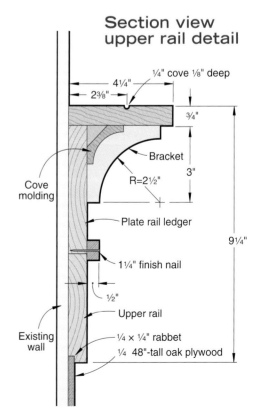

Section view upper rail detail

- ¼" cove ⅛" deep
- 4¼"
- 2⅜"
- ¾"
- Bracket
- R=2½"
- 3"
- Cove molding
- Plate rail ledger
- 9¼"
- 1¼" finish nail
- ½"
- Upper rail
- ¼ × ¼" rabbet
- ¼ 48"-tall oak plywood
- Existing wall

or so, go ahead—no one will notice the difference. As for the height, plan for the plate rail to perch about 6' above the floor.

START SHAPING THE PIECES

Measure the thickness of your plywood before you begin shaping the rabbets on the mullions. Sometimes ¼" plywood is less than ¼" thick. The panels must fit snugly in the rabbets for the project to look its best.

If your wall has windows with interior trim that won't match your new paneling, replace the trim with a flat frame of oak. These trim pieces were cut 4" wide. Rather than working on the wall, use a biscuit joiner to assemble each frame in the shop, carry it to a window, and nail it in place. Doing it that way helps ensure square corners and tight miter joints.

The plate rail brackets were made from 8/4 lumber, but you could laminate pieces of 4/4 stock. Cut a template to match the shape shown in the Section view upper rail detail drawing, opposite. Trace that shape onto each piece of stock, saw close to the line, and finish up with a drum sander.

A pneumatic brad nailer speeds up a big project such as this one. When

This is one project where a brad nailer really pays off in speed and neat installation.

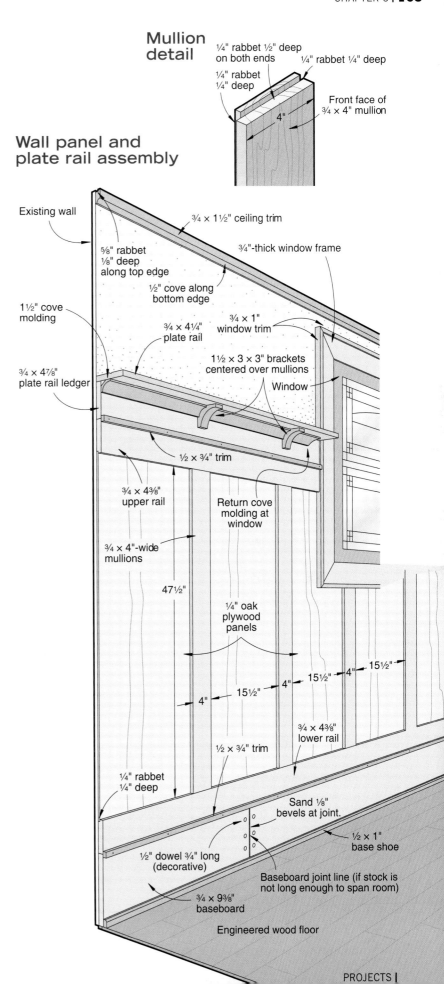

Mullion detail

Wall panel and plate rail assembly

WALL PANELING *(CONTINUED)*

you're finished stain and varnish everything before filling the brad holes with putty that matches the stained wood. Then apply a second coat of varnish.

SIX STEPS TO INSTALLATION

1 **BASE.** Begin building at the bottom with a big, solid-looking baseboard. We used ¾" boards 9⅜" wide, cut a slight chamfer on the edge of any boards that butt together, and used a biscuit joiner to keep those joints lined up. Use a level to keep the boards straight despite an uneven floor.

A ¾" board 4⅜" wide sits on top of the baseboard and serves as the lower rail for the panel frames. Nail those boards into the wall studs. If you plan on new flooring, wait to install the base shoe.

2 **PANELING.** Temporarily set the mullions in place, as shown in **PHOTO A.** Mark their locations on the wall. Use a strip of masking tape at the top end so the marks will stand out. The inset photo shows you how to hold the mullions while you make sure everything is lined up properly. Drive a screw into the wall just above the rabbeted tongue. The screw head keeps the board in place. Then make matching alignment marks on the tape and the board. Once they're all up and the layout looks good, cut the panels to fit.

Stock up on construction adhesive because you will quickly empty those tubes from this point on. Starting at one end of a wall, fasten the first mullion into place, keeping it square with the baseboard. Apply a wavy bead of adhesive down its back and two nails through the tongue of the upper rabbet.

Apply a wide, wavy bead of adhesive to a panel, slip it into the rabbet of the baseboard, as shown in **PHOTO B,** and then slide it into the side rabbet of the mullion and press it against the wall. When you come to the new window frame, cut panels to fit snugly.

Leave a ¾" gap for trim between the window frame and the face of each mullion, as seen in **PHOTO C.**

3 **WINDOW TRIM.** Cover the seam between the window frame and the wall panel with a ¾"×1" strip. As shown in **PHOTO D,** you'll cut a notch on the side strips that's ¼" deep and runs from the lower end of the trim strip to the top edge of the paneling. The strip along the bottom of the window is ¾"×¾". Nail these trim pieces to the frame with brads.

A

Align the mullions to check your layout. The inset shows how to hold them before you're ready to nail.

B

Apply construction adhesive and slide the panels into place.

C

D

Leave a gap between the window frame and adjacent mullions and fit the window trim pieces.

E Set the plate rail ledger atop the upper rail and fasten with finish nails.

F A homemade gauge is more reliable than measuring for keeping the trim aligned.

4 **UPPER RAIL AND LEDGER.** Mirroring the baseboard design an upper rail and a plate rail ledger run across the top of the paneling. The rabbet along the bottom edge of the upper rail mates with the panels and the rabbeted end of each mullion. The plate rail ledger sits atop the upper rail, as shown in **PHOTO E.** Fasten both of those boards to the wall studs with finish nails.

A ½"×¾" trim strip covers the seam between the ledger and upper rail, and another strip of the same dimensions covers the seam between the baseboard and lower rail. **PHOTO F** shows a homemade gauge that helps you install each trim piece perfectly straight. Glue two scraps together to form a gauge that hangs on the top edge of the ledger and locates the top edge of the trim. Make another for the narrower lower rail.

G Pocket-screw holes fasten the brackets in place. The shelf covers the opening.

5 **BRACKETS.** Drill pocket-holes (see page 55) in the top of each bracket and center a bracket above each full-length mullion, using a square to mark the location on the ledger. Align the top surface of each bracket with the top edge of the ledger to support the plate rail shelf.

Hold a small square against the bracket to keep it lined up while you nail through the lower end. Then drive a self-tapping pocket screw through the hole, as shown in **PHOTO G.** (If you don't have a pocket-hole jig, you can toenail the bracket in place from the top.)

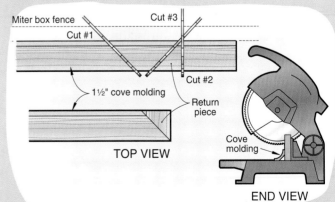

H Cove trim fits between the brackets to add depth and dimension to the shelf.

6 **PLATE RAIL SHELF.** Nail the plate rail shelf to the ledger and the support brackets. The final bit of trim consists of 1½" oak cove molding, readily available at home centers. Cut pieces to fit exactly between the brackets and nail them in place, as shown in **PHOTO H.**

When we came to the windows, we cut the end piece of molding to make a "return." See box at right for cutting details. Glue the return to the molding as shown. It sits 2" from the end of the shelf.

Cutting the cove return piece

Miter box fence

Cut #1

Cut #3

1½" cove molding

Cut #2

Return piece

TOP VIEW

Cove molding

END VIEW

FAUX CEILING BEAMS

THIS EASY PROJECT IS AN IDEAL WAY TO DRESS UP A DINING ROOM OR FAMILY ROOM CEILING, GIVING A ROOM A DISTINCT LOOK THAT SETS IT APART FROM THE REST OF THE HOUSE.

Faux ceiling beams are easy to build and install—truly a project you can complete in a couple of weekends. The beams shown in this project use dimensional lumber—no ripping any long pieces.

As you plan check the location of your ceiling joists. For surest support run your faux beams perpendicular to the joists. However the joists might not be exactly where you want your beams. If for appearance's sake you need to run the beams parallel to the joists, you have a couple of alternatives. If you have access from the attic above, add 2× blocking between the joists into which you can fasten the nailer for the beam. If there is no access from above, you can install toggle bolts through the 1×6 nailer every 16".

It is tough working above your head, so this project is organized to do as much as possible at sawhorse level. Consider finishing your lumber in advance so

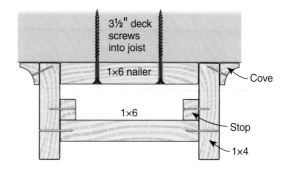

you won't have to add the finish in situ. You'll do a neater job and won't have to climb any ladders to do your painting. In addition drill pilot holes and start fasteners before you attach components in place.

You should be able to find lumber up to 16' in length, enough to span a typical dining room. If your beams will be longer, use a scarf joint (see page 91).

A Using a stud finder (see page 13), locate each ceiling joist and mark it with painter's tape. Measure in two places for the edge of the backerboard and tack in 8d nails.

B Set the nailer against the 8d nails. Fasten the board with two 3½" deck screws at every joist. If you cannot find a joist (sometimes the case along walls), add a toggle bolt.

C Once the sides have been cut to length, attach the stop that will hold the bottom piece. A homemade guide assures that the stop is positioned correctly.

D Be sure that your pilot holes for attaching the sides are no more than ½" from the edge so you can cover them with molding later.

1 **MARK FOR THE NAILERS.** Work out the space you want between beams. Halve that space between beams and parallel walls. Mark for the beam location by measuring out from the wall at two points, each a couple of feet from where the ends of the beams will be. Mark the centers of each beam location and then measure 2¾" to one side of the centerline. Tack an 8d nail at that point. This will give you something to push the nailers against as you place them. Mark the joist or blocker locations with painter's tape **[PHOTO A]**. Transfer these measurements to each nailer, making an X on the joist side of the mark.

2 **INSTALL THE NAILERS.** Cut the 1×6 backer board to length less ¼"—the board will be covered, so there is no need for an exact fit. Drill a pilot hole and start two 3½" deck screws at each joist location. Make two T-supports with 2×2s and a scrap of plywood. Cut them so they are slightly longer than needed so you can bow them in place to hold the nailer in place as you fasten it, as shown in **PHOTO B**.

3 **PREPARE THE BEAM SIDES.** Carefully measure for the length of the first beam and cut a 1×4 side piece to length. Test the fit; by bowing it slightly you can snap it in place. When satisfied with the fit, cut the second side, the cove molding, and the bottom piece from 1×6 stock. Make a guide for installing the parting stop with scrap plywood. Using this guide glue and nail the stop **[PHOTO C]**.

4 **INSTALL THE SIDES.** To attach the sides to the backer board, drill pilot holes ½" from the edge and start 1½" square-drive finish screws **[PHOTO D]**. Using your T-braces or a willing helper, position each side piece and attach it.

5 **INSTALL THE BOTTOM.** Test-fit the bottom piece, then apply glue to the stops and push the bottom piece in place **[PHOTO E]**. Again using your T-brace to hold it, shoot 1½" brads into the stop or fasten with 4d finish nails.

6 **ADD TRIM.** To cover the fastener heads and complete the project, attach the cove molding **[PHOTO F]**. Putty the nail holes.

E Test the bottom piece. If you are satisfied with the fit, add glue and push the bottom piece into place. Fasten with brads or 4d finish nails.

F Add cove molding to the upper edge of the beam. It will conform to any variations in the ceiling and neatly cover the gap between the beam and the ceiling.

COLUMNS AND ARCHES

HERE'S A PROJECT THAT WILL BRING BEAUTIFUL CRAFTSMAN STYLE TO YOUR HOME AND PROVIDE A GENTLE DIVIDER TO OTHERWISE WIDE OPEN SPACES.

These ornamental columns, connected to a gently arched soffit, were designed to finish off the room divider cabinets shown on pages 190–197, but they can be adapted to suit most any situation. How can you plan and build an arch? And what's the best way to form a column?

FASHION A SOPHISTICATED SWEEP

First consider the framing to which the arch will be attached. Owners of the home shown added wall studs and blocking between ceiling joists to provide solid attachment points for the arch. If you don't plan to tear into the walls and ceiling as you remodel, consider placing the arch to take advantage of the existing framing.

Start with graph paper when you're laying out an arch. Draw the area to scale, then design a gentle, symmetrical curve that's pleasing to the eye. This arch flows from a 12" height at the ends to 6¼" at the middle of a 108" span, as shown in **DRAWING 1.**

To transfer that curve to ¾" plywood or to particleboard, mark the end points and center point on the sheet goods with a pencil. Drive a nail halfway in at each point. Cut a ⅛" strip of scrap wood long enough to contact all three nails and use it as a fairing stick. Place it against the end points, then push the middle up to the center point. Mark the resulting curve with a pencil.

Cut the resulting line carefully with a jigsaw to form the upper arch (A). If your arch is longer than a single sheet, mark the curve on sheets butted together. Keep it as smooth as possible, but remember that minor flaws will disappear under the drywall that's still to come. Save the waste material for later use.

If you make your arch in two pieces, join them with ¾" plywood about 12" long and slightly narrower than the center portion of the arch. Attach this glue block (B) with glue and screws, as shown in **DRAWING 2.** Trim the ends so that the arched pieces fit perfectly in place between the walls. Then cut two ¾" plywood end dividers (C) to fit between the arches ¾" from each end. The ones shown measure 12"×14". Add ¾" plywood dividers (D) between the sides, spaced approximately 2' apart. Screw the sides and dividers together to form the boxlike structure shown in **DRAWING 2.** Finally attach a bottom (E) made with two layers of ¼" plywood.

Because the vertical columns would meet a horizontal surface, the mini-soffits seen in **DRAWING 2** were added. We formed the sides (F) from the scraps left by cutting the arches, so the curves match. Cut each ¾" plywood end (G) 10" long and wide enough to match the sides. Then cut the bottom (H) 10" wide and 29⅞" long. Screw each mini-soffit together and use a belt sander to bevel parts G and H to match the sides. Attach these units to the upright arch with screws from inside the upright arch.

To make the mounting plates shown in **DRAWING 2A,** cut two pieces of ¾" plywood (I) to fit between the sides of the arch. Apply construction adhesive to both sides, then drive screws through the plates and into the studs. Find a helper and slide the arch structure into place. Drive screws through the arch sides and into the mounting plates, then toenail through the sides and into the ceiling joists or blocking.

The entire assembly received a layer of ⅜" drywall. You'll have no trouble bending drywall to the large radius of the arch. You'll need flexible corner bead to cover the curved edges, followed by joint compound.

Centerline (joint line)

*If arch is less than 96", it can be cut from one 4 × 8' sheet of plywood.

*108"

54"

Ⓐ Upper arch

6¼"

12"

¾" fir plywood

Ⓕ Mini-soffit side

Ⓕ Mini-soffit side

Waste   Waste

30⅝"

30⅝"

Stock cut from upper arch

Curve can be marked with a long stick laid across nails located at ends and at centerline.

Drawing 1 Arch layout

¾" plywood mounting plate

Apply construction adhesive to both sides of mounting plate before mounting.

Ⓘ

#8 × 3" deck screws driven into a wall stud

#8 × 2½" drywall screws

Ⓐ Ⓒ

Ⓓ

Assembled arch

Ⓐ Ⓔ

Ⓕ

Drawing 2 Arch exploded view

¾" plywood dividers

#8 × 1¼" F.H. wood screw

¾" plywood glue block glued and screwed to arch at joint

Drawing 2A Mounting plate detail

*If arch is less than 96", it can be cut from a sheet of 4 × 8' plywood.

Place end divider ¾" from end of arches (for mounting plate).

*108"

Ⓐ Ⓑ Ⓒ

Ⓓ

Ⓑ

Ⓓ

Ⓐ Ⓓ

Ⓐ

Ⓒ

Bevel bottom edge of dividers to match the curve of the arch.

Ⓐ

#8 × 1½" F.H. wood screws

¾" plywood arch

#8 × 2½" drywall screw

15½"

#8 × 1¼" F.H. wood screws

Ⓔ

Two layers of ¼" plywood (Might require multiple pieces if longer than 8'; stagger joints on each layer.)

#8 × 1¼" F.H. wood screws

¾" plywood bottom

Ⓕ Ⓗ

Ⓖ

#8 × 1½" F.H. wood screw

¾" plywood cut from upper arch

Ⓕ

15½"

Mini-soffits

¾" plywood end

Sand or cut bevel on edge of Ⓖ to match arch.

Ⓕ Ⓖ

Sand or cut bevel on end of Ⓗ to match arch.

Ⓗ Ⓕ

30⅝"

11½"

CLASSIC COLUMNS ON COMMAND

You can buy hollow columns 8' long in a wide range of diameters. Wood species offered may include cherry, mahogany, maple, oak, walnut, and several exotics. The columns shown in this project are 45" tall, but you could use the same procedures to go from floor to ceiling.

COLUMNS AND ARCHES *(CONTINUED)*

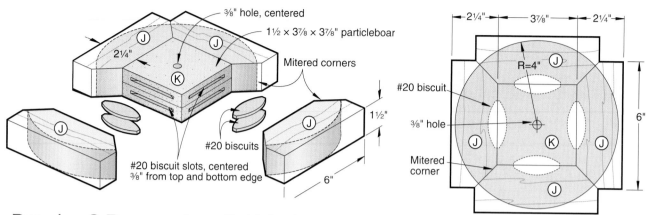

Drawing 3 Base and capital blank assembly

Don't plan for a pair of columns slightly over 4', if you could keep them shorter, because you'll waste most of an 8' piece. The manufacturer uses several thin plies of poplar to make the tube. Then a handsome, hardwood veneer goes on the outside, with the grain running the length of the column. The total wall thickness of the larger ones is about ¼". These cherry columns, 6" in diameter, cost less than $20 per foot (see Resources, pages 236–237).

MAKING THE TOP AND BOTTOM

The bottom end of each column nests inside a round, profiled hardwood base 8" in diameter. An identical piece serves as a capital at the top of the column. Square, hardwood blocks at the bottom and top, respectively, are properly called the plinth and the entablature, and these complete the assembly.

The base and capital are made of 1½" stock and measure 8" in diameter. You'll shape them from the blanks [DRAWING 3]. Using 1½"-thick hardwood of the same species as the columns, cut four sides

2¼" wide and 6" long (J). Cut a partial miter on all of the ends, making the short edge 3⅞". Then make a center square (K) from plywood or particleboard, laminated to a 1½" thickness. Cut it to 3⅞" on each side. Using two biscuits per joint, glue and clamp the four sides and the center into a single block.

The groove that receives the column must be cut to the exact diameter of that column. A circle cutter works well for this task (see Resources, pages 236–237). Mount the wing cutter in your drill press, clamp a piece of scrap on the table, and make a test cut. When the column fits snugly into place, you've found the right cutter setting. Form a groove ⅜" deep in the top of the base and the bottom of the capital [PHOTO A]. Widen the groove by shortening the cutting arc of the wing cutter. The bottom of the groove should be at least as wide as the column's wall thickness.

Place a compass in the center hole and draw a circle 8" in diameter. Cut close to the line on your bandsaw [PHOTO B], then carefully sand to the line on a disc

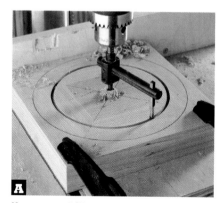

A Keep your drill press speed low and make sure the workpiece is clamped securely when using a circle cutter.

B Leave the pencil line as you cut the workpiece into a rough circle. Take the piece to a disc sander to true it up.

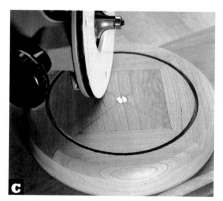

C Mount a cove-and-bead bit in your router and set it so that it rounds over the edge without cutting a shoulder.

sander. A ³⁄₈" radius cove-and-bead router bit (again see Resources, pages 236–237) was used to make the profile around the base and capital.

Stick a piece of cloth-backed, double-faced tape on the top of the workpiece and press the piece, top-down, onto a piece of scrap at least 6" wide and 15" long. Run a 2" screw through the center hole and into the scrap. Then clamp the scrap to your workbench.

Set the bit to cut a round-over profile only and rout counterclockwise around the workpiece. Hold the ball-bearing pilot firmly against the wood as you rout. Then remove the screw, flip the workpiece over, stick a new piece of double-faced tape on the bottom, and screw the workpiece to the scrap piece once again, and you'll produce the results shown in **PHOTO C.**

Now complete the profile. Make two or three passes, lowering the bit slightly each time, until you've reached the working depth of the bit, as shown in **PHOTO D.** A flat area will remain between the round-overs. Sand lightly to add some curvature there.

For the plinth and entablature, shown in **DRAWING 4,** cut enough 1½"-thick stock 2¾" wide to make eight mitered pieces (L), each one 9" on its longer edge. Glue these pieces into two squares, using a pair of biscuits at each corner.

CUTTING, ASSEMBLING THE COLUMN

It would be tough to make a solid column the exact length needed and then slide it into place. Fortunately you don't have to do that. The secret to a snug, secure placement lies hidden inside each of our finished columns.

To prepare a place for each column to stand, drop a plumb line from one side of the mini-soffit and make a mark on a piece of masking tape. Use that as a reference point for locating the plinth.

Attach the plinth with screws, as shown in **PHOTO E.** Locate the screws where the column base and capital will hide them.

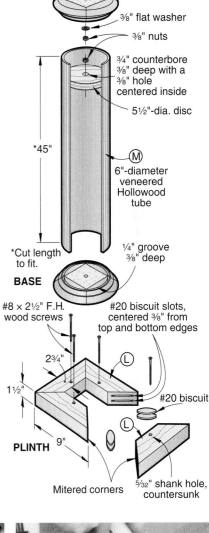

Drawing 4
Column
exploded view

Drawing 4A
Cross-section detail

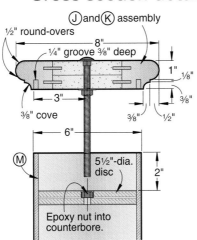

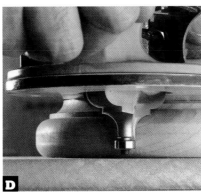

D Here the final profile appears to the left. On the right side, you see the result of the previous shallower pass.

E When setting the plinth locate the screws where they'll be hidden by the base and capital.

F

A long bolt allows you to adjust the height of the column. A shaped hole and epoxy prevent the nut from turning.

G

Apply epoxy at both ends, then slip the column assembly onto the plinth. Turn the capital to lock everything in place.

Use a tape measure to find the distance from plinth to entablature, as shown in **DRAWING 5.** Subtract 2³⁄₁₆" to determine the length for the Hollowood tube. This dimension will give you enough room to slide the column assembly into place. Cut the tube (M) to length, making sure to keep the saw perpendicular to the workpiece.

Now start building the internal assembly, shown in **DRAWINGS 4** and **4A,** that makes installation a snap. Using your bandsaw and disc sander, shape a scrap of particleboard or plywood into a 5½" disc that fits snugly into the tube.

Drill a ³⁄₈" hole through the center of the disc, then counterbore with a spade bit or Forstner bit to make a hole just slightly smaller than a ³⁄₈" hex-head nut. Shape this hole with a chisel to accept the corners of the nut, so that it fits snugly and won't turn. Spread epoxy around the sides of the hole and insert the nut, making sure to keep the adhesive out of the threads. Wait for the epoxy to harden.

Spread yellow glue around the inside of the tube, 2" below the rim. Slide the disc into place and let the glue dry.

You could wait until after installation to apply a finish, but it's more easily done now. Finish-sand all of the components and apply two or three coats of polyurethane varnish to all of the exposed surfaces, sanding lightly between coats with 220-grit sandpaper.

Now set the column in its base on the floor. Run a ³⁄₈" carriage bolt, 6" long, through the capital from above and tighten it to the capital with a ³⁄₈" nut and

washer. Start the bolt into the disc inside the column, as shown in **PHOTO F.**

Turn the capital clockwise, as viewed from above, until the tube bottoms out in the groove. Apply a thin layer of 2-hour epoxy to the bottom of the base and the top of the capital. Set the assembly on the plinth, align the base joints with the plinth joints, and have a helper hold it in place. Turn the capital clockwise, as viewed from below, until it contacts the entablature **[PHOTO G].** Make it snug and align the miter joints.

Check to see whether the finish needs any touch-up where the column moved against the base and capital. If so sand that area lightly and apply another coat of finish to the entire column.

Drawing 5 Column length detail

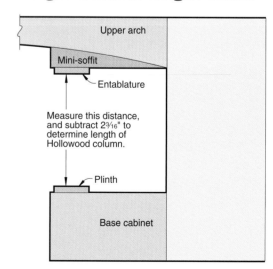

Upper arch

Mini-soffit

Entablature

Measure this distance, and subtract 2³⁄₁₆" to determine length of Hollowood column.

Plinth

Base cabinet

SHELVES AND BOOKCASES

WHETHER FOR BOOKS OR COLLECTIBLES, SHELF SPACE ALWAYS COMES IN HANDY. TRY THESE PROJECTS DESIGNED TO PUT THINGS IN THEIR PLACE.

OFF-THE-SHELF UPGRADE

You can buy a perfectly good off-the-shelf bookcase for less than it would cost you to purchase the lumber to build it. By adding a face frame, crown molding, and a kick plate to it, you can put together a bookcase with a substantial, built-in look. This project uses shelf units from IKEA, but you can vary the size and configuration to suit the ready-made shelves available to you. The face frame was made of birch.

Assemble the shelf units, fasten them together with trimhead screws, and experiment with a cardboard mock-up of the faceplate until you like the shape.

1 **LAY OUT THE ARCH.** On the 1×10, mark the width of the unit plus ¼" less the width of the side pieces. (The ¼" will extend the face frame slightly beyond the bookcases.) Using the jig

A

Exploded view

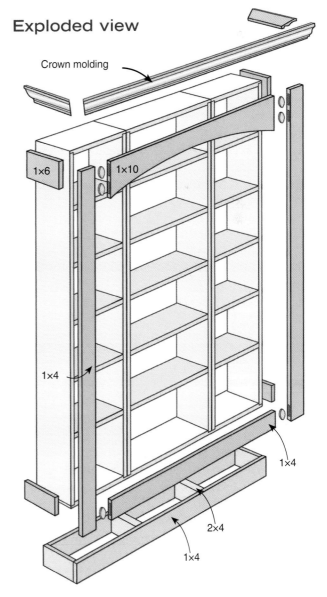

Crown molding

1×6

1×10

1×4

1×4

2×4

1×4

SHELVES AND BOOKCASES *(CONTINUED)*

arrangement shown in **PHOTO A** on page 175, bend and clamp a strip of wood roughly in the shape of your arch. To flatten the arc, you might have to clamp blocks in place as shown. When the arc matches your cardboard mock-up, trace along it and cut the arc with a jigsaw or bandsaw.

2 PREFAB THE BASE. Use 1×4 stock to make the base. Use hardwood for the front and sides and 2× pine for the interior bracing. Assemble as shown in **PHOTO B**.

3 ASSEMBLE THE FACE FRAME. Cut the bottom 1×4 and lay it and your arch on the shelf unit to mark the side pieces. Cut them to length with a tablesaw, power mitersaw, or circular saw. Carefully set the frame on the bookcase for a dry fit. Use a biscuit joiner (see pages 64 and 94–95) for making the joints. Place waxed paper beneath each joint to catch excess glue. Glue and place the biscuits and clamp the face frame **[PHOTO C]**. Use a carpenter's square to check for square. Let it dry overnight.

4 FASTEN FRAME TO CASE. Glue and fasten it in place and add the side pieces to the top **[PHOTO D]**. Attach crown molding **[PHOTO E]** following the directions on pages 147–150.

FINAL INSTALLATION

Fasten a 2×4 to the floor as a nailer for the kick plate. Use a stud finder to locate wall studs. Mount a 1×4 inside the upper part of the shelf unit and fasten it with 3" trimhead screws.

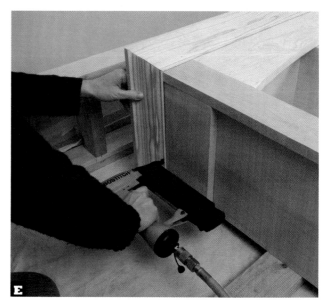

BUILT-IN CABINET IN THE CRAFTSMAN STYLE

FOR DISPLAY AND STORAGE THIS BEAUTY CAN BE ADAPTED TO YOUR SITUATION.

Chances are you have any number of ideal locations in your home for a built-in bookcase like the one at right. These rock-solid storage and display cases look great flanking a fireplace or entertainment center, tucked into a nook, or lining the walls of your home's study area. They're easy to make and add lasting value to your home. *Note: You'll need to adjust the dimensions to fit your location.* Quartersawn oak and straight-grained oak plywood were used in this project, but you can substitute other woods.

FIRST BUILD THE CABINET CASE

1 **CUT THE CASE PARTS.** Cut the cabinet sides (A), top and bottom (B), fixed shelf (C), and fixed-shelf edge banding (D). See the Materials List on page 179 for our dimensions. To make the most of your materials, consult the cutting diagram on page 178.

Before taking the next steps, check the 2×4 framed opening in your wall. If the opening is plumb, level, and square, the outside dimensions of the case should be ⅛" smaller in width and length than the opening. Cut the back (E) to size and check whether it will fit into the opening before proceeding.

2 **MARK THE GROOVE POSITIONS.** Mark positions for the shelf standards (see **DRAWING 1B**). Use a straightedge, router, and ⅝" straight bit set ³⁄₁₆" deep to rout the grooves. Stop the groove so the fixed shelf covers its rounded end.

3 **CUT HOLES FOR THE LIGHTS.** Using a 2⅛" hole saw, cut holes for the lights where shown on **DRAWING 1**.

4 **PREPARE CABINET PARTS.** Adjust your biscuit joiner's fence so the machine cuts a centered slot in the edge of ¾"-thick stock. Set its cutting depth for the #10 biscuits used throughout this project. (If you don't own a biscuit joiner, you can use rabbets and stopped dadoes, going with a slightly longer fixed shelf, top, and bottom.)

Cut the biscuit slots for joining the ends of the sides (A) and top and bottom (B) as shown in the box on page 179. (See pages 64 and 94–95 for more on using a biscuit joiner.)

5 **CUT SLOTS FOR SHELF EDGING.** Cut biscuit slots for joining the fixed-shelf edge banding (D) to the fixed shelf (C). Next cut the slots for joining the fixed shelf to the sides. To do this use the fixed shelf as a reference and straightedge for aligning and positioning the slots in the sides (A).

Mark with tape
Sanding pencil marks off open-grained woods, such as oak, can be challenging. Our solution: Mark the biscuit positions on masking tape, then peel away the tape before you clamp the joints.

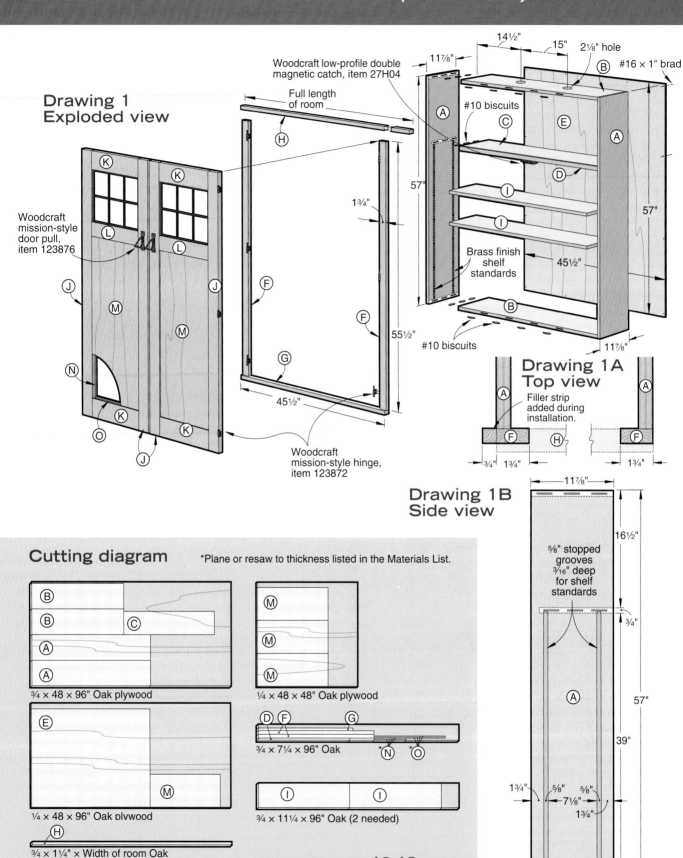

Drawing 1
Exploded view

Woodcraft low-profile double
magnetic catch, item 27H04

Full length
of room

14½"

15"

2⅛" hole

#16 × 1" brad

11⅞"

#10 biscuits

57"

57"

45½"

Brass finish
shelf
standards

Woodcraft
mission-style
door pull,
item 123876

1¾"

55½"

45½"

#10 biscuits

11⅞"

Woodcraft
mission-style hinge,
item 123872

Drawing 1A
Top view

Filler strip
added during
installation.

¾"   1¾"

1¾"

Drawing 1B
Side view

11⅞"

⅝" stopped
grooves
³⁄₁₆" deep
for shelf
standards

16½"

¾"

57"

39"

1¾"

⅝"   ⅝"

7⅛"

1¾"

¾"

Cutting diagram

*Plane or resaw to thickness listed in the Materials List.

¾ × 48 × 96" Oak plywood

¼ × 48 × 48" Oak plywood

¼ × 48 × 96" Oak plywood

¾ × 7¼ × 96" Oak

¾ × 11¼ × 96" Oak (2 needed)

¾ × 1¼" × Width of room Oak

¾ × 7¼ × 60" Oak (4 needed)

¾ × 9¼ × 96" Oak

MATERIALS LIST

Case Part		FINISHED SIZE T	W	L	Matl.	Qty.
A	sides	¾"	11⅞"	57"	OP	2
B	top & bottom	¾"	11⅞"	44"	OP	2
C	fixed shelf	¾"	10¾"	44"	OP	1
D	fixed-shelf edge banding	¾"	1"	44"	O	1
E	back	¼"	45½"	57"	OP	1
F	vertical face frames	¾"	1¾"	55½"	O	2
G	lower trim	¾"	1¼"	45½"	O	1
H	upper trim	¾"	1¼"	*	O	1
I	adjustable shelves	1"	11¼"	43 3/16"	LO	2

Door Part		FINISHED SIZE T	W	L	Matl.	Qty.
J	door stiles	1"	3"	55¼"	LO	4
K	upper & lower rails	1"	3⅞"	14⅞"	LO	4
L	center door rails	1"	3"	14⅞"	LO	2
M	door panels	½"	15¼"	34"	LP	2
N	vertical panel stops	¼"	¼"	34⅛"	O	4
O	horizontal panel stops	¼"	¼"	15⅜"	O	4
P	vertical glass stops	¼"	⅜"	11⅜"	O	4
Q	horizontal glass stops	¼"	⅜"	15⅜"	O	4

Material key: O–oak, LO–laminated oak, LP–laminated plywood, OP–oak plywood.

Supplies: #10 biscuits, 48" brass-finish shelf standards (4), shelf clips with nails (8), ¾" brad nails, 1" brad nails, stain, clear finish.

* Upper trim runs full length of room across both bookcases, bookcases, and is installed after bookcase is in place.

6 ATTACH EDGE BANDING. Glue and clamp edge banding to the fixed shelf. Then glue and clamp together parts A, B, and C/D, checking for square.

7 CUT THE BACK. Cut the back (E) according to the Materials List, making sure it is square. Lay the A/B/C/D assembly on its front face and attach the back with 1" brads. (If you prefer pneumatic nailers, use 1" narrow-crown staples. Air-driven brads will not hold the back sufficiently.)

8 CUT FACE FRAMES. Lay the assembled case on its back. Cut the vertical face frames (F) and lower trim (G) to size. Biscuit-join, glue, and clamp these in place. Cut the biscuit slots for the upper trim (H).

As shown in **DRAWING 1A,** one of the vertical face frames is ¾" wider than the other so it can be scribed to fit the wall (more on that later). Cut the adjustable shelves (I) to size. Set aside for now.

MAKE THE DOORS

Note: Before cutting your door stiles and rails in the next step, check the size of the face-frame opening. Allow for these clearances: 3/32" between the doors and the face frame along the hinged edges, ⅛" at the tops and bottoms of the doors, and 1/16" between the doors.

How to cut three types of joints found in the carcass

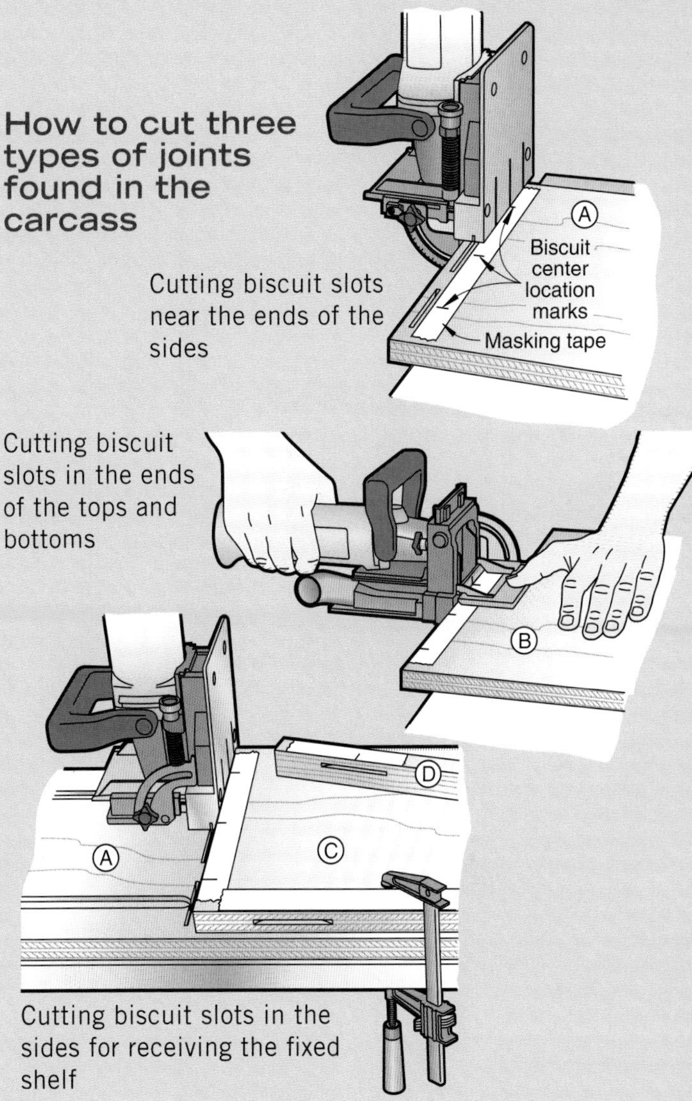

Cutting biscuit slots near the ends of the sides

Cutting biscuit slots in the ends of the tops and bottoms

Cutting biscuit slots in the sides for receiving the fixed shelf

1 CUT DOOR PARTS. From 5/4 stock cut the door stiles (J), upper and lower door rails (K), and center door rails (L) to size. Because 5/4 quartersawn oak is hard to find, we laminated 4/4 boards and planed the laminations to 1" thick.

2 MARK SLOT LOCATIONS. Mark where the rails and stiles meet. Cut two slots for #10 biscuits at each joint.

3 ASSEMBLE THE DOORS. Use glue, biscuits, and clamps to assemble the cabinet case. Keep the door flat by working on a flat surface and make sure that the glue-up is square by measuring diagonally. To precisely space the center door rails, use spacers, as shown in **DRAWING 2A** on page 180.

Drawing 2 Door
(viewed from behind)

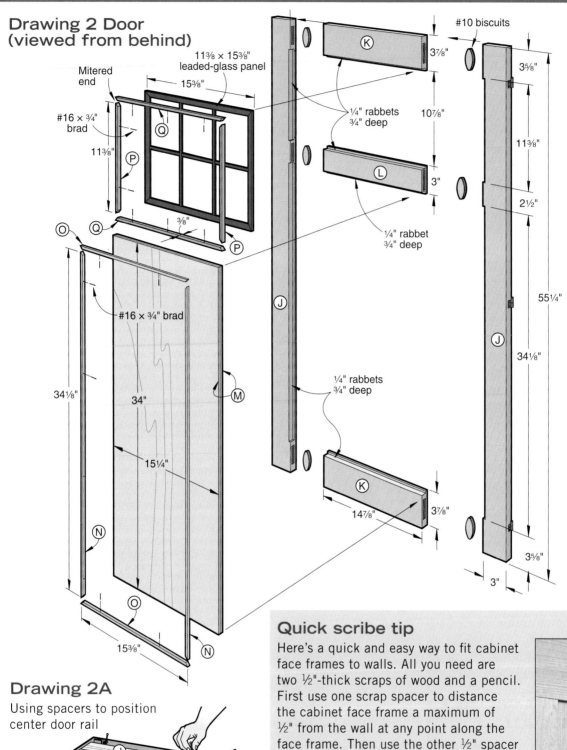

11³⁄₈ × 15³⁄₈"
leaded-glass panel

Mitered end

15³⁄₈"

#16 × ³⁄₄" brad

11³⁄₈"

Ⓠ

Ⓟ

Ⓞ

Ⓠ

³⁄₈"

Ⓟ

#16 × ³⁄₄" brad

34¹⁄₈"

34"

15¹⁄₄"

Ⓜ

Ⓝ

Ⓞ

Ⓝ

15³⁄₈"

Ⓚ

3⁷⁄₈"

¼" rabbets
¾" deep

10⁷⁄₈"

Ⓛ

3"

¼" rabbet
¾" deep

Ⓙ

¼" rabbets
¾" deep

Ⓚ

14⁷⁄₈"

3⁷⁄₈"

#10 biscuits

3⁵⁄₈"

11³⁄₈"

2½"

Ⓙ

55¼"

34¹⁄₈"

3⁵⁄₈"

3"

Drawing 2A
Using spacers to position
center door rail

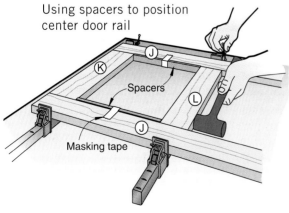

Ⓚ

Ⓙ

Spacers

Ⓛ

Ⓙ

Masking tape

Quick scribe tip

Here's a quick and easy way to fit cabinet face frames to walls. All you need are two ½"-thick scraps of wood and a pencil. First use one scrap spacer to distance the cabinet face frame a maximum of ½" from the wall at any point along the face frame. Then use the other ½" spacer and a pencil to scribe the wall contour onto the face frame or a filler strip edge-glued to the face frame, as shown at right. (In this instance we used a filler strip to fill the void between the edge of the face frame and the wall panel.) Simply plane or cut along the scribed line for a perfect fit to the wall.

A Rout the rabbeted panel and glass openings in the doors in three passes for accurate, chip-free results.

B The opening for the bookcase should include blocking that supports the bottom along its front and back edges.

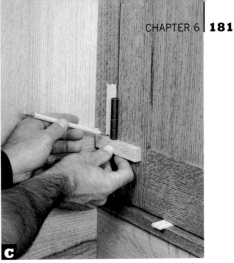

C Use a scrap of wood and sharp pencil to transfer the hinge position to a piece of masking tape on the vertical face frame.

4 **CUT RABBET.** Using a router and a bearing-piloted rabbeting bit, cut a ¼" rabbet, ¾" deep around the inside openings of the door, taking three successively deeper passes **[PHOTO A].** For the most chip-free results, move the router counterclockwise (this is a "climb cut"). Square the corners with a chisel.

5 **LAMINATE DOOR PANELS.** Laminate the door panels (M) from two pieces of ¼" plywood. (You'll likely have to laminate these because of the difficulty of finding ½" plywood with two good faces.) Place the panels in their openings.

6 **CUT PANEL STOPS.** Cut vertical (N) and horizontal panel stops (O) to fit the panel opening. Miter their ends and secure in position with ¾" brads. To prevent the stop from splitting, drill pilot holes through them with a like brad. Or attach the stops with a pneumatic brad nailer. Cut and fit the vertical stops for the glass (P) and the horizontal glass stops (Q). You will attach them later.

7 **APPLY FINISH.** Apply stain and clear finish to the entire project. The finish shown is Minwax Aged Oak Gel Stain, topped with two coats of Minwax Fast Drying Satin Polyurethane.

INSTALL THE CABINET INTO YOUR WALL

Attach the 2× blocking needed to hold the cabinet securely in position. Slide the cabinet into its opening, as shown in **PHOTO B**. Temporarily position the doors in the openings with spacers to set the clearances. Check the squareness of the case against the doors and shim around the edges of the case to make it fit the doors. The case should sit plumb and level.

Scribe the vertical face frames to fit adjoining walls. Place the bookcase back into its opening. Secure it by driving nails through the cabinet sides or face frames and into surrounding blocking or other sturdy supports. This bookcase was secured with nails driven into the baseboard directly below the bottom front edge of the cabinet, as well as into the framing directly above the top front edge of the cabinet.

Install the light fixtures. Low-voltage fixtures with long-life halogen bulbs are a good choice. (See Resources, pages 236–237.) Glue, biscuit-join, and nail the upper trim (H) in place.

ATTACH THE DOORS

Mark the locations of the top and bottom hinges onto the door where shown on **DRAWING 2**, opposite. Center the middle hinge between the top and bottom hinges. Attach the nonmortise hinges with the supplied screws.

Position the doors in the cabinet opening and place ⅛"-thick spacers underneath them. Transfer the locations of the hinges onto the vertical face frame, as shown in **PHOTO C**. Attach the other halves of the hinges to the face frame at the marked locations.

Lift the doors off the installed hinges. Attach door pulls and magnetic catch where shown on **DRAWING 1**, page 178.

FINAL TOUCHES

Cut the brass-finish shelf standards to length with a hacksaw and nail them into the ⅝" grooves in the cabinet sides. Use needle-nose pliers to hold the tiny shelf-standard nails as you drive them with a hammer.

Place the shelf clips where desired and install the adjustable shelves. Secure the 11⅜"×5⅜" glass panels with the P and Q stops and ¾" brads. This project has a leaded-glass panel to accentuate the Arts and Crafts look of the bookcase, but a single pane of glass would work fine. Hang the doors—that's it.

UNDERSTAIR BUILT-IN CABINETS AND DRAWERS

IT'S ALWAYS GREAT TO PUT WASTED SPACE TO USE; SELDOM CAN YOU DO SO AS ATTRACTIVELY AS THIS.

You can always use more storage space, right? Here's a simple way to get it by tapping into those roomy pockets behind the walls of your home. No matter what your available space, you can mix and match these boxes, drawers, doors, and shelves to fit under a stairwell or into a knee wall or dormer.

CREATE A PLAN THAT SUITS YOUR SPACE

These adaptable built-ins are designed around two box sizes—a 14"-high "short" box and a 28"-high "tall" box—to accommodate different wall areas, storage needs, and looks. Typical installation areas for these units include a sloping stairwell wall (above) and, as shown in the box opposite, a dormer area or a knee wall. The width of our boxes is 14", which allows them to fit between wall studs, commonly spaced at 16" on center. If the spacing between your studs is not 16" on center, don't worry; simply adjust the width of your boxes and size the other parts as necessary to fit the space.

For safety's sake before starting this project make sure that there are no electrical outlets in the wall and that the wall cavities are free of water or gas pipes, air ducts, and pass-through wiring. For a staircase wall installation, also check the location of the stair stringer to see whether it will interfere with a cabinet. If so you might be able to avoid the interference by locating the cabinets closer to the floor. (We set ours at 8" above.)

After completing your inspection prepare a sketch of your layout to determine the number of short and tall boxes that you need and your total material requirements for the project.

PREPARE THE BOX OPENINGS

1 PLAN THE LOCATION. Refer to "Uncovering wasted space," opposite, for general layout guidelines.

2 LOCATE YOUR WALL STUDS using a magnetic or electronic stud finder or by driving a 6d finish nail into the wall at various points. Your studs should be 16" on center, leaving approximately 14½" of space between them. Draw the outline of the studs on the wall.

3 MARK THE LOCATION. Using a level and a straightedge, draw a line on the wall for the location of the bottom of the boxes. From this line measure up a distance equal to the height of the boxes plus ¼" and draw a line for the top of each box opening. The added ¼" will give you room to adjust the boxes. The gaps will be covered by trim.

4 CUT OUT THE OPENINGS for the boxes using a drywall saw. See **PHOTO A**, page 185.

MAKE THE BOX

1 CUT THE ¾" OAK PLYWOOD. Cut the box tops and bottoms (A), short sides (B), and long sides (C) to size.

2 RIP EDGING. From the ¾"-thick stock (in this project oak was used for all edging, trim, and face parts), rip six ¾"×83" blanks to form the top and bottom edging (D), short side edging (E), and long side edging (F). Each strip provides enough edging for one box.

MATERIALS LIST

Case Part		T	W	L	Matl.	Qty.
A	tops & bottoms	¾"	11¾"	12½"	OP	12
B	short sides	¾"	11¾"	14"	OP	4
C	long sides	¾"	11¾"	28"	OP	8
D	* top & bottom edging	¾"	¾"	12½"	O	12
E	* short side edging	¾"	¾"	14"	O	4
F	* long side edging	¾"	¾"	28"	O	8
G	short backs	¼"	14"	14"	OP	2
H	long backs	¼"	14"	28"	OP	4

Drawers		T	W	L	Matl.	Qty.
I	sides	½"	5½"	11"	C	8
J	fronts & backs	½"	5½"	11"	C	8
K	bottoms	¼"	11"	10½"	OP	4
L	faces	¾"	6⅛"	12⁵⁄₁₆"	O	4

Doors		T	W	L	Matl.	Qty.
M	stiles	¾"	2"	12⁵⁄₁₆"	O	6
N	rails	¾"	2"	12⁵⁄₁₆"	O	6
O	vertical glass stops	¼"	¼"	22¹³⁄₁₆"	O	6
P	horizontal glass stops	¼"	¼"	8¹³⁄₁₆"	O	6
Q	door stops	¾"	¾"	1"	O	3

Shelves		T	W	L	Matl.	Qty.
R	shelves	¾"	10¾"	12¼"	OP	8
S	edging	¾"	1"	12¼"	O	8

Wall Trim		T	W	L	Matl.	Qty.
T	sill	¾"	1¼"	68½"	O	1
U	bottom horizontal trim	½"	2½"	67"	O	1
V	vertical trim	½"	3"	13"	O	1
W	vertical trim	½"	3"	27"	O	1
X	vertical trim	½"	3"	41"	O	1
Y	vertical trim	½"	3"	55"	O	2
Z	top horizontal trim	½"	2½"	16¾"	O	3
AA	top horizontal trim	½"	2½"	20½"	O	1

*Parts initially cut oversize. See the instructions.

Material key: OP–oak plywood, O–oak, C–choice of poplar or maple.

Supplies: ¼" hardboard, #8×1" flathead wood screws, #8×1¾" flathead wood screws, 1½" machine screws, #18×½" wire brads, #17×1" nails, 8¾×22¾" glass (3), 4d and 6d finish nails, wood shims, adhesive-backed rubber bumpers, glue, stain, clear finish.

Hardware: 107° hinges, no. B075T1650 (6); hinge-mounting clips, no. B175H919 (6); 10" full-extension drawer slides, no. KV8400 B10 (4 pair); ¼" spoon shelf supports (nickel), no. HB28C25 (2); 1¼" polished chrome knobs, no. A04271 26 with 1" screws (7). Order from Woodworker's Hardware, P.O. Box 180, Sauk Rapids, MN 56379; call 800/383-0130 or go to www.wwhardware.com.

Uncovering wasted space

Perhaps instead of wasted space beneath your stairway, you have—as is often the case—another stairway. Don't give up. You might find other spots ripe for a variation on this project. Dormers and knee walls are prime candidates. The same warnings apply however: Especially in the case of the knee wall, check first for plumbing stacks, wiring, and perhaps even a chimney!

DORMER INSTALLATION

Transform unused space in a dormer area into useful storage with these units. This drawing shows two tall boxes with shelves and doors installed in the dead space between sidewalls.

KNEE WALL INSTALLATION

Gain storage and good looks by installing units in a knee wall. This drawing shows two side-by-side tall boxes with shelves and doors, located next to two short boxes (stacked) holding drawers.

UNDERSTAIR BUILT-IN CABINETS AND DRAWERS *(CONTINUED)*

Drawing 1 Carcasses

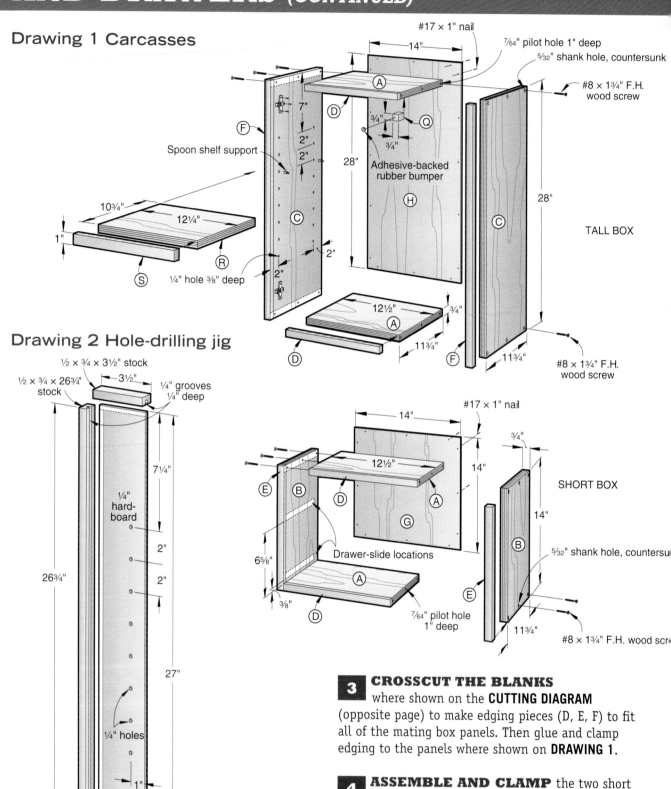

#17 × 1" nail

$\frac{7}{64}$" pilot hole 1" deep

$\frac{5}{32}$" shank hole, countersunk

14"

#8 × 1$\frac{3}{4}$" F.H. wood screw

7"

2"

2"

$\frac{3}{4}$"

$\frac{3}{4}$"

28"

Adhesive-backed rubber bumper

Spoon shelf support

28"

TALL BOX

10$\frac{3}{4}$"

12$\frac{1}{4}$"

1"

$\frac{1}{4}$" hole $\frac{3}{8}$" deep

2"

2"

12$\frac{1}{2}$"

$\frac{3}{4}$"

11$\frac{3}{4}$"

11$\frac{3}{4}$"

#8 × 1$\frac{3}{4}$" F.H. wood screw

A, D, F, Q, H, C, R, S

Drawing 2 Hole-drilling jig

$\frac{1}{2}$ × $\frac{3}{4}$ × 3$\frac{1}{2}$" stock

$\frac{1}{2}$ × $\frac{3}{4}$ × 26$\frac{3}{4}$" stock

3$\frac{1}{2}$"

$\frac{1}{4}$" grooves $\frac{1}{4}$" deep

7$\frac{1}{4}$"

$\frac{1}{4}$" hard-board

2"

2"

26$\frac{3}{4}$"

27"

$\frac{1}{4}$" holes

1"

$\frac{1}{2}$"

3$\frac{1}{4}$"

#17 × 1" nail

14"

12$\frac{1}{2}$"

14"

$\frac{3}{4}$"

SHORT BOX

14"

6$\frac{5}{8}$"

Drawer-slide locations

$\frac{3}{8}$"

$\frac{5}{32}$" shank hole, countersu

$\frac{7}{64}$" pilot hole 1" deep

11$\frac{3}{4}$"

#8 × 1$\frac{3}{4}$" F.H. wood scr

E, B, D, A, G

3 **CROSSCUT THE BLANKS** where shown on the **CUTTING DIAGRAM** (opposite page) to make edging pieces (D, E, F) to fit all of the mating box panels. Then glue and clamp edging to the panels where shown on **DRAWING 1.**

4 **ASSEMBLE AND CLAMP** the two short boxes using a top and bottom (A) and two short sides (B) for each. Check for square. Then drill pilot and countersunk shank holes through the short sides into the tops and bottoms for screws where shown. Drive the screws.

With the box locations marked on the wall, cut out the openings with a drywall saw.

5 **CUT THE SHORT BACKS** (G) from ¼" oak plywood to the size listed and attach them to the back of the short boxes with #17×1" nails where shown. *Note: It's easiest to finish the boxes and the backs before attaching the backs.*

6 **MAKE THE HOLE-DRILLING JIG,** **DRAWING 2.** To ensure equally spaced holes for the shelf supports in the long sides (C), make a hole-drilling jig. Chuck a ¼" bit in your drill and set a depth stop (we used masking tape) ⅝" from the end of the bit. (This depth allows for the ¼" thickness of the jig and the ⅜" depth of the hole.) As shown in **PHOTO B**, page 186, place the jig on the inside face of a long side panel against the top edge and a long edge and drill the first row of holes. Then reposition the jig against the opposite long edge of the panel and drill the second row of holes. Repeat this procedure on all long sides (C).

7 **ASSEMBLE AND CLAMP** the four tall boxes, referring to **DRAWING 1**, using a top and bottom (A) and two long sides (C) for each. After checking for square drill pilot and countersunk shank holes through the long side panels into the top and bottom panels for the screws where shown. Drive the screws.

8 **CUT THE LONG BACKS** (H) from ¼" plywood to the size listed and attach them to the back of the tall boxes with #17×1" nails where shown.

Cutting diagram

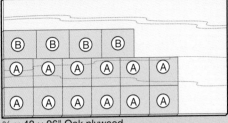

¾ × 48 × 96" Oak plywood

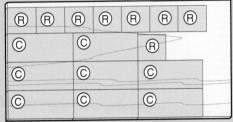

¾ × 48 × 96" Oak plywood

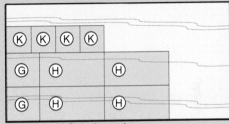

¼ × 48 × 96" Oak plywood

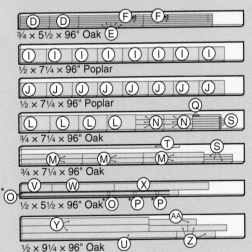

¾ × 5½ × 96" Oak

½ × 7¼ × 96" Poplar

½ × 7¼ × 96" Poplar

¾ × 7¼ × 96" Oak

¾ × 7¼ × 96" Oak

½ × 5½ × 96" Oak

½ × 9¼ × 96" Oak
*Plane or resaw to thickness listed in the Materials List.

UNDERSTAIR BUILT-IN CABINETS AND DRAWERS *(CONTINUED)*

MAKE THE DRAWERS

1 **CUT DRAWER SIDES/BOTTOMS.**
From ½"-thick stock of your choice (we used poplar), cut the drawer sides (I) and front and back pieces (J) to the sizes listed. From ¼" plywood cut the drawer bottoms (K) to size.

2 **CUT THE GROOVE.** Referring to
DRAWINGS 3 and **3A,** cut the ¼" groove in the sides (I) and front and back pieces (J) to receive the drawer bottoms (K). Using the same setup cut the two ¼" dadoes in the drawer sides (I) to receive the rabbeted ends of the drawer front and back (J).

3 **CUT THE RABBETS.** Referring to
DRAWING 3B attach an auxiliary fence to your tablesaw fence and position the fence adjacent to your ¼" dado blade. Now cut the rabbets in the ends of the drawer fronts and backs (J).

4 **DRY-ASSEMBLE THE DRAWERS**
(I, J, K) and check that the parts fit together correctly. Then glue and clamp the drawer assemblies, checking for square.

5 **MAKE THE DRAWER FACES.**
From ¾"-thick oak, cut the drawer faces (L) to the size listed. Place a drawer face on the front (J) of a drawer assembly and center it side-to-side and top-to-bottom with the front. Clamp the

B

To drill uniformly spaced shelf-support holes in the box's long side panels, use a hole-drilling jig and a depth stop.

Drawing 3 Drawer

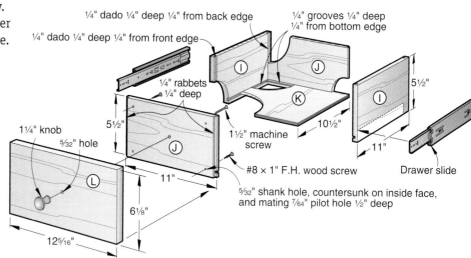

¼" dado ¼" deep ¼" from back edge
¼" dado ¼" deep ¼" from front edge
¼" grooves ¼" deep ¼" from bottom edge
¼" rabbets ¼" deep
1¼" knob
5/32" hole
5½"
5½"
10½"
11"
11"
1½" machine screw
#8 × 1" F.H. wood screw
5/32" shank hole, countersunk on inside face, and mating 7/64" pilot hole ½" deep
Drawer slide
6⅛"
12 5/16"

Drawing 3A Drawer dado detail

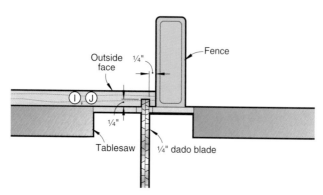

Outside face
Fence
¼"
I, J
¼"
¼" dado blade
Tablesaw

Drawing 3B Drawer rabbet detail

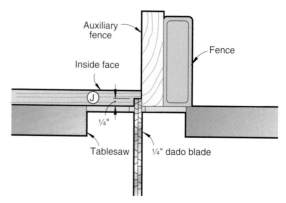

Auxiliary fence
Fence
Inside face
J
¼"
¼" dado blade
Tablesaw

face to the drawer, making sure that the face does not move. Now drill four pilot and countersunk shank holes through the drawer front into the face for the mounting screws where shown on **DRAWING 3**. Drive the screws. Also in the center of the drawer face, drill a ⁵⁄₃₂" hole for the knob attachment screw (you will need a 1½"-long machine screw) through the face and the drawer front. Install the knob. Assemble the drawer faces and attach knobs to the other drawers.

6 **POSITION THE DRAWER SLIDES** against the sides (I), flush to their front and bottom edges. Attach the slides using the screws supplied with the slides. Disconnect the outer part of the slides from the drawer-mounted part and attach these pieces to the short box sides where shown on **DRAWING 1**.

FABRICATE THE DOORS

1 **CUT DOOR STILES/HALF LAPS.** From ¾"-thick oak, cut the door stiles (M) and rails (N) to the sizes listed. Cut the 2" mating half laps on the ends of the stiles (M) and rails (N) where shown on **DRAWING 4**.

2 **GLUE AND CLAMP** the door frames, checking for square.

3 **ROUT A ¼" RABBET** ⅜" deep around the back inside edges of the door for the glass and vertical and horizontal glass stops (O, P) where shown. To prevent tear-out cut the rabbet depth in three passes, removing ⅛" of material with each pass. Square the corners of the rabbets with a chisel.

4 **BORE THE HOLES.** Chuck a 1⅜" (35mm) Forstner bit in your drill and bore the two ½"-deep holes in the back of the door stiles (M) for the 107-degree hinges where shown on **DRAWING 4**. Install the cup part of the hinges in the door stiles. Install the mating hinge-clip mounting plates inside the tall boxes as directed in the manufacturer's instructions. When locating the mounting plates, make sure that the front face of the door frame is flush with the front of the box edging (D, F) and that there is an equal reveal all around. Remove the door frames after mounting.

Drawing 4 Door

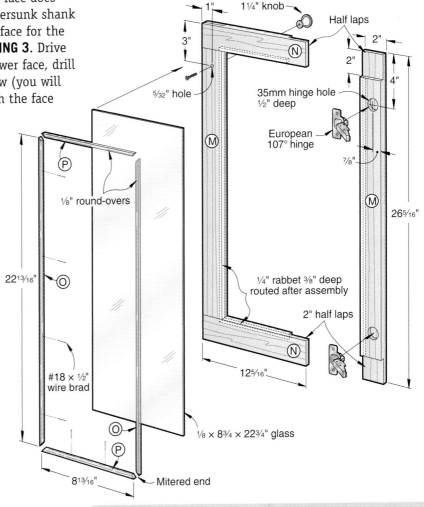

1"
1¼" knob
Half laps
3"
2"
2"
⁵⁄₃₂" hole
35mm hinge hole ½" deep
European 107° hinge
4"
⅞"
26⁵⁄₁₆"
¼" rabbet ⅜" deep routed after assembly
2" half laps
12⁵⁄₁₆"

22¹³⁄₁₆"
⅛" round-overs
#18 × ½" wire brad
⅛ × 8¾ × 22¾" glass
8¹³⁄₁₆"
Mitered end

An ounce of prevention...

To prevent bending brads and possibly splitting a glass stop when attaching the thin, hard-oak stops to the door, predrill holes in the stops. Simply cut the head off a brad and use the remaining piece as a drill bit to bore the holes. Also to avoid scratching or possibly breaking the glass when nailing the stops, put a piece of cardboard or poster board on top of the glass and flush against the stops. This will protect the glass from hammer slips.

UNDERSTAIR BUILT-IN CABINETS AND DRAWERS (CONTINUED)

5 **MAKE THE GLASS STOPS.** To form the vertical and horizontal glass stops (O, P), shown on **DRAWING 4**, thickness-plane a 1/2"×2"×68" oak blank to 1/4". With a 1/8" round-over bit chucked in your table-mounted router, rout the two long edges of the blank; then rip a 1/4"-wide strip from each side of the blank. Repeat this process to make a third strip. Each strip makes all of the glass stops for one door. Next miter-cut the strips to make the glass stops fit the openings in the back of the doors. *Note: It is easiest to finish the doors before installing the glass and the glass stops.*

6 **SECURE THE GLASS.** Place a 1/8"×83/4"×223/4" piece of glass in a door opening. Secure the glass by installing the glass stops (O, P) using #18×1/2" wire brads. Repeat this procedure for the remaining doors.

7 **ADDING THE DOORKNOB.** Drill a 5/32" hole through the door stiles (M) where shown on **DRAWING 4** for the knob. Attach all knobs using the screws provided.

8 **CUT DOOR STOPS.** From 3/4"-thick oak, cut the door stops (Q) to size. Glue and clamp the stops to the top (A) and long side (C) of the tall boxes, in the corner opposite the door-hinge side of the box, where shown on **DRAWING 1**. Position the stop back from the front of the edging (D, F) a distance equal to the thickness of the door plus a rubber bumper (an adhesive-backed bumper of your choice).

PREPARE THE SHELVES

1 **CUT THE SHELVES.** From 3/4" plywood cut the shelves (R) to the size listed.

2 **EDGE THE SHELVES.** From 3/4"-thick oak, cut the shelf edging (S) to size. Then glue up and clamp the edging, making it flush with the top front edge of the shelves where shown on **DRAWING 1**. (The edging overhangs each shelf's bottom face.)

INSTALL THE BOXES

1 **POSITION A BOX IN ITS WALL OPENING,** resting it on the bottom of the opening. As shown in **PHOTO C**, insert shims along the sides of the box to fill the gaps and make it plumb. Also using a straightedge check that the front edge of the box is flush with the face of the wall. Then secure the box by driving #8×13/4" wood screws through the box and shims into the studs.

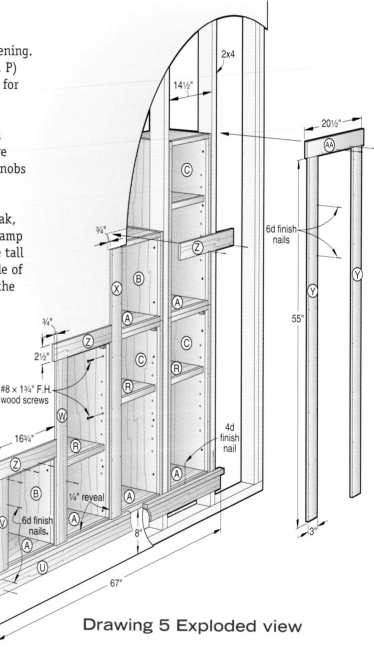

Drawing 5 Exploded view

To make the box plumb in its wall opening, insert shims between the box and the wall studs.

INSTALL THE REMAINING BOXES
using the same alignment process. Between adjacent boxes check that the distance between the outer edges of the boxes remains constant from top to bottom. This also shows that the boxes are plumb.

ADD THE TRIM

Note: Stain and finish the trim before installing.

CUT THE SILL. From ¾"-thick oak, cut the sill (T) to the size listed. Also from ½"-thick oak, cut the bottom horizontal trim (U) to size.

POSITION THE BOTTOM TRIM. Bring the horizontal trim (U) on the underside of the sill (T) flush with the back edge and centered end to end, where shown on **DRAWING 5**. Attach the sill to the bottom with 4d finish nails.

POSITION THE SILL/TRIM assembly (T/U) on the wall, centering it end to end with the outer boxes and leaving a ¼" reveal at the top of the box bottoms (A). Attach the assembly by driving 6d finish nails through the trim into the wall studs.

ADD VERTICAL TRIM. From ½"-thick oak, cut the vertical trim pieces (V, W, X, Y) to the sizes listed. Place the vertical trim (V) in position where shown on **DRAWING 5**, leaving a ¼" reveal on the left side of the short box. Attach the trim to the front of the box using 6d finish nails. Place vertical trim (W) in position between the short

box and adjacent tall box. Fasten, leaving a ¼" reveal on both boxes.

ADD TOP HORIZONTAL TRIM. From ½"-thick oak, cut the top horizontal trim pieces (Z, AA) to size. Referring to **DRAWING 5** and to **PHOTO D**, position a top horizontal trim piece (Z) above the short box and nail it to the front of the box.

ADD REMAINING VERTICAL TRIM. Install the remaining vertical trim pieces (X, Y) and top horizontal trim pieces (Z, AA) where shown. Center the last top horizontal trim piece (AA) over the two vertical trim pieces (Y).

APPLY THE FINISH

FINISH-SAND all areas not previously sanded with 220-grit sandpaper. Remove dust with a tack cloth.

APPLY A STAIN of your choice and protect with a satin polyurethane finish. Sand and remove dust between coats.

INSTALL THE DOORS, DRAWERS, rubber bumpers on the door stops (Q), shelf supports, and shelves.

Position all vertical and horizontal trim to leave a ¼" reveal around the boxes.

ROOM DIVIDER
A DEGREE OF SEPARATION BETWEEN ROOMS CAN MAINTAIN OPENNESS WHILE DIVIDING SPACES. HERE IS A HANDSOME CRAFTSMAN APPROACH.

Modeled after the room dividers found in Craftsman bungalows, this project is not only a stunning feature, it provides plenty of room for storage and display. The design utilizes glass for the doors and shelves and includes lights inside the cabinet. The result functions to divide the space while letting you display favorite treasures.

After building the cabinets give them the crowning touch by making an archway and a pair of columns as described in the project on pages 170–174.

Note: The following directions cover the construction of the right-hand cabinet of the pair shown at right. If you build a pair, remember that the left cabinet is a mirror image, not identical. As you plan this project, you might want to change the width of these cabinets to suit your home. One key dimension: Be sure to leave a clear walkway of at least 36" between the cabinets.

ASSEMBLE THE CARCASS

1 **CUT SIDES AND TOP.** Referring to the Materials List on page 192, rip and crosscut the sides (A) and the top/bottom (B) from cherry plywood. On these parts the best-looking side faces the cabinet's interior. Using an adjustable circle cutter or a Forstner bit chucked into your drill press, and referring to **DRAWING 1** and the directions furnished with your lighting kit, lay out and drill the holes for the halogen puck lights. (Similar light kits can be purchased at most home centers.) Lay out and drill the shelf-pin holes in the sides (A).

2 **CUT RABBETS.** Install a ¾" dado blade in your tablesaw and raise it for a ¼"-deep cut.

Screw a scrap-wood face to your rip fence and position it so the inner edge of the dado blade just touches the scrap-wood face. Cut the rabbets at the top end of the sides (A) where shown on **DRAWING 1**. Move the rip fence and make the dado near the lower end of each side.

3 **GLUE AND CLAMP THE SIDES** (A) and the top/bottom (B), flushing their edges. Drill the pilot and countersunk shank holes in the sides

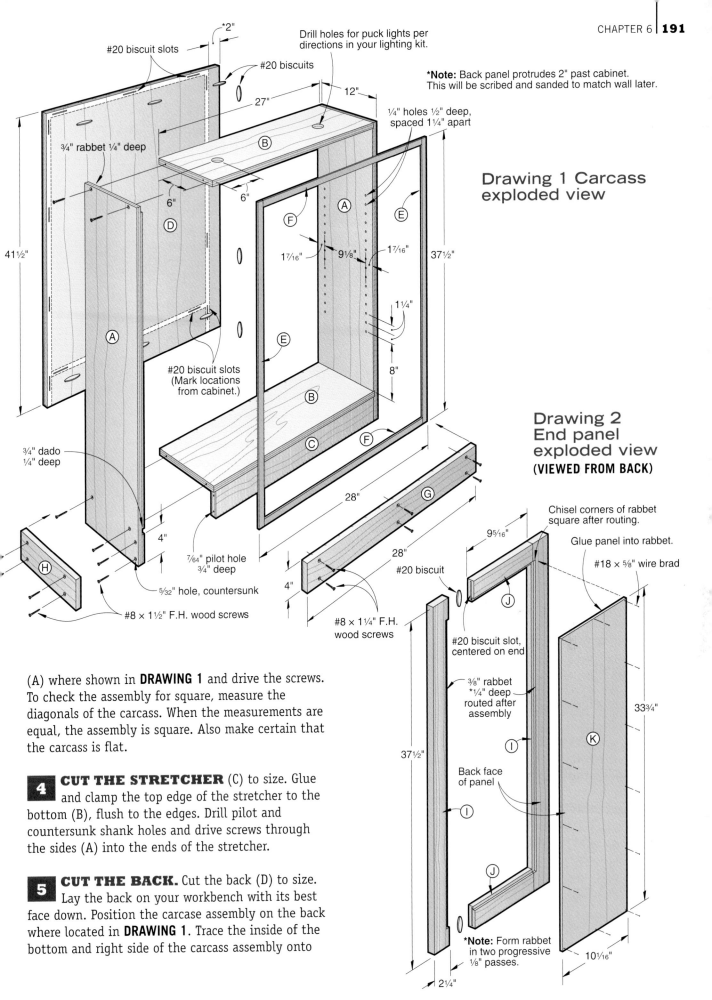

#20 biscuit slots

*2"

#20 biscuits

Drill holes for puck lights per directions in your lighting kit.

27"

12"

¾" rabbet ¼" deep

¼" holes ½" deep, spaced 1¼" apart

Note: Back panel protrudes 2" past cabinet. This will be scribed and sanded to match wall later.

Drawing 1 Carcass exploded view

6"

6"

41½"

B

D

A

F

A

E

E

1⁷⁄₁₆"

9⅛"

1⁷⁄₁₆"

37½"

1¼"

8"

E

B

¾" dado ¼" deep

#20 biscuit slots (Mark locations from cabinet.)

C

F

Drawing 2 End panel exploded view
(VIEWED FROM BACK)

28"

G

28"

Chisel corners of rabbet square after routing.

Glue panel into rabbet.

9⁵⁄₁₆"

#18 × ⅝" wire brad

4"

7⁄₆₄" pilot hole ¾" deep

5⁄₃₂" hole, countersunk

#8 × 1½" F.H. wood screws

H

4"

#20 biscuit

#8 × 1¼" F.H. wood screws

#20 biscuit slot, centered on end

⅜" rabbet *¼" deep routed after assembly

Back face of panel

J

I

I

J

37½"

33¾"

K

10¹⁄₁₆"

2¼"

*Note: Form rabbet in two progressive ⅛" passes.

(A) where shown in **DRAWING 1** and drive the screws. To check the assembly for square, measure the diagonals of the carcass. When the measurements are equal, the assembly is square. Also make certain that the carcass is flat.

4 **CUT THE STRETCHER** (C) to size. Glue and clamp the top edge of the stretcher to the bottom (B), flush to the edges. Drill pilot and countersunk shank holes and drive screws through the sides (A) into the ends of the stretcher.

5 **CUT THE BACK.** Cut the back (D) to size. Lay the back on your workbench with its best face down. Position the carcase assembly on the back where located in **DRAWING 1**. Trace the inside of the bottom and right side of the carcass assembly onto

ROOM DIVIDER *(CONTINUED)*

MATERIALS LIST

Part		T	W	L	Matl.	Qty.
		FINISHED SIZE				
A	sides	¾"	12"	41½"	CP	2
B	top/bottom	¾"	12"	27"	CP	2
C	stretcher	¾"	4"	26½"	CP	1
D	back	¾"	30"	41½"	CP	1
E	vertical bands	¼"	¾"	37½"	C	2
F	horizontal bands	¼"	¾"	26½"	C	2
G	subbase front	¾"	4"	28"	C	1
H	subbase side	¾"	4"	13½"	C	1
I	panel stiles	¾"	2¼"	37½"	C	2
J	panel rails	¾"	2¼"	9⁵⁄₁₆"	C	2
K	panel	¼"	10¹⁄₁₆"	33¾"	CP	1
L	scribe strips	¾"	2"	41½"	C	2
M	upper top	¾"	13⁵⁄₁₆"	30½"	CP	1
N	front/back bands	¾"	1½"	31¼"	C	2
O	end band	¾"	1½"	14¹³⁄₁₆"	C	1
P	side spacers	¾"	2"	30½"	CP	2
Q	end spacer	¾"	2"	9⁵⁄₁₆"	CP	1
R	baseboard front/back	¾"	4"	31½"	C	2
S	baseboard side	¾"	4"	15"	C	1
T	door stiles	¾"	2¼"	37¼"	C	4
U	door rails	¾"	2¼"	11¹³⁄₁₆"	C	4
V	vertical stops	¼"	⅜"	33½"	C	4
W	horizontal stops	¼"	⅜"	10⅛"	C	4

Material key: C–cherry, CP–cherry plywood.

Supplies: (for a single cabinet) #8×1¼" flathead wood screws, #8×1½" flathead wood screws, #20 biscuits, #18×⅝" wire brads, #17×1" wire brads, 2-lamp halogen lighting kit, double-strength glass, ¼"-thick glass.

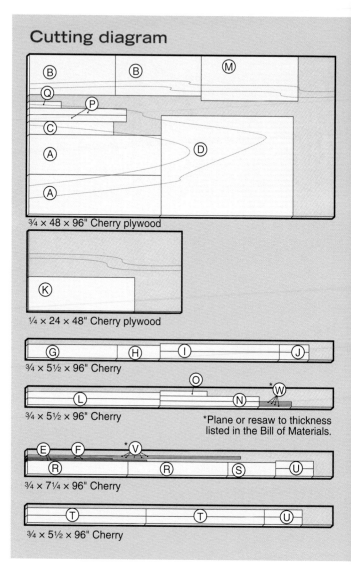

Cutting diagram

¾ × 48 × 96" Cherry plywood

¼ × 24 × 48" Cherry plywood

¾ × 5½ × 96" Cherry

¾ × 5½ × 96" Cherry

*Plane or resaw to thickness listed in the Bill of Materials.

¾ × 7¼ × 96" Cherry

¾ × 5½ × 96" Cherry

Easy on the power driver

Use a slow speed on your power driver when you're screwing into the edge of plywood so that you can stop as soon as the screw's head seats into its countersink. If you try to use too much speed or power, the screw's threads can spin after the fastener's head seats, chewing away the wood fibers. This dramatically reduces the screw's holding power.

the back, making light pencil lines in the position indicated by the dashed lines in **DRAWING 1**. Mark the location of the biscuit slots on the back (D) and also mark mating locations around the perimeter of the carcase assembly (A/B/C). Adjust your biscuit joiner to cut a slot centered in the thickness of your ¾"-thick plywood. Cut all the slots into the back edges of the carcase assembly. Also cut all slots along the upper end of the back (D) and its left side. To cut the remaining slots into the back, stand the biscuit joiner on end, as shown in **PHOTO A**. After you cut the slots, glue, biscuit, and clamp the back (D) to the carcase assembly.

Note: To make a left-hand cabinet, position the 2" scribing allowance on the cabinet's opposite end.

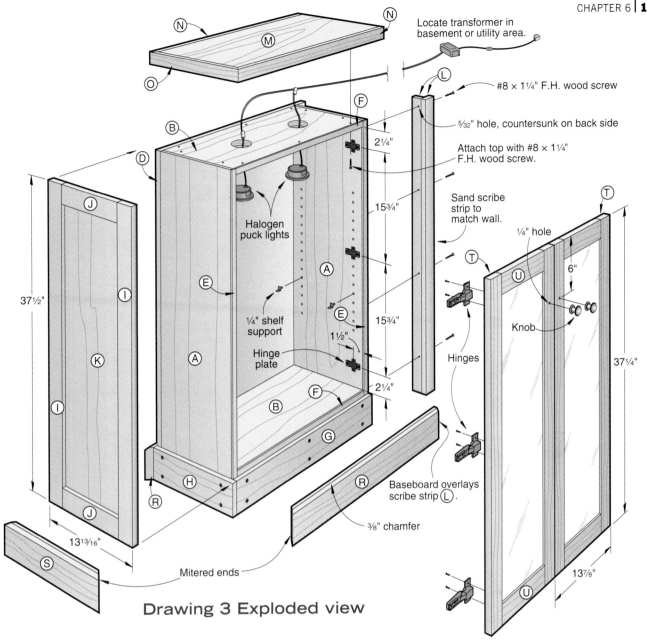

Locate transformer in
basement or utility area.

#8 × 1¼" F.H. wood screw

⁵⁄₃₂" hole, countersunk on back side

Attach top with #8 × 1¼"
F.H. wood screw.

Sand scribe
strip to
match wall.

¼" hole

6"

Knob

Hinges

Baseboard overlays
scribe strip (L).

Halogen
puck lights

¼" shelf
support

Hinge
plate

2¼"

15¾"

15¾"

1½"

2¼"

37½"

37¼"

13¹³⁄₁₆"

13⅞"

⅜" chamfer

Mitered ends

Drawing 3 Exploded view

**Clamping a straightedge to the back (D) creates a fence for
positioning the biscuit joiner when cutting the biscuit slots
along its bottom and right side.**

6 **RIP AND CROSSCUT** to size the vertical
bands (E) and the horizontal bands (F). After
applying glue to these parts, use masking tape to
hold them in place while the glue dries. From solid
cherry stock rip and crosscut the subbase front (G)
and the subbase side (H) to size. Referring to
DRAWING 1 glue and screw these parts to the carcass.

DRESS THE CARCASE WITH A PANEL AND A SCRIBE STRIP

1 **CUT THE PANELS.** Referring to the
Materials List, opposite, rip and crosscut the
panel stiles (I) and the panel rails (J) from solid
cherry stock. Cut slots for #20 biscuits where shown
on **DRAWING 2,** then glue and clamp the assembly.

2 **RABBET THE FRAME.** With the glue
dry chuck a rabbeting bit into your table-

ROOM DIVIDER *(CONTINUED)*

mounted router and rout the rabbet into the back inner perimeter of the frame. Form the ¼"-deep rabbet in two progressive ⅛" passes. Use a chisel to square the corners. Cut the panel (K) to fit the rabbeted opening. After test-fitting the panel, apply glue sparingly to the rabbet, insert the panel, and secure it with #18×⅝" wire brads.

3 ASSEMBLE THE END PANEL.
Referring to **DRAWING 3**, glue and clamp the end-panel assembly (I/J/K) to the carcass assembly, flushing the back edge and the top end. The end-panel assembly extends ⁷⁄₁₆" beyond the front of the carcass assembly.

4 PREPARE SCRIBE STRIPS. Referring to the Materials List on page 192, cut the scribe strips (L) to size from solid cherry. Referring to **DRAWING 3,** glue and clamp the scribe strips into an L-shaped assembly. Clamp this assembly to the carcass so that it's flush with the subbase front (G) and protrudes ¾" past the front edge of the right side (A). Drill pilot and countersunk shank holes through the scribe strip assembly into the side, then glue and screw it to the carcass assembly.

ADD THE TOP AND BASEBOARDS

1 CUT THE BANDS. Referring to the Materials List, cut the upper top (M) from ¾"-thick plywood. Cut the front/back bands (N) and the end band (O) from solid cherry. Referring to **DRAWING 4** miter the ends to fit around the upper top (M). Cut the biscuit slots into the upper top (M) and into the bands (N, O) and glue and clamp the top assembly.

2 PREPARE THE UPPER TOP ASSEMBLY. Referring to the Materials List, cut the side spacers (P) and the end spacer (Q). Glue and clamp the spacers to the upper top. (The spacers provide clearance to run the wiring for the lights inside the cabinet.) Set aside the upper top assembly for now; you'll attach it after installing the cabinet.

3 PREPARE THE BASEBOARDS.
Referring to the Materials List, rip solid cherry 4" wide for the baseboard front and back (R) and the baseboard side (S). Rout a ⅜" chamfer along the top edge of these parts. Make this cut in several passes to avoid chip-out. Referring to **DRAWING 3** miter the ends of the baseboards (R) and (S) to fit around the

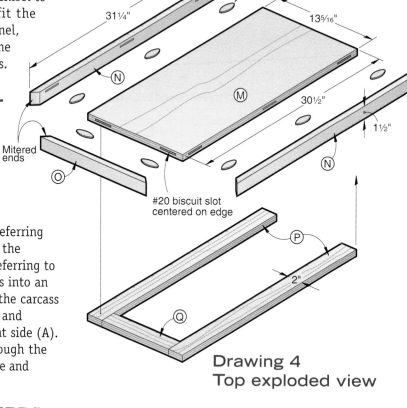

#20 biscuit slot
⅜"
#20 biscuit
31¼"
13⁵⁄₁₆"
N
M
30½"
1½"
N
Mitered ends
O
#20 biscuit slot centered on edge
P
2"
Q

Drawing 4
Top exploded view

bottom of the carcass assembly. Glue and clamp them in place.

BUILD THE DOORS

1 CUT DOOR STILES AND RAILS. Rip and crosscut the door stiles (T) and the door rails (U) to size. Chuck a ¼" Forstner bit into your drill press and drill a series of overlapping holes to form the mortises in the stiles (T) where shown on **DRAWING 5A**. Use a chisel to smooth the walls of the mortise and to square the corners.

2 MAKE THE TENONS. To set up for cutting the tenons, screw a ¾"×4"×18" extension to your tablesaw's miter gauge. Install a ¾" dado head into your tablesaw and raise it for a ¼"-deep cut. Referring to **DRAWING 5B** clamp a stop block to the miter-gauge extension and make test cuts in scrap lumber to check the thickness of the tenon in the mortise. After you cut the cheeks of all the tenons, raise the dado head to make the ½"-deep shoulder cut at the top and bottom of each tenon. Check the joints with a dry assembly, then glue and clamp the door assemblies.

Drawing 5 Door exploded view

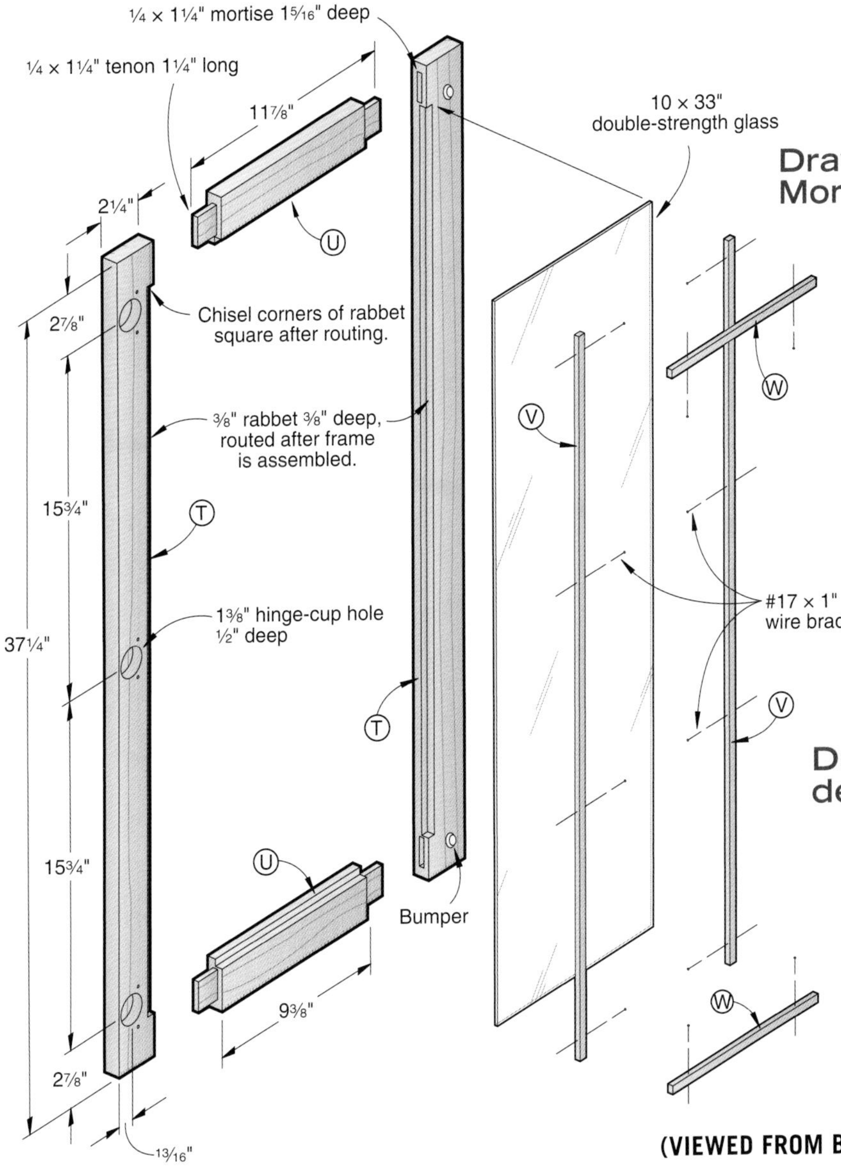
1/4 x 1 1/4" mortise 1 5/16" deep
1/4 x 1 1/4" tenon 1 1/4" long
11 7/8"
2 1/4"
U
10 x 33" double-strength glass
2 7/8"
Chisel corners of rabbet square after routing.
3/8" rabbet 3/8" deep, routed after frame is assembled.
15 3/4"
T
1 3/8" hinge-cup hole 1/2" deep
37 1/4"
T
V
W
#17 x 1" wire brads
V
15 3/4"
U
Bumper
9 3/8"
W
2 7/8"
13/16"

(VIEWED FROM BACK)

Drawing 5A Mortise detail

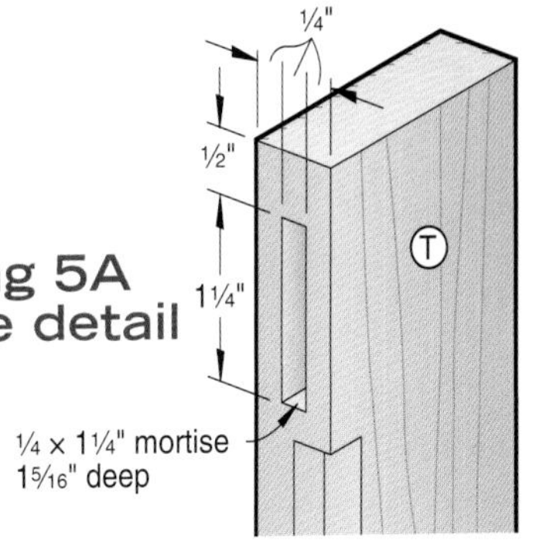
1/4"
1/2"
1 1/4"
T
1/4 x 1 1/4" mortise 1 5/16" deep

Drawing 5B Tenon detail

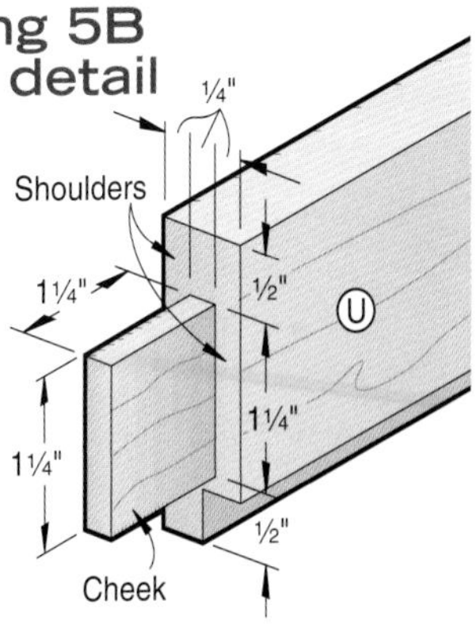
1/4"
Shoulders
1 1/4"
1/2"
U
1 1/4"
1 1/4"
1/2"
Cheek

Drawing 5C Hinge-drilling detail

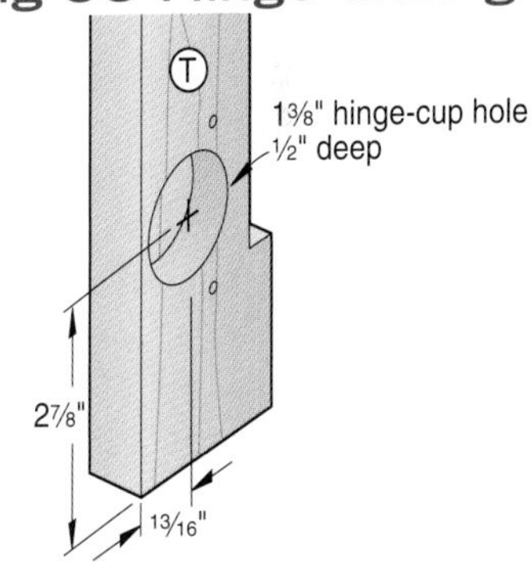
T
1 3/8" hinge-cup hole
1/2" deep
2 7/8"
13/16"

3 **RABBET THE FRAMES.** Chuck a 3/8" rabbeting bit into your table-mounted router and rout a rabbet around the inner perimeter of each door's back. To help prevent chip-out, rout the 3/8"-deep rabbet in progressive 1/8" passes. Use a chisel to square the corners of each rabbet.

4 **ADD THE HINGES.** Referring to **DRAWINGS 5** and **5C**, drill the doors' hinge-cup holes, using a 35mm or 1 3/8" Forstner bit, and install the hinges. Using the holes in the hinge-cup flanges as guides, drill pilot holes and drive the screws. Mount the plates in the carcass where shown in **DRAWING 3** and test-fit the doors. Then remove the hinges and plates.

5 **INSTALL THE GLASS.** Take the completed door assemblies to a glass shop and have double-strength glass cut about 1/8" smaller than the size of the rabbeted opening. (An art-glass shop can create the leaded-glass design.) Have the glass shop cut the 1/4"-thick cabinet shelves and have them seam the edges. When you get home store the glass safely until after applying the finish to the doors. Cut and fit the vertical and horizontal glass stops (V, W) and drill holes for the brads. Set these parts aside for now. Referring to **DRAWING 3** drill the mounting holes for the knobs.

TIME TO FINISH THINGS OFF

1 **APPLY FINISH.** Apply your choice of clear finish to the wood. We first brushed on one coat of Minwax gloss polyurethane varnish, then when dry sanded it with 220-grit sandpaper. After removing the dust with a tack cloth, apply a second coat, switching to Minwax satin polyurethane varnish.

2 **FINAL TOUCHES.** Add the doors, bumpers, and top after you've installed the cabinet.

INSTALLING THE CABINETS

At first the idea of installing the divider cabinets sounds easy enough. But when you check the installation site, you realize that the framing crew who built your house didn't own a level. And so many things happen over time to even the most carefully built house: Joists shrink, studs bow, and foundations settle. Fortunately our installation procedure helps you overcome wavy floors and less-than-perfect walls.

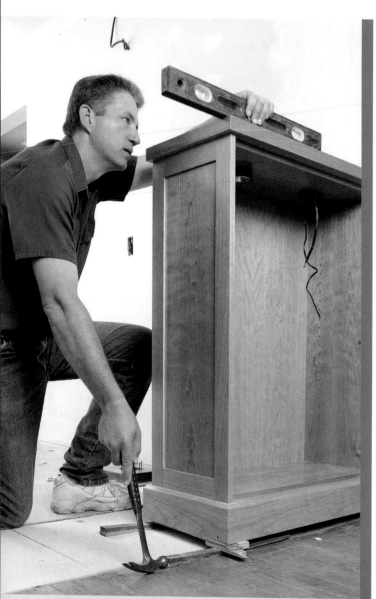

When installing built-ins don't assume level floors and plumb walls. Settling, joint compound buildup, and less-than-perfect framing mean that you have to bring things up to a new standard.

FIND THE HIGH SPOTS ON THE FLOOR

1 **SET BOTH CABINETS INTO POSITION** but don't even reach for your level or square yet. Using chalk or a lumber crayon, outline each cabinet's footprint onto the floor. Then move both cabinets well out of the way.

2 **PUT YOUR LEVEL** on the floor and find the highest spot within one footprint. To do this move your level parallel to the wall, perpendicular to the wall, and diagonally across the footprint. Mark an "**X**" at the highest point and repeat the process within the other footprint.

3 **PLACE A STRAIGHTEDGE** between the points, putting your level atop the straightedge, to discover which of the two marked points is higher. You'll install the first cabinet on the side with the higher mark.

Leveling over a ridge

If there's a crown in your floor between the two high points, simply place a scrap block of 2×4 at each high point, then bridge your straightedge between the blocks.

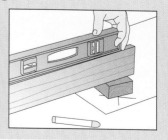

PREPARE THE CABINETS FOR INSTALLATION

1 **SET THE FIRST CABINET** onto its footprint, then level the cabinet from side to side by sliding tapered softwood shims (home centers have them by the bundle) below the base of the cabinet. Keep the cabinet snugly against the wall as you level it. After you level the cabinet side to side, check it from front to back, tapping in the shims until the cabinet is level in both directions.

2 **USE A FRAMING SQUARE** to check that the front and back of the cabinet are square to the wall. If your wall is curved, adjust the cabinet so that the square has the same reading at the front and back. Use duct tape to secure the shims to the floor.

3 **SET YOUR SCRIBE** 1/16" larger than the biggest wall-to-cabinet gap. Run a strip of masking tape down each end of the cabinet that touches the wall. Run the scribe down the wall to mark along the tape.

4 **RECRUIT A HELPER** and lift the cabinet straight up and off the shims. Use brads to fasten the shims to the floor inside the cabinet's marked footprint. Lay the cabinet on its paneled end and use a belt sander to remove stock to the scribed line. Slightly tilt the sander toward the

center of the cabinet to undercut for a snug fit against the wall. Repeat for the line scribed along the back.

SECURE THE CABINETS IN PLACE

1 **REPLACE THE CABINET** on the shims and push it against the wall. Run the wire for the lights through a hole in the wall that will be covered by the upper top. Drill angled pilot and counterbored shank holes close to the floor through the cabinet's baseboards. Toe-screw the cabinet to the floor, making sure the screw heads do not protrude. Trim the shims flush to the baseboards.

2 **SPAN A LEVEL STRAIGHTEDGE** from the installed cabinet's top to the opposite wall and make a mark. Shim the second cabinet so its top edge aligns with the line marked on the wall. Use a straightedge to align its front and back with the first cabinet. As with the first cabinet, secure the shims, scribe, and fasten the second cabinet in place.

3 **INSTALL THE LIGHTS,** following the manufacturer's instructions. Set the upper tops on the cabinets, centered front to back, with their ends against the walls. Apply tape, scribe the ends to the walls, and belt-sand to the scribed lines. Drive #8×1¼" flathead screws from inside the cabinets to secure the tops. Make molding with the same chamfered top as the baseboards. It should be tall enough to cover the toe-screw heads. Miter-cut it to length and nail it to the cabinets' bases. Fill the nail holes, sand the filler smooth, and finish the molding. Put in the shelves and attach the doors.

ENTERTAINMENT CENTER

THE FINAL CONFIGURATION OF THIS CABINET IS UP TO YOU. ITS DESIGN CAN FLEX TO SUIT YOUR SPACE AND STORAGE REQUIREMENTS.

Whether low and long, wide and high, equipped with cabinets or doors, or any combination thereof, this clever design can morph into the configuration that you need.

The Materials List and **CUTTING DIAGRAMS** (both on page 200) show parts for a pair of long and short sides, a single and double base and top, one door box (add the drawer shelf to make a drawer box), one door, and two drawers. To develop a cutting list for the configuration that you want to build, draw your design on paper and then count the components needed.

For example the unit in the large photo at right consists of two pairs of tall sides, eight shelves (two of which are bottom shelves), one double base, one double top, six boxes with four drawer shelves, two doors, and four pairs of drawers. The chest of drawers, opposite upper right corner, is made up of one pair of short sides, three shelves (one of which is a bottom shelf), a single base, single top, four boxes with four drawer shelves, and four pairs of drawers.

BUILD THE CARCASE

1 **CUT SIDES AND SHELVES.** From ¾" plywood cut the sides (A) and shelves (B) to the sizes shown on the Materials List. You'll need five shelves for a tall unit and three for a short unit.

2 **RIP THE SIDE BANDING** (C), bottom banding (D), and the shelf edging (E) to width and cut them about ½" longer than their mating plywood panels. Glue and clamp the banding to the sides and bottom shelf. Glue and clamp the edging to the remaining shelves where shown on **DRAWING 1**. See the tip "Reduce banding sanding" (page 203) for a timesaving method for applying the banding.

3 **SAND.** With the glue dry sand the banding flush with the faces of the sides and the bottom shelf. Sand the edging flush with the shelves' top faces. Trim the banding and edging ends flush with their respective panels' ends.

4 **MARK THE BOTTOM END** of each side (A/C). Lay out the locations of the 25mm holes for the knockdown fitting cam housings on the sides (A/C) where dimensioned on **DRAWING 3**. Measure the locations for the top pair of 25mm holes from the top end. Measure all the other vertical locations from the bottom end, as indicated on the drawing. See the tip "Fast, foolproof marking" (page 202) for a good marking method.

ENTERTAINMENT CENTER *(CONTINUED)*

Cutting diagrams

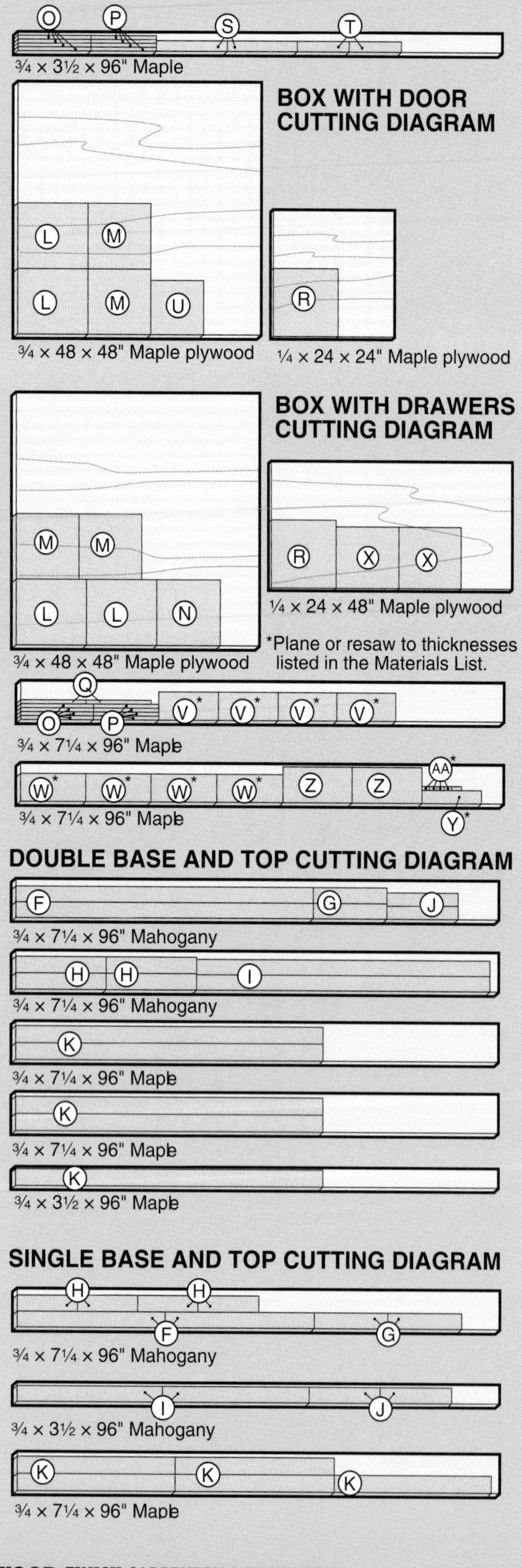
¾ x 3½ x 96" Maple
BOX WITH DOOR CUTTING DIAGRAM
¾ x 48 x 48" Maple plywood
¼ x 24 x 24" Maple plywood
BOX WITH DRAWERS CUTTING DIAGRAM
¼ x 24 x 48" Maple plywood
*Plane or resaw to thicknesses listed in the Materials List.
¾ x 48 x 48" Maple plywood
¾ x 7¼ x 96" Maple
¾ x 7¼ x 96" Maple
DOUBLE BASE AND TOP CUTTING DIAGRAM
¾ x 7¼ x 96" Mahogany
¾ x 7¼ x 96" Mahogany
¾ x 7¼ x 96" Maple
¾ x 7¼ x 96" Maple
¾ x 3½ x 96" Maple
SINGLE BASE AND TOP CUTTING DIAGRAM
¾ x 7¼ x 96" Mahogany
¾ x 3½ x 96" Mahogany
¾ x 7¼ x 96" Maple

MATERIALS LIST

Case Part		T	W	L	Matl.	Qty.
		FINISHED SIZE				
A	sides–tall	¾"	13¼"	61¾"	MP	2
A	sides–short	¾"	13¼"	31¼"	MP	2
B	shelves–tall	¾"	13¼"	28"	MP	5
B	shelves–short	¾"	13¼"	28"	MP	3
C*	side banding–tall	¾"	¾"	61¾"	M	4
C*	side banding–short	¾"	¾"	31¼"	M	4
D*	bottom banding	¾"	¾"	28"	M	2
E*	shelf edging–tall	¾"	1⅛"	28"	M	8
E*	shelf edging–short	¾"	1⅛"	28"	M	4
Base and Top		**T**	**W**	**L**	**Matl.**	**Qty.**
F	base stretchers–single	¾"	3"	29½"	MY	2
F	base stretchers–double	¾"	3"	59"	MY	2
G	base sides	¾"	3"	14¾"	MY	2
H*	feet–single unit	3"	3"	2¼"	LMY	4
H*	feet–double unit	3"	3"	2¼"	LMY	6
I	reveal stretchers–single	¾"	2¾"	29"	MY	2
I	reveal stretchers–double	¾"	2¾"	58½"	MY	2
J	reveal sides	¾"	2¾"	14¼"	MY	2
K*	top–single	¾"	15¾"	30½"	EM	1
K*	top–double	¾"	15¾"	60"	EM	1
Boxes		**T**	**W**	**L**	**Matl.**	**Qty.**
L	sides	¾"	12½"	14"	MP	2
M	top/bottom	¾"	12½"	12½"	MP	2
N	drawer shelf	¾"	12½"	12½"	MP	1
O*	side banding	¾"	¾"	14"	M	4
P*	top/bottom banding	¾"	¾"	12½"	M	4
Q*	drawer shelf banding	¾"	¾"	12½"	M	2
R	back	¼"	13"	13"	MP	1
Door		**T**	**W**	**L**	**Matl.**	**Qty.**
S	stiles	¾"	2"	13⅞"	M	2
T	rails	¾"	2"	10⅜"	M	2
U	panel	¾"	10⅜"	10⅜"	MP	1
Drawers		**T**	**W**	**L**	**Matl.**	**Qty.**
V	fronts/backs	½"	5⅜"	11¾"	M	4
W	sides	½"	5⅜"	13"	M	4
X	bottoms	¼"	11¾"	12½"	MP	2
Y*	slide cleats	¼"	2½"	12"	M	2
Z	faces	¾"	6⅞"	13⅞"	M	2
AA*	glides	⅜"	¾"	1½"	M	4

*Parts initially cut oversize. See the instructions.

Material key: MP-maple plywood, M-maple, MY-mahogany, LMY-laminated mahogany, EM-edge-joined maple.

Supplies: #8×¾" flathead wood screws, #8×1¼" flathead wood screws, #8×1½" flathead wood screws; #8×2" flathead wood screws; 8-32×1½" roundhead machine screws.

Using the jig

There is no substitute—certainly not hand-measuring the location of each hole—that can compete with a simple jig.

To use the one shown, push its right stop against the shelf's right edge. Clamp the drilling jig in place and drill the first hole. Unclamp, shift the jig so its left stop is against the shelf's left edge, and drill the second hole. This way no matter what the dimensions of the workpiece, the fastener holes will be a consistent distance from the edges.

5 **BORE CAM-HOUSING HOLES.** Chuck a 25mm Forstner bit in your drill press, set the fence 1½" from the bit's center, and adjust the depth stop to drill ½" deep. Drill the cam-housing holes at their marked locations.

6 **TO DRILL THE PILOT HOLES** in the ends of the shelves for the knock-down fitting screw studs, build the jig shown in **DRAWING 2**. When drilling the 5mm guide holes in the drill guide, use your drill press and a fence fitted with a stop block for maximum accuracy. Clamp the jig to the shelves with their top faces up. Chuck a 5mm bit in your drill so it protrudes 3" from the chuck. Slip a #10 flat washer over the bit and drill the stud pilot holes as shown in the box above. The chuck acts as a depth stop, and the washer protects the jig from the chuck's jaws.

7 **FINISH SIDES AND SHELVES.** Rout a 1/32" chamfer on all the banding and edging where shown on **DRAWING 1**. Finish-sand the

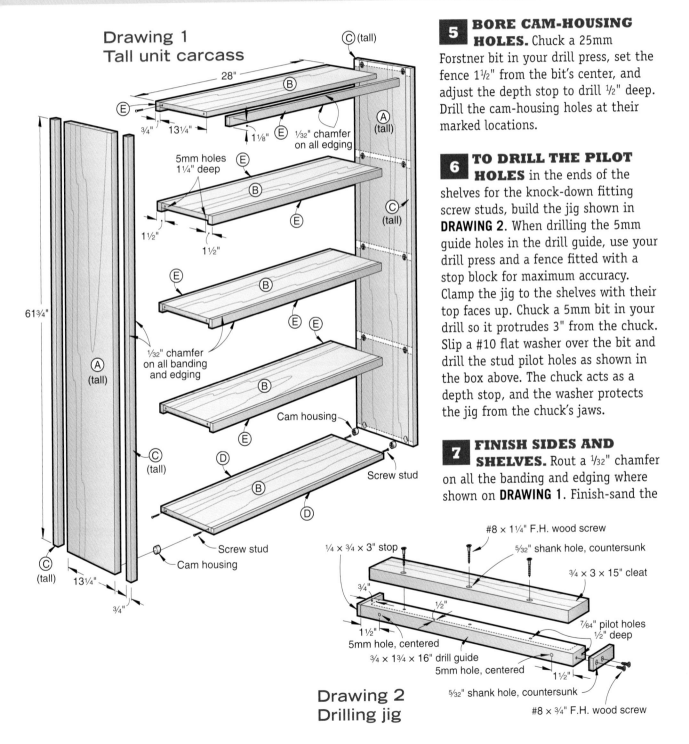

Drawing 1
Tall unit carcass

Drawing 2
Drilling jig

sides and shelves to 220 grit. Apply two coats of satin polyurethane, sanding lightly with 220-grit sandpaper between coats.

8 **PRESS THE CAM HOUSINGS** into their holes so they are flush with the surface. Engage the end of your combination square in the housings' slots to rotate them into alignment. Orient the stud holes to the sides' top, except for the bottom pairs. These stud holes are oriented toward the bottom.

9 **DRIVE IN THE STUDS** with a screwdriver until the stud's flange seats on the shelf's end.

ADD A BASE AND TOP

1 **PREPARE BASE STRETCHERS AND SIDES.** Miter-cut the single or double unit base stretchers (F) and base sides (G) to size. Glue and clamp them into a rectangular frame, as shown on **DRAWING 4**.

2 **TO MAKE THE SIX FEET** (H) for a double-wide unit, cut four ¾"×3⅛"×18"

A

Putting it together
Insert the shelf studs in the cam-housing sockets. Turn the cams with a phillips screwdriver to lock the shelves in place.

mahogany boards and laminate them into a 3"-thick blank. For the four feet for a single-wide unit, use four ¾"×3⅛"×12" boards. With the glue dry joint and plane the blank to 3" wide, then crosscut the 2¼"-long legs. Rout a ⅛" chamfer around the bottom of each leg.

3 **CLAMP THE LEGS** to the base frame with their edges flush with the edges of the base stretchers (F) and base sides (G) where shown on **DRAWING 4**. Drill pilot and countersunk shank holes and glue and screw the legs to the frame. Sand the mating edges smooth.

4 **CUT THE REVEALS.** Miter-cut the reveal stretchers (I) and reveal sides (J) to size. Glue and clamp them into the lower and upper reveal frames. With the glue dry glue and clamp the lower reveal frame to the base. The reveal frame sits in ¼" all around from the base frame's edge.

5 **SAND AND STAIN.** Finish-sand the base assembly and the upper reveal frame to 220 grit. Apply stain if desired and let it dry for 24 hours. We used Bartley Pennsylvania cherry gel stain.

6 **MAKE THE TOP.** For the single- or double-unit top (K), edge-join ¾"-thick boards to make a blank about 1" wider and 1" longer than shown on

Fast, foolproof marking

To speed the repetitive layout of the cam-housing holes, mark the desired measurements on a piece of masking tape applied to your tape measure blade. The masking tape does not interfere with the operation of your tape measure. As long as you always measure from the bottom edge of the workpiece, you won't accidentally mismark the location of a hole.

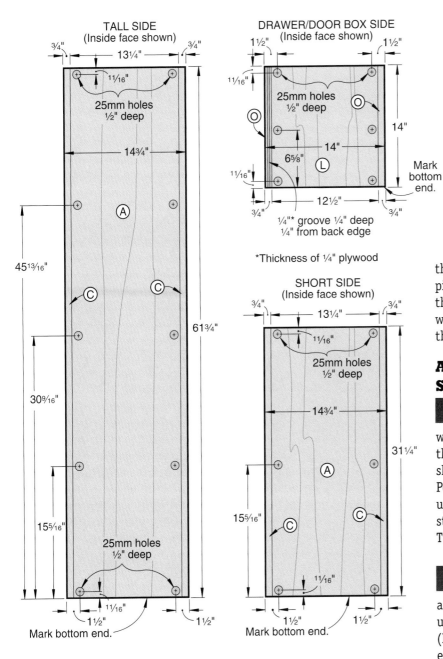

TALL SIDE
(Inside face shown)

¾" 13¼" ¾"

11/16"

25mm holes
½" deep

14¾"

Ⓐ

45¹³⁄₁₆"

Ⓒ Ⓒ

61¾"

30⁹⁄₁₆"

15⁵⁄₁₆"

25mm holes
½" deep

11/16"
1½"
Mark bottom end. 1½"

DRAWER/DOOR BOX SIDE
(Inside face shown)

1½" 1½"

11/16"

25mm holes
½" deep

Ⓞ Ⓞ

Ⓞ Ⓞ

14"

14"

6⅝"

Ⓛ

11/16"

12½"

¾" ¾"

Mark
bottom
end.

¼"* groove ¼" deep
¼" from back edge

*Thickness of ¼" plywood

SHORT SIDE
(Inside face shown)

¾" 13¼" ¾"

11/16"

25mm holes
½" deep

14¾"

Ⓐ

31¼"

15⁵⁄₁₆"

Ⓒ Ⓒ

11/16"

1½" 1½"
Mark bottom end.

Drawing 3 Sides

the Materials List. With the glue dry cut the top to size and sand to 220 grit.

7 **FINISH** with two coats of satin polyurethane on the base assembly, upper reveal frame, and top.

8 **APPLY THE REVEAL FRAME.** With the finish dry clamp the upper reveal frame to the top. The reveal frame sits back from the top's edge ¾" all around. Drill pilot and countersunk shank holes through the reveal frame into the top where shown on **DRAWING 4**. Drive in the screws.

ASSEMBLE THE SHELF UNIT

1 **ADD THE SHELVES.** Lay one side (A/C) on the floor with the cam housings up. Insert the shelves (B/E) and the bottom shelf (B/D), as shown in **PHOTO A**. Position the other side on the upturned shelves, engaging the shelf studs in the cam-housing sockets. Turn the cams to lock in the shelves.

2 **CLAMP THE BASE ASSEMBLY** (F/G/H/I/J) and top assembly (I/J/K) to the shelf unit. The base stretcher/side frame (F/G) is flush with the shelf unit's edges. The top (K) overhangs ½" all around. If you are building a double unit, tightly clamp the units together

Reduce banding sanding

To reduce sanding time when applying banding, carefully plane your banding stock to just a paper-thickness thicker than your plywood. Lay your panel and banding across your bar clamps, as shown in the photo, right. Apply white glue for longer working time. Starting at one end and working down the panel's length, first clamp the banding flush with the panel using a pair of quick-action clamps, then draw it tight with a bar clamp.

With the glue dry make a couple of passes with a cabinet scraper followed by a couple of swipes with a sanding block to create flush edges.

ENTERTAINMENT CENTER *(CONTINUED)*

Drawing 4 Exploded view

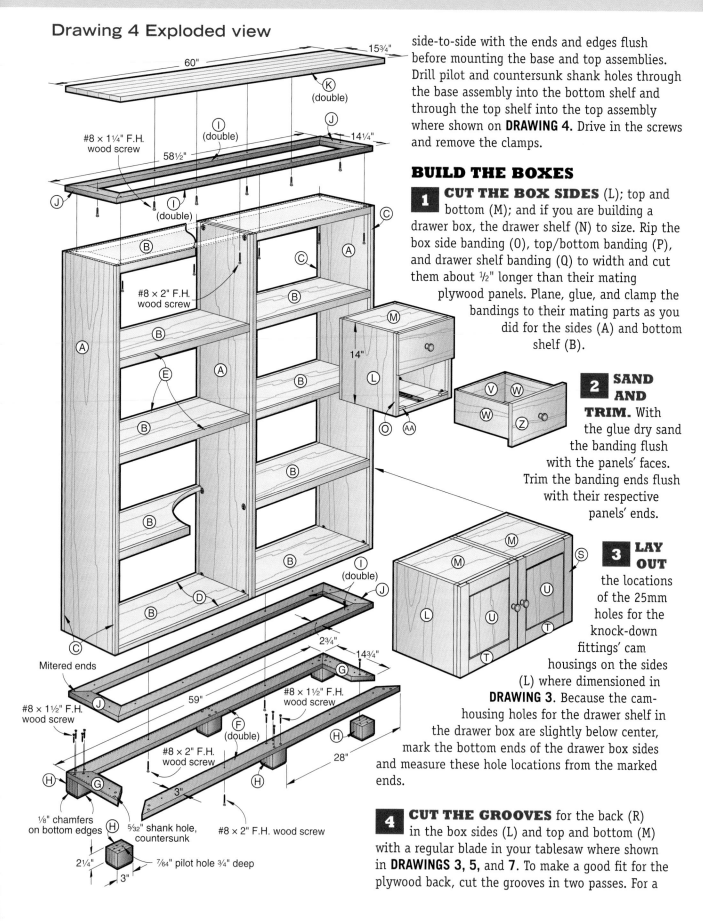

side-to-side with the ends and edges flush before mounting the base and top assemblies. Drill pilot and countersunk shank holes through the base assembly into the bottom shelf and through the top shelf into the top assembly where shown on **DRAWING 4**. Drive in the screws and remove the clamps.

BUILD THE BOXES

1 **CUT THE BOX SIDES** (L); top and bottom (M); and if you are building a drawer box, the drawer shelf (N) to size. Rip the box side banding (O), top/bottom banding (P), and drawer shelf banding (Q) to width and cut them about ½" longer than their mating plywood panels. Plane, glue, and clamp the bandings to their mating parts as you did for the sides (A) and bottom shelf (B).

2 **SAND AND TRIM.** With the glue dry sand the banding flush with the panels' faces. Trim the banding ends flush with their respective panels' ends.

3 **LAY OUT** the locations of the 25mm holes for the knock-down fittings' cam housings on the sides (L) where dimensioned in **DRAWING 3**. Because the cam-housing holes for the drawer shelf in the drawer box are slightly below center, mark the bottom ends of the drawer box sides and measure these hole locations from the marked ends.

4 **CUT THE GROOVES** for the back (R) in the box sides (L) and top and bottom (M) with a regular blade in your tablesaw where shown in **DRAWINGS 3, 5,** and **7**. To make a good fit for the plywood back, cut the grooves in two passes. For a drawer box pair up the drawer box sides as right- and left-hand sides.

5 ADD FASTENERS. As before press the cam housings into the sides. Use the jig to drill stud pilot holes in the top, bottom, and drawer shelf ends. Drive in the studs. Clamp a box together and check the groove-to-groove dimensions. Cut the box back (R) to size. Note that the grain runs vertically.

6 COMPLETE THE DRAWER SHELF. To make the rear edge of the drawer shelf (N/Q) fall inside the drawer box back (R), rip ½" off its rear edge, giving the drawer shelf assembly a finished width of 13½".

7 SAND AND FINISH. Rout a 1/32" chamfer on all the banding edges and ends. Sand the box parts to 220 grit and apply the finish.

MAKE A FRAME-AND-PANEL DOOR

1 CUT STILES (S) and rails (T) to size. Install a ¼" dado blade in your tablesaw and cut ¼"-deep grooves centered in the thickness of the rails and stiles, shown in **DRAWING 6**. To ensure centered grooves make test cuts in scrap the same thickness as your parts, adjusting the fence as necessary. When the fence is correctly positioned, cut the grooves in the stiles (S) and rails (T).

2 MAKE THE TENONS. Install a ¼" dado blade in your tablesaw and form the tenons on the ends of the rails (T). Test-fit the rail tenons in the stile grooves by first making cuts in your scrap piece.

3 CLAMP YOUR DOOR FRAME together and check the groove-to-groove dimensions.

Cut the panel (U) to size. With a 3/8" dado blade in your tablesaw, form a centered tongue on the panel that fits the frame parts' grooves and leaves a 1/8" reveal. To eliminate chipping veneer at the corners, first form the cross-grained tongues, then the parallel-grained tongues. Sand the panel to 220 grit.

4 TO ENHANCE THE REVEAL stain the panel's tongue with the same stain used on the mahogany parts. Apply masking tape to the tongue's shoulder to keep stain from bleeding onto the panel's surface. With the stain dry squeeze glue into the grooves. Use glue sparingly so it does not squeeze out into the reveal. Clamp the door together, making certain that it is square and flat.

5 MARK THE HINGE-CUP LOCATIONS on the back of the door's stile where shown on **DRAWING 5**. With a 35mm Forstner bit, drill the ½"-deep holes. Drill the 3/16" knob hole where shown. Sand the door to 220 grit and apply the finish.

6 DRILL HOLES FOR HINGE PLATES. Mark horizontal and vertical centerlines for the hinge plates on one side (L/O) where shown in **DRAWING 5**. Position the plates on the centerlines and drill the pilot holes.

PUT TOGETHER A PAIR OF DRAWERS

1 PREPARE FRONTS/BACKS. Plane enough lumber to ½" thick for the drawer fronts/backs (V) and sides (W). Cut the parts to size. Install a ¼" dado blade in your tablesaw and cut the rabbets in the fronts/backs and the dadoes in the sides to form the lock-rabbet joint shown in **DRAWING 7A**. Cut the ¼"-deep grooves in the parts for the

The beauty of a knock-down

This project owes its versatility to special knock-down hardware. Unlike the type of cams you might have encountered with out-of-the-box knock-down furniture, these are much less obtrusive. Simply insert the screw stud into the cam housing's socket. Turn the cam clockwise to lock the stud in place.

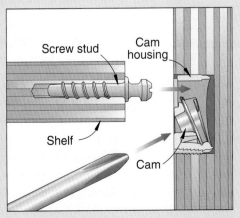

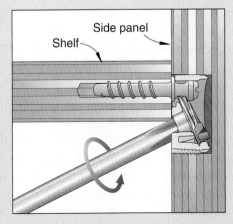

ENTERTAINMENT CENTER *(CONTINUED)*

Drawing 5
Door box

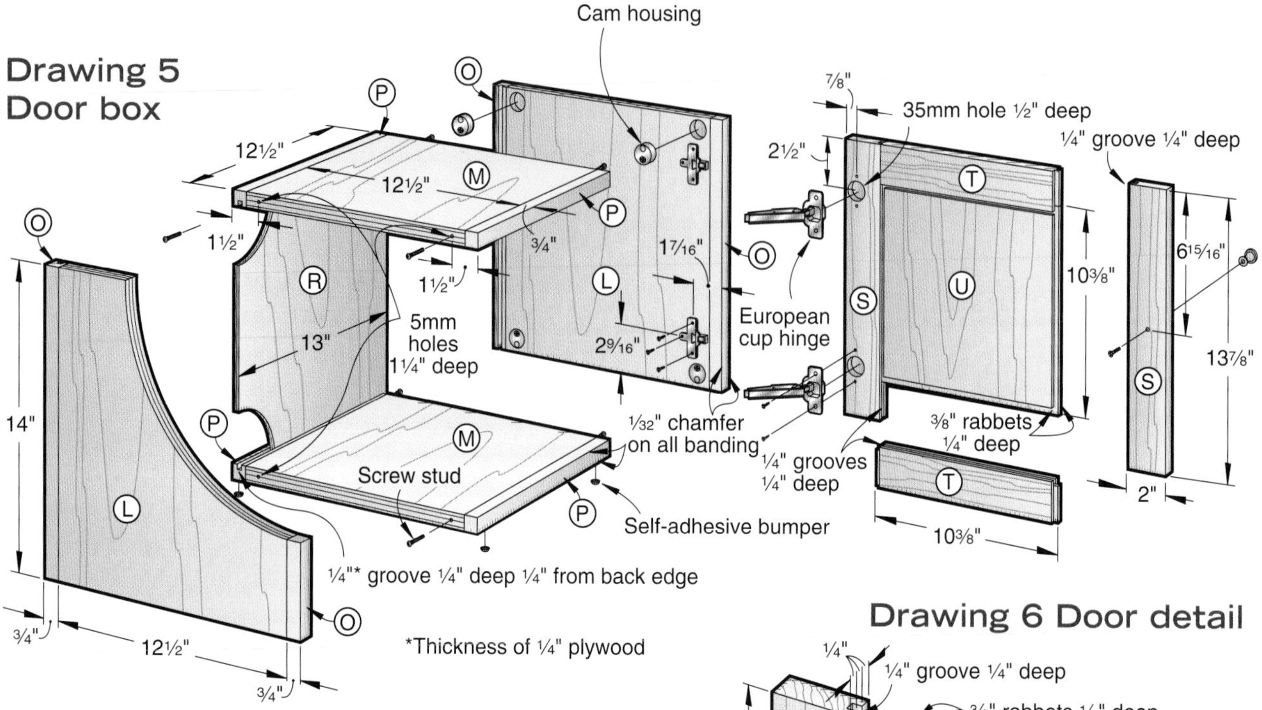
Cam housing
O
P
12½"
12½"
M
7/8"
35mm hole ½" deep
¼" groove ¼" deep
2½"
T
P
O
1½"
¾"
1⅞"
O
R
1½"
L
S
U
10⅜"
6¹⁵⁄₁₆"
5mm
holes
1¼" deep
European
cup hinge
13"
2⁹⁄₁₆"
13⅞"
S
14"
P
1/32" chamfer
on all banding
⅜" rabbets
¼" deep
M
¼" grooves
¼" deep
Screw stud
T
2"
L
P
Self-adhesive bumper
10⅜"
¼"* groove ¼" deep ¼" from back edge
O
¾"
12½"
*Thickness of ¼" plywood
¾"

Drawing 6 Door detail

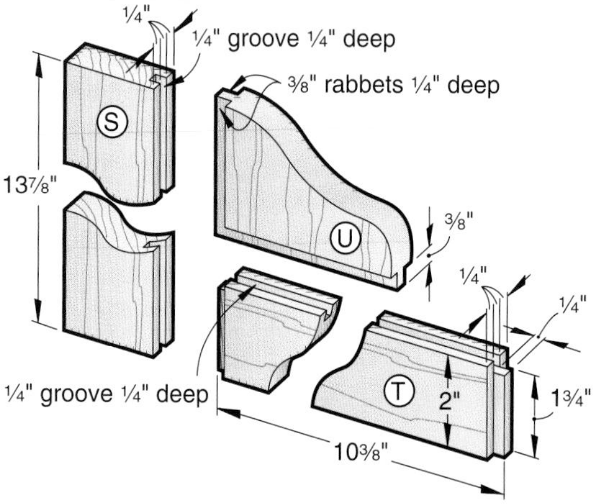
¼"
¼" groove ¼" deep
⅜" rabbets ¼" deep
S
13⅞"
⅜"
U
¼"
¼"
¼" groove ¼" deep
T
2"
1¾"
10⅜"

bottoms (X), shown in **DRAWING 7**. Use a regular blade in your tablesaw, making two passes to match the thickness of the ¼" plywood.

2 **DRILL AND SAND.** Drill the four 5/16" holes in the fronts (V) for mounting the drawer faces (Z) where shown. The faces are fastened to the drawers with washer-head screws. The oversize holes allow you to adjust the faces' positions during final assembly. Sand all the drawer parts to 220 grit.

3 **DRY-ASSEMBLE DRAWER PARTS** to check their fit, measure for the bottoms (X), and cut the bottoms to size. Apply glue to the lock-rabbets and grooves and clamp the drawers together.

4 **PREPARE CLEATS.** Resaw a ¾"×2½"×12" board in half and plane it to ¼" thick for the drawer slide cleats (Y). Glue and clamp them to the drawer bottoms, centered as shown in **DRAWING 7**.

5 **CUT THE DRAWER FACES** (Z) to size and drill centered 3/16" holes for the knobs. Sand the faces to 220 grit. Apply finish to all the drawer parts.

6 **RESAW AND PLANE** a ⅜"×¾"×8" blank for the glides (AA). Cut them to length and drill centered countersunk shank holes.

ASSEMBLE THE BOXES

1 **POSITION THE GLIDES** (AA) on the drawer box bottom (M/P) and drawer shelf (N/Q) where shown in **DRAWING 7**. Drill pilot holes and screw the glides in place.

2 **REMOVE THE OPTIONAL REAR BRACKET** from the undermounted drawer slides and separate the drawer and carcass members. Carefully centering the carcass members and keeping their front ends flush with the front edges of the bottom and shelf, screw them in place.

3 **ADD SHELF STUDS.** Insert the top, bottom, and drawer shelf studs in the cam housings of one side of the door and drawer boxes. Lock them in place. Slide the backs into the grooves.

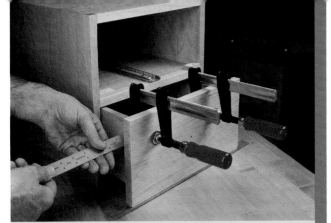

Attach the drawer faces

Place a ¹⁄₁₆"-thick spacer underneath the drawer face and clamp it, centered, to the drawer. The upper drawer is removed to show the placement of the slide's carcass member and the glides (AA).

Mate the other sides with the protruding srew studs and lock the cams.

4 **INSTALL HINGES.** Screw the hinge plates to the door box. Press the hinges into the cup holes and using the holes in the cup flanges as guides, drill the pilot holes. Drive the screws. Install the knob and snap the hinges onto the plates. Turn the adjustment screws to center the door on the box.

5 **TURN THE DRAWERS UPSIDE DOWN.** Carefully centering the slides' drawer members and keeping their front ends flush with the drawers' front edges, screw them in place. Slide the drawers into the box and check that they are square

in their openings. If not the slides' slotted holes provide adjustment.

6 **TO MOUNT THE LOWER DRAWER FACE** (Z), place the drawer box on a flat surface. Pull the bottom drawer out far enough to accommodate the heads of small C-clamps or bar clamps. Clamp a drawer face to the drawer, as shown in box at left. Remove the drawer and, centering the bit in the ⁵⁄₁₆" holes in the drawer front (V), drill pilot holes into the drawer face (Z). Drive in washer-head screws and remove the clamps.

7 **MOUNT THE UPPER DRAWER FACE** in the same manner, this time placing the upper face on a ¹⁄₈"-thick spacer resting on the top edge of the lower drawer face. Clamp, drill, and drive in the screws.

8 **CHECK THE ALIGNMENT** of the drawers and faces with the drawer box and each other. Make any necessary adjustments to the positions of the drawer slides and drawer faces. When you are satisfied with the alignment, using the holes in the drawer faces as guides, drill the knob-screw holes through the drawer fronts. Using the 1½"-long machine screws that come with them, screw the knobs in place. To keep the door and drawer boxes from slipping around on the shelves, attach four self-adhesive bumpers to the bottom of each box.

Drawing 7 Drawer box

Drawing 7A Lock-rabbet joint

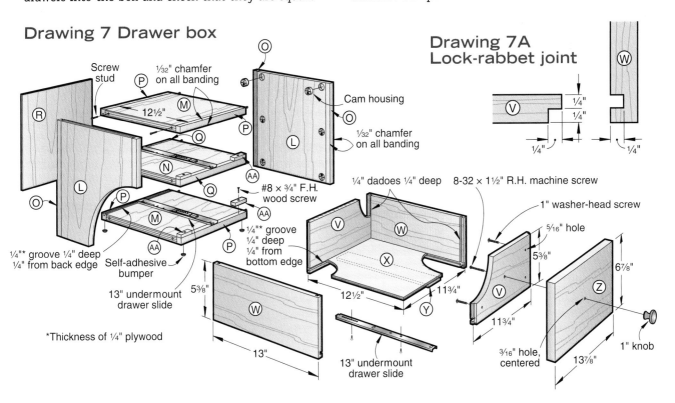

KITCHEN CABINETS

THEY CAN COST A BUNDLE IF YOU HAVE THEM CUSTOM-MADE, AND OFF-THE-SHELF TYPES MIGHT NOT HAVE THE QUALITY YOU WANT. FORTUNATELY DOING IT YOURSELF CAN DELIVER THE BEST OF BOTH WORLDS.

Sure you could go to the store and buy new cabinets when it's time to remodel your kitchen. But a woodworker with a bit of experience does have another choice and a big advantage. Examine the quality of those factory-built units. Check the prices. You probably can beat the big manufacturers on both counts by building your own cabinets.

This project requires only basic woodworking tools and some special jigs that you can make yourself. Still there's no denying that it's a major undertaking. Make sure you have the time and patience to get it done in a reasonable fashion. Feeling confident on that score? Then here are the basics that will make the job go smoothly.

PLAN TO THE LAST DETAIL

This is not a project that you can jump into with a few rough sketches. You need to make precise measurements and drawings that are detailed enough to let you visualize both the construction procedures and the results. You can do it all on graph paper, but computer-aided design software is a great help.

Wheelchair access or a strong personal preference for lower or higher countertops might enter into your planning. Otherwise stick with standard specifications. The typical kitchen countertop is 36" off the floor; base cabinets are 24" deep; upper cabinets are 12" to 13" deep; and the upper cabinets perch 18" above the countertop. Plan for a 1/8" gap on each side of an appliance.

We're going to build boxes of manageable size and set them side by side, so you need to figure out logical widths for those boxes. For example the sink base might be 42" wide, a standard storage unit might

be 30", and a cabinet housing a stack of drawers might be 18". Measure existing kitchens and look at the cabinet manufacturers' brochures at home centers for examples.

We'll show you how to build slightly modified Eurostyle cabinets. These give you a contemporary look, and the absence of face frames makes them easier to build than more traditional styles.

Place hardware high on your planning list too. If you can't find everything you need at your favorite home center, get a detailed catalog from an online hardware supplier—or peruse their website.

You have a huge array of pulls, hinges, and drawer slides to choose from, and those choices do make a

Think ahead to the kind of hardware you want. Specialty items can take a while to be delivered. More important the type of door you want might affect the kind of hinge required.

difference. For example standard drawer slides mount on the drawer sides, usually requiring ⅛" clearance on each side. An undermounted style, which is hidden from view, allows for a slightly wider drawer too.

Also spend some time considering specialized hardware, such as pullout trays, drawer inserts, wastebasket racks, storage baskets, and the like. Remember you'll have to size some cabinets to accommodate those choices.

QUALITY OF MATERIAL MATTERS

Don't settle for common materials when you're aiming for top-notch results. It's worth the extra cost to go with professional quality when you select sheet goods, fasteners, and hardware.

You'll need enough solid-wood stock to build doors, drawers, and various trim pieces. Cherry was used for these cabinets. The door panels were made out of ¼" cherry plywood, with two good faces.

You can buy melamine-coated sheet material at any home center, but a better option is to go to a builder's supply outlet and buy "thermo-fused" melamine. It's a higher-quality product with a shiny white coating that's more durable and easier to keep clean than the dull kind that most home centers carry.

This project uses sheet goods with thermo-fused melamine on one face and a brown gluing surface on the other. Each sheet comes oversize at 49"×97", allowing for space lost to saw kerfs. You can expect to pay about $30 per sheet.

You'll use ¾" sheets for the sides and bottom of each base cabinet and for the sides, top, and bottom of each upper cabinet. Buy enough ¼" sheet stock, also with thermo-fused melamine on one side and a gluing surface on the other, to cover the backs of all the cabinets.

Fastening fibercore

Special cabinet-connecting screws are available from such suppliers as McFeely's (800/443-7937 or mcfeelys.com). Unlike wood screws, where the collar diameter narrows above the threads, the collar below the heads of these screws is as wide as the threads to help hold the screw in place while the threads gently grip the edges of the pilot hole, as shown in the cutaway view below. This fastener also can be used to connect pieces of melamine-covered particleboard.

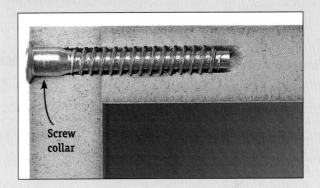

Screw collar

Also buy enough ¾" sheet material with melamine on both sides to make shelves for all of your cabinets. You can use the two-sided type of sheet goods for the whole project, but you'll have to sand off the melamine coating on the bottom of each upper cabinet so that veneer will adhere to it.

Cover the melamine's exposed edges with wood-veneer tape. Look for it in 8' rolls at home centers, or you can order it online. Plan for some waste, because it's best to avoid using splices.

START WITH A BASE CABINET

You need only basic woodworking skills to build the standard cabinet box. Let's start with a typical base cabinet, as shown in **DRAWING 1.** Vary the dimensions and the number of drawers to make nearly any cabinet unit you want.

To avoid chipping the melamine, outfit your tablesaw with a sharp, 80-tooth blade. Then cut a sheet in half lengthwise and cut one half into three equal pieces, each approximately 24"×32".

One piece at a time, clamp each sheet of melamine to your workbench, white face up. This white surface will be visible inside the cabinet. Equip your router with an edge guide and a ¼" straight bit and rout a groove ⅜" deep and 9⁄16" from the edge, as shown in **PHOTO A** and **DRAWING 1.** This edge will serve as the back edge of the cabinet sides and bottom.

KITCHEN CABINETS *(CONTINUED)*

A

Equip your router with a good edge guide before you start making grooves for cabinet backs. Set the guide and then do all the backs at once.

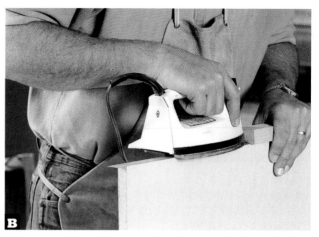

B

All you need to apply veneer is an inexpensive household iron. If you plan to do a lot of cabinetwork, you can buy veneer tape in 250' rolls.

Now cut the two sides to 23¼"×30½". Make the cabinet bottom 23¼" deep and as wide as the finished width of the cabinet minus 1½". From the same material cut two rails for the top and a drawer divider, each piece 5" wide and as long as the bottom's width. Rout a groove in the back rail, sized and located to match the grooves in the sides.

Now because they will show on the finished cabinet, put veneer tape on the front edges of the sides, bottom, and rails. We used cherry veneer to match the solid wood used for the doors and drawer fronts.

Apply veneer tape with a common household iron, as shown in **PHOTO B**. Secure the workpiece vertically in a vise or in a handscrew clamp that is, in turn, clamped to the top of your workbench. Cut enough tape to protrude beyond both ends of the piece. With your iron set at medium heat, run it along the length of the piece. This melts enough of the adhesive backing to hold the tape in place.

Then go over the tape again, holding the iron in place for 3 or 4 seconds in each spot. Move an iron's length ahead and also press a wood block on the previous spot. The wood absorbs some of the heat, and the pressure helps to set the veneer in place.

Score the tape from beneath at one end of the workpiece, using the wood block as a backing surface. Snap off the veneer, then sand it flush with medium-grit sandpaper on a sanding block. Repeat at the opposite end.

Use a veneer-trimming tool, shown in **PHOTO C**. Or you can shave the veneer flush with a sharp chisel.

See the box on page 215 for details about making a drilling jig that you'll use to position shelf holes on the cabinet sides. Use this jig to drill a series of holes in each area where you want to place a shelf, to allow for some adjustment in shelf spacing.

Most factory-built cabinets have holes from the top of the cabinet clear down to the bottom, but there's no need to do that. Your cabinets will look better on the inside with fewer holes. In addition you won't wind up with a hole, or half a hole, near the bottom, where liquids could splash into the particleboard core and cause damage.

Attach the sides to the bottom with #20 biscuits and #8×2" production screws. Keep it simple by lining up the edge of the biscuit joiner with the edge of the cabinet side, as shown in **PHOTO D,** and then the edge of the bottom. That way you don't even need to make pencil marks. Use four biscuits per edge.

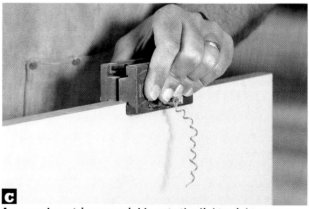

C

A razor-sharp trimmer quickly cuts the lightweight veneer. This spring-loaded model handles both sides at once and works on stock of various thicknesses.

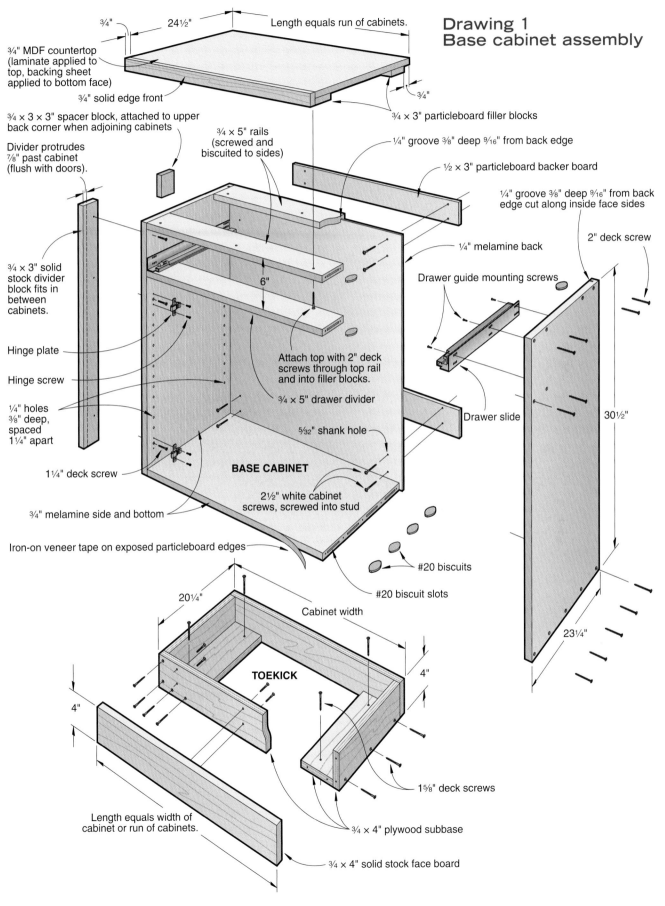

Drawing 1
Base cabinet assembly

¾" 24½" Length equals run of cabinets.

¾" MDF countertop (laminate applied to top, backing sheet applied to bottom face)

¾" solid edge front

¾" ✕ 3 ✕ 3" spacer block, attached to upper back corner when adjoining cabinets

¾ ✕ 5" rails (screwed and biscuited to sides)

¾ ✕ 3" particleboard filler blocks

¾"

¼" groove ⅜" deep ⁹⁄₁₆" from back edge

½ ✕ 3" particleboard backer board

Divider protrudes ⅞" past cabinet (flush with doors).

¼" groove ⅜" deep ⁹⁄₁₆" from back edge cut along inside face sides

2" deck screw

¾ ✕ 3" solid stock divider block fits in between cabinets.

¼" melamine back

Drawer guide mounting screws

6"

Hinge plate

Hinge screw

Attach top with 2" deck screws through top rail and into filler blocks.

Drawer slide

¼" holes ⅜" deep, spaced 1¼" apart

¾ ✕ 5" drawer divider

30½"

⁵⁄₃₂" shank hole

1¼" deck screw

BASE CABINET

¾" melamine side and bottom

2½" white cabinet screws, screwed into stud

#20 biscuits

Iron-on veneer tape on exposed particleboard edges

#20 biscuit slots

23¼"

20¼"

Cabinet width

TOEKICK

4"

4"

1⅝" deck screws

Length equals width of cabinet or run of cabinets.

¾ ✕ 4" plywood subbase

¾ ✕ 4" solid stock face board

KITCHEN CABINETS *(CONTINUED)*

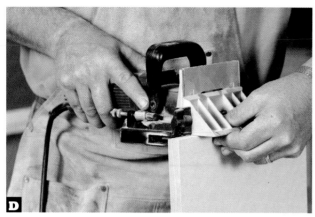

D

Keep joinery simple and avoid measurements completely when possible. Here the biscuit joiner is lined up with the edge of the cabinet side.

E

Make a simple jig to guide your biscuit joiner for the drawer divider slots and label it. Again you eliminate the need for measurements.

Also cut biscuit slots for the drawer divider. Use a shop-made jig for this, consisting of a square piece of particleboard, 5" on each side, with wider guide boards screwed to two adjoining sides. Fit and clamp the jig against the corner of a cabinet side, line up the biscuit joiner as shown in **PHOTO E,** and you're ready to cut, again without measuring or marking.

Attach the sides to the bottom with biscuits and yellow glue. Before that glue has set, install the drawer divider and front top rail, as shown in **PHOTO F,** with biscuits and glue. Rails provide all the strength you need, and the extra access area makes installation easier than it would be with a full top.

Slide the back into its grooves from above, as shown in **PHOTO G.** Spread the corners just enough to fit the back top rail and its biscuits into place. Add five

#8×2" self-tapping, flathead screws along each bottom edge and two screws into each end of each rail. Drill a ⅛" countersunk starter hole for each screw.

Lay the cabinet on its face to install the top and bottom backerboards, made from ½" particleboard. Cut them 3" wide and the same length as the rails. You'll drive screws through these pieces when you install the cabinets.

Glue the backerboards in place with yellow glue. Press down on each board as you drive brads through the cabinet sides and into the ends of the board, as shown in **PHOTO H.** The pressure closes any gap on the visible side of the back, and the brads hold the boards in place while the glue dries. The brads, like the screw heads, won't be visible once the cabinets are set in place.

F

After you've attached the sides to the bottom, there's still enough "give" to allow the installation of the drawer divider and top front rail.

G

Slide the back into place without glue. That flexibility will come in handy if you need to adjust the cabinet slightly for squareness during installation.

Drawing 2
Wall cabinet assembly

¾" melamine (particleboard) cabinet top and bottom

#20 biscuit slots

¼" groove ⅜" deep 9/16" from back edge cut along inside face of top, sides, and bottom

#20 biscuits

¾ × 3 × 3" spacer block, attached to upper back corner when joining cabinets

12"

#8 × 1¼" deep

½ × 3" particleboard backerboard

Divider protrudes ⅞" past cabinet (flush with doors).

Iron-on veneer tape on exposed particleboard edges

3" typical (less for short doors)

⅛"

12"

Drill pilot hole to fit hinge screws.

1⅜" hole ½" deep ⅛" from edge of door

3" white cabinet screws, screwed into stud

¼" melamine back

30" for soffit
42" for full-height

Inside dimension of door frame + ⅞"

¼" plywood panel

¾ × 3" solid stock divider block fits in between cabinets.

5/32" shank holes

Inside dimension of door frame + ⅞"

¼" groove ½" deep

Hinge plate

2¼"

Hinge

*¼" holes ⅜" deep spaced 1¼" apart

Hinge screws

#20 biscuit slot

#20 biscuit

5/32" shank hole

2" deck screws

2¼"

¼" groove ½" deep

*Use ¼" hole template to locate and space holes.

Size door to fit outside of cabinet (less reveal).

Veneer glued to bottom of cabinet after assembly.

¾ × 2¼" frames

Drawing 2A
Tenon detail

¼"   ¼"

½"   ¼"

2¼"

2"

¼ × 2" tenon ½" long

¼" groove ½" deep, centered along edge

Drawing 2B Door and divider detail/top view

Door

Cabinet

¾" divider

Reveal

Cabinet

Door

KITCHEN CABINETS *(CONTINUED)*

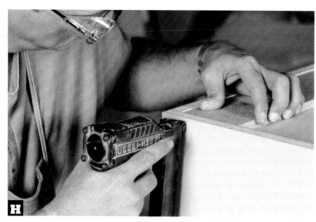

Glue the backerboards in place, then add small fasteners to hold them while the glue dries. Use a pneumatic gun or tap in some brads with a hammer.

A featherboard adds a lot to your accuracy when you're cutting grooves on the edges of the door rails and stiles.

Eurostyle cabinets are designed to butt against each other, but we modified that arrangement. We attached a ¾" solid-wood divider between each adjacent pair of cabinets. Each divider protrudes ⅞" from the front edge of the cabinet. That measurement puts the dividers flush with the cabinet doors, which are held ⅛" away from the cabinet by their hinges.

Most of your cabinets will be covered on the sides by a wall, an adjoining cabinet, or an appliance. Cover any visible side with a rail-and-stile, flat-panel assembly. Follow the procedures outlined in the section on door-making that follows.

BUILDING A WALL CABINET

The wall cabinets are a shallower, simpler version of the base cabinets. All you need is the basic box and shelves—you don't have to deal with drawers. See the details in **DRAWING 2** on page 213.

For the sides cut ¾" melamine 12" wide and to the length needed. Cut the top and bottom 12" wide and to a length equal to the finished width of the cabinet minus 1½". Rout a groove for the back, as in the base cabinets. Drill the shelf-support holes, again assuming two shelves per cabinet.

Make two biscuit slots per joint. Assemble the bottom and sides with biscuits and yellow glue, slide the back into its grooves, and add the top. Add four screws per joint, following the procedure described above. Cover the bottom of each upper cabinet with cherry veneer.

To make each shelf cut ¾" melamine the same length as the width of the cabinet opening and ¼" narrower than the inside depth of the cabinet.

Cover the exposed edge on the front of each shelf by ironing on white PVC tape, available at home centers.

MAKING THE DOOR

We built frame-and-panel cabinet doors with flat panels and exposed, stub tenons joining rail to stile. Solid cherry makes up the frames, and ¼" cherry plywood the panels. A 90-degree profile was maintained around the outside edges to match the cabinet dividers. See **DRAWINGS 2** and **2A** for the basic door dimensions and construction details. For other door and hinge options, see page 217.

For a single-door cabinet, make the door width ¼" less than the width of the cabinet itself. Plan on double doors for any cabinet that's more than 22" wide. In that case subtract ⅜" from the cabinet width and divide the result by 2 to get the width of each door.

Rip enough solid stock 2¼" wide to make the rails and stiles for your doors. Then take some time to choose the straightest pieces for the stiles. Straight stiles produce flat, good-fitting doors. If you're making cabinets of various heights cut the longest stiles to length first, then the remaining stiles, and finally the rails. To determine the length of the rails, subtract 4½" (the combined width of two stiles) from the finished door width and add 1" to account for the tenons.

With a standard blade on your tablesaw, cut a groove on the inside edges of the stiles and rails, as shown in **PHOTO I**. Make it ½" deep and just wide enough to accept the plywood. Usually ¼" plywood won't measure exactly ¼" so run some test cuts on scrap pieces first. Cut the length of the piece and

Drawing 3
Drawer assembly

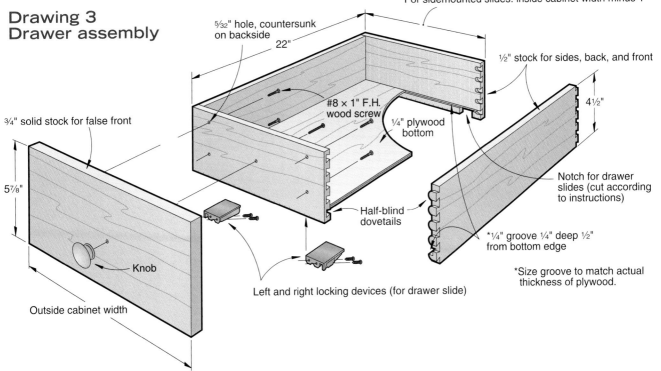

For undermounted slides: inside cabinet width minus ½"
For sidemounted slides: inside cabinet width minus 1"

5/32" hole, countersunk on backside

22"

½" stock for sides, back, and front

¾" solid stock for false front

#8 × 1" F.H. wood screw

¼" plywood bottom

4½"

5⅞"

Notch for drawer slides (cut according to instructions)

Knob

Half-blind dovetails

*¼" groove ¼" deep ½" from bottom edge

*Size groove to match actual thickness of plywood.

Left and right locking devices (for drawer slide)

Outside cabinet width

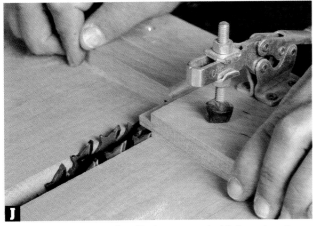

J

This shop-made tenoning jig features a hold-down toggle clamp. Make your own carriage-style jig or use a miter gauge.

flip the other face against the fence and cut in the opposite direction. This step centers the groove on the workpiece. Adjust the fence until the width is perfect.

Equip your tablesaw with a dado set and cut ½"-long tenons on both ends of each rail, sized to fit the grooves. We used a sliding carriage that rides in the miter gauge slots, and a hold-down clamp, as shown in **PHOTO J**.

To improve the appearance of the door, ease the inside edges of the grooves with 150-grit sandpaper on a block. Another benefit: The softened edges will take finish better than sharp ones would.

Make a shelf-hole jig

To make sure your shelf holes line up accurately, you need a drilling jig. Make the simple one shown here out of scrap material, and you'll be all set to construct any standard cabinetry.

To use the jig fit its guide boards against one top corner of a cabinet side. Mark the guide holes you want to use, set a depth stop on your ¼" brad-point bit, then drill the shelf holes ⅜" deep. Flip the jig over to fit against the opposite top corner, mark the correct holes, and drill again, being careful not to enlarge the guide holes.

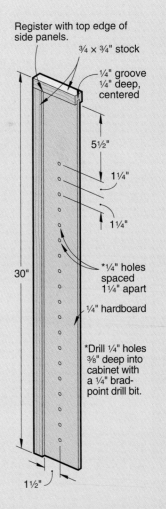

Register with top edge of side panels.

¾ × ¾" stock

¼" groove ¼" deep, centered

5½"

1¼"

1¼"

30"

*¼" holes spaced 1¼" apart

¼" hardboard

*Drill ¼" holes ⅜" deep into cabinet with a ¼" brad-point drill bit.

1½"

K

Before the glue sets measure across the diagonals of each door. Equal measurements mean that the corners are square.

L

Buy an affordable dovetail jig and practice with it so you'll be able to make the drawer joints quickly.

Dry-fit the doors, measure for the panels, and then cut the panels with a plywood blade mounted on the tablesaw. Allow for a 1/16" gap at each side and each end to make for a smooth assembly. Ease the edges of this panel too, with 150-grit sandpaper on a block. Rounded edges slip easily into the grooves without catching and possibly damaging the veneer. When everything fits perfectly glue the tenons in place with yellow glue and clamp each door with pipe clamps or bar clamps. Again use 150-grit sandpaper to ease the exposed edges of the rails and stiles next to the panel. Check the door for square by measuring the diagonals, as shown in **PHOTO K.**

Drive two 5/8" brads into each tenon from the backside of the door and remove the clamps. Lay each door on a flat surface and weight it down with more doors, or boards, while the glue dries. Crisscross the doors as you stack them; otherwise squeeze-out at the joints could glue them together.

Use cup-style hinges, which are unseen when the doors are closed and allow for adjustments too. You'll need a 1 3/8" Forstner bit to make the cup holes in the doors.

DESIGN THE DRAWERS

The typical cabinet drawer is 22" deep. Its width depends not only on the opening but also on the kind of slides you choose. The height must be at least 1/4" less than the height of the opening but might have to be reduced, again depending on the slides. See **DRAWING 3** for the dimensions and details of a typical drawer in this project. Maple is a good choice for the sides, front, and back of the drawer box.

Any of the popular dovetail jigs, along with a router and dovetail bit, will produce the half-blind dovetails desirable in a quality drawer. Our setup is shown in **PHOTO L.** Of course you might choose another type of joint that's easier to make.

For a clean look install undermounted drawer slides, which don't show on the sides of the drawers. Following the manufacturer's directions mount the guides on the 3/4" melamine divider rail that separates the drawer compartment from the rest of the cabinet. These undermounted slides require just 3/16" clearance on each side. A good hardware catalog will specify the side and height clearances for each style of slide.

BUILD THE TOE-KICK

The 3" setback at the bottom of a base cabinet lets you get right up close without stubbing your toes. Furniture factories build this "toe-kick" into their cabinets.

Use a separate toe-kick assembly that's easy to adjust on the site, just in case the floor isn't perfectly level. Once you adjust the toe-kick, you can place the cabinets on top and know that they're sitting level.

To make the toe-kick cut scraps of 3/4" particleboard or plywood to a 4" width. For each run of cabinets, you'll need two pieces the length of that run and enough 18 3/4" pieces to make the vertical and horizontal cross members set at 16" intervals. Join the cross members into L-shaped structures with screws, as shown in **DRAWING 1,** then screw on the sides, making a support 20 1/4" wide.

Apply a durable, clear finish to the solid wood surfaces. Polyurethane varnish stands up to handling and spills.

INSTALLING HINGES

AS BEAUTIFULLY CRAFTED AS YOUR CABINET DOOR MIGHT BE, IF IT BINDS WHEN IT SHUTS, YOUR FINE WORK IS DOWN THE TUBES. HERE'S HOW TO GET THE HANG OF HINGES.

You're near the cabinetmaker's moment of truth: You've fastened the last hinge in place and sent your door arcing closed. When it stops you'll know whether you've achieved excellence or exasperation. Relax. Armed with the shop-tested information here, you can make sure this moment of truth ends in triumph.

PLAN AROUND YOUR DOOR STYLE

The type of door you choose will determine the techniques and hardware you'll need for installation success. Most cabinets feature one of three types of doors:

• Full-overlay and partial-overlay doors mount in front of the cabinet frame and opening. Full-overlay doors cover all but a roughly ⅛" space around the frame. Partial-overlay doors, like the ones typically used on kitchen cabinets, leave a ½"- to 1"-wide view of the frame around the edges of the door. Fitting these doors to your cabinet doesn't demand quite the level of precision you'll need for the other two styles, but hinges still need to be positioned so that the door rests uniformly against the frame and so that facing doors line up with each other.

• Lipped, or partial-inset, doors feature a rabbet around the back edge of the door that allows the panel to drop partway into the cabinet frame, eliminating a visible gap between door and cabinet. The lip conceals minor out-of-square problems, but you'll still need to leave a consistent ⅛" gap between the lip and the frame to leave room for the offset hinges.

• The front face of an inset door rests flush with the face of the frame or cabinet, with a consistent 1/16" to 3/32" gap around all four sides. Inset doors require exacting measurements and dead-on-square glue-ups. But they also provide a sophisticated, clean look that's a testament to your craftsmanship.

SUCCESS HINGES ON HINGES

Once you zero in on a door type, you're ready to choose the appropriate hinges. You'll find a sampling of different types on page 38. Some hinges only work with a specific rabbet size or stock thickness. For example the most common offset hinges for partial inset doors work with a ⅜" rabbet around the back face of the door. Other hinges, such as a partial-wrap hinge, fit common ¾" stock.

Major door styles and the hinges they use

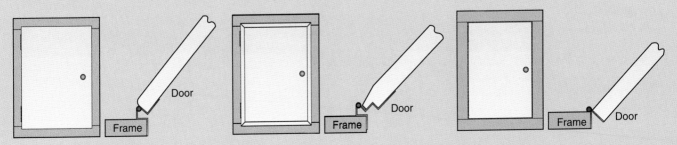

Door · Frame · Door · Frame · Door · Frame · Door

INSTALLING HINGES *(CONTINUED)*

No set rules exist for scaling hinge size to door size. Most cabinet and furniture doors have stiles and rails 2" to 2½" wide, so it's common to opt for no-mortise leaf hinges with a 2" barrel.

The number of hinges to use varies with the size and weight of the door. A rule of thumb suggested by one hinge manufacturer calls for two hinges on doors up to 36" high or 15 pounds, three hinges for doors up to 65" high and 15 to 30 pounds, and four hinges for doors 85" high and 30 to 45 pounds.

Other characteristics that might influence your hinge choice include finish, weather resistance, and adjustability. Many of the most commonly used hinges come in a choice of bright or antique brass, chrome or nickel, bronze, pewter, copper, and black finishes. For outdoor use though you'll want a hinge with either a painted finish, zinc-coated finish, or chrome finish.

Eurostyle concealed hinges have the edge on adjustability. Most models allow you to adjust the cabinet door up and down, from side to side, and in or out of the frame or cabinet opening. (See page 220 for tips on installing these hinges.)

Some traditional leaf-style choices also offer easy-adjustment installation. Instead of the usual three holes per leaf, no-mortise hinges use two vertical slots and one round screw hole on one leaf and two horizontal slots or a slot and hole on the other leaf. They get their "no-mortise" name because the two leaves fold together to form a single thickness. This automatically leaves a ¹⁄₁₆" gap between the door stile and the frame on an inset door, eliminating the need to chisel or rout a mortise to recess the hinge leaf flush with the surrounding wood.

For more information on installing an inset door using no-mortise hinges, see the six-step method in the box below.

Six steps to installing an inset door

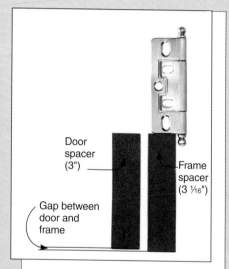

Door spacer (3")

Frame spacer (3 ¹⁄₁₆")

Gap between door and frame

1 Tailor a pair of spacers to the dimensions of your hinges and to where you want them mounted on the cabinet. For example to position the hinges on our computer desk's overhead cabinet, we cut strips of hardboard scrap ¾" wide. From this we cut a 3¹⁄₁₆" spacer to use on the edge of the frame and a 3" spacer for the edge of the cabinet door. Combined these two sizes leave a ¹⁄₁₆" gap between the door and the frame using this particular no-mortise hinge.

2 Tape a spacer to the frame edge as shown. Then clamp the hinge to the frame of the cabinet so that the barrel rests against the front edge of the frame. This leaves your hands free to drill the pilot holes using a spring-loaded centering bit or to mark their position with a self-centering punch. Place the pilot holes at the centers of the two slots but do not drill a hole beneath the round center hole for the third screw until after you've made the final alignments.

3 Tape your door spacer on the edge of the door at one end, as shown above. Turn the hinge upside down to use the barrel as an alignment guide against the front face of the door. As on the frame drill the pilot holes at the centers of the two slots to allow for adjustments. Here we're using a self-centering, spring-loaded drill bit. Then flip the hinge over and screw it into place. Repeat this procedure for the remaining hinges.

PREPARE FOR THE JOB

Regardless of the door type or hardware you choose, a few tools and preparations will simplify the installation job. Begin by working on a solid, dead-flat surface. An irregular work surface can cause the cabinet carcass to rack, making doors hard to fit and mount.

Minor off-square mistakes can escalate into bigger problems. A door that's off-plumb by just 1/32" needs to be planed by that much along the two stile edges, ultimately adding 1/16" to the gap. That doesn't sound like much until you recall that inset doors should have a gap of only 1/32" to 1/16".

These shop-made accessories and specialty tools increase your chances for success:
• A precise try square or combination square ensures square glue-ups. Use a precision steel rule and a fine-lead pencil or crafts knife for exact marking.
• Centering bits automatically position your pilot holes at the center of the hinge hole. A less-expensive alternative is a self-centering screw-hole punch that marks where to drill your pilot hole (see page 113).
• A 1⅜" or 35mm Forstner bit lets you drill flat-bottom holes for Eurostyle hinges.
• An assortment of spacers allows you to consistently position your hinges on both the door and frame, as shown in the box below. These can be custom-cut from ⅛"- or ¼"-thick scrap—hardboard is ideal.

If you're installing multiple doors, avoid confusion by marking which are right-hand or left-hand doors and which end you want at the top. In the case of flat-panel doors, also indicate the side that should face out. If you're making several cabinets, label which doors go in each individual cabinet.

To avoid marring a finished door, temporarily mount your hinges after the doors and cabinet have been sanded to their final thickness but not stained and finished (except for the center panel). Remove the hinges before the final finish is applied and finally place them after the finish has dried.

4 Clamp a long, straight scrap to the cabinet, extending it beyond the end of the lower rail. The top edge of this temporary support should rise approximately 1/16" above the lower rail to accommodate the gap. Rest the door on this support, as shown above, while driving top and bottom screws into the hinges. When installing bright brass hinges, you might want to cover the face with masking tape to avoid accidental scratches while driving the mounting screws.

Adjust these screws to raise or lower the door within the opening.

Adjust these screws to move the door forward or back within the opening.

5 Remove the temporary support scrap from the bottom rail and close the door. Check the gap around all four sides and use the hinge adjustment slots, shown above, to reposition the doors as needed. Once you achieve an even gap on the top and bottom and the door rests flush with the frame, drill a centered pilot hole and add a fifth screw to anchor the hinge in place on the frame. This still allows you to adjust the slant of the door within the frame.

Protruding corner

6 In time the door or cabinet frame might change shape with different humidity conditions or as tensions within the wood are released. Use the adjustment slots on the hinges to correct for these problems as needed. To fix the protruding corner on the cabinet shown above, for example, slide the door away from the barrel of the lower hinge. For additional strategies to correct out-of-alignment doors, see "Getting the hang of it" on page 221.

INSTALLING HINGES *(CONTINUED)*

EUROSTYLE HINGE TRICKS

It's no wonder Eurostyle concealed hinges have become so popular. With simple up-down, in-out, and side-to-side adjustability, they're just the ticket for finetuning the fit of inset or overlay cabinet doors. The key to installing these hinges lies in accurately boring the 35mm hinge-cup holes in the door stile. Here are two tips for doing just that.

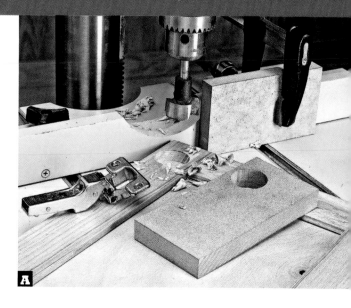
A

TIP 1: USE A POSITIONING GUIDE.

To get started cut a ¾"×3"×7" piece of plywood, particleboard, or medium-density fiberboard. Lay out the center of the hinge-cup hole where shown in the drawing, below right. The result is a quick and accurate hole-cutting guide as shown in **PHOTO A**. Simply chuck a 35mm Forstner bit into your drill press and bore a hole through the guide. (Don't have a 35mm Forstner bit? See the next tip for a solution.) Now position the fence and stop block, adjust the drill-press depth stop to the required depth, and bore hinge-cup holes, as shown in the three photos below.

Note: The backset and depth of hinge-cup holes vary for other types and brands of hinges. Check the instructions included with the hinges. Use the 1⅜" endset noted on the drawing for the short doors of a workbench cabinet. For longer doors, such as kitchen cabinet doors, use a 3" endset.

TIP 2: SUBSTITUTE A 1⅜" BIT. Suppose you
don't have a 35mm Forstner bit. A 1⅜" Forstner bit is only .003" smaller than 35mm (about the thickness of a sheet of paper) and works just fine.

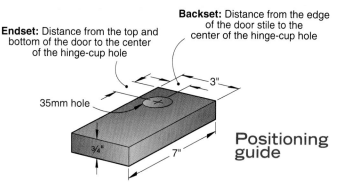

Endset: Distance from the top and bottom of the door to the center of the hinge-cup hole

Backset: Distance from the edge of the door stile to the center of the hinge-cup hole

35mm hole

3"

¾"

7"

Positioning guide

Drill precision hinge-cup holes in 3 easy steps

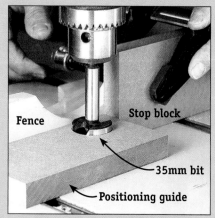

Fence

Stop block

35mm bit

Positioning guide

1 With the bit in the guide hole, position the fence so it touches the back edge of the guide. Place a stop block at the right end.

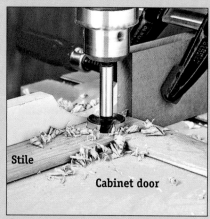

Stile

Cabinet door

2 Set the drill-press depth stop to the required depth and bore hinge-cup holes in all of your doors for the first hinge.

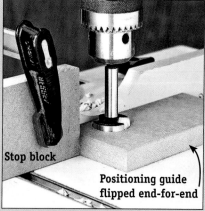

Stop block

Positioning guide flipped end-for-end

3 Flip the guide end-for-end, insert the bit, and reposition the stop block. Now drill hinge-cup holes for the second hinge.

GETTING THE HANG OF IT

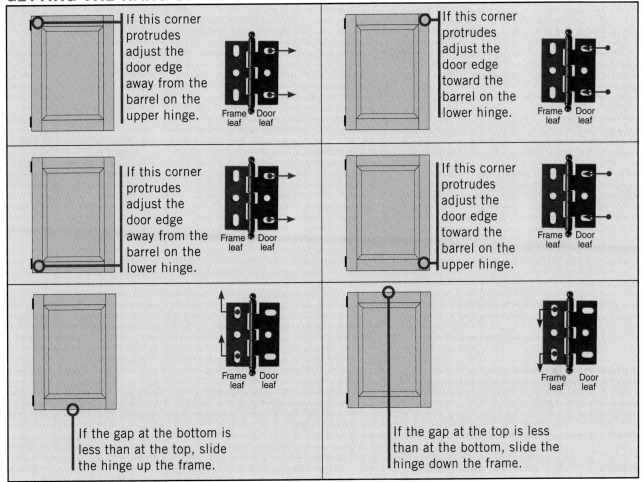

If this corner protrudes adjust the door edge away from the barrel on the upper hinge.

Frame leaf Door leaf

If this corner protrudes adjust the door edge toward the barrel on the lower hinge.

Frame leaf Door leaf

If this corner protrudes adjust the door edge away from the barrel on the lower hinge.

Frame leaf Door leaf

If this corner protrudes adjust the door edge toward the barrel on the upper hinge.

Frame leaf Door leaf

If the gap at the bottom is less than at the top, slide the hinge up the frame.

Frame leaf Door leaf

If the gap at the top is less than at the bottom, slide the hinge down the frame.

Frame leaf Door leaf

MORE TIPS FOR HANGING DOORS QUICKLY AND ACCURATELY

• Use screw-in levelers, like the one shown at left, for cabinet legs on uneven floors to prevent racking that can cause doors to stick.
• Don't use a sander to finetune the fit of your door; it's not a dimensioning tool.

A sharp hand plane gives you greater control without rounded edges and wavy spots. Use your tablesaw and jointer only if you have the skill to be able to remove amounts of wood no greater than 1/64".
• For doors that are wider than they are high, mount hinges within one hinge length of the top edge to avoid excess stress from the weight of the door.
• Keep seasonal changes in mind when you're mounting doors. Depending on where you live, a 1/32" gap that looks tight but acceptable in the cool, dry air of January might disappear some hot, humid

day in July. A rule of thumb for inset door gaps is 1/16", or roughly the thickness of a nickel. This allows for seasonal and humidity changes. Give your door at least two coats of a film finish to slow the transfer of moisture into and out of the wood.
• Add the cabinet back last. This gives you access to the interior for installing hinges and door catches or latches.
• On projects with several doors, slight differences in door sizes are sometimes unavoidable. If an opening is slightly undersize or oversize for one door, try others to see whether you can make those door size variations work to your advantage.
• If your door is slightly off plumb and the cabinet's vertical frame pieces are parallel, cut a shim the size and shape of your hinge leaf from a business card. If the door tilts clockwise, place the shim behind the lower hinge leaf that mounts on the cabinet. If it tilts counterclockwise shim the same leaf on the upper hinge.

DISPLAY CABINET

CAST A FAVORABLE LIGHT ON YOUR CURIOS WITH THIS ADAPTABLE DESIGN.

Is there one wall cabinet that meets all needs? If so you might be looking at it. It was designed with a cove top, halogen lights, and a towel bar so that it fits right into a kitchen or bathroom. But leave off the towel bar, and this beauty looks perfect in a living room, family room, or dining room. You could even skip the lights, cove top, and radiused sides and replace the glass with wood panels to make utility cabinets for the laundry room or shop.

MAKE THE SIDES AND SHELVES

1 **EDGE-JOIN** cherry lumber (refer to the Materials List on page 225) into slightly oversized blanks for the sides (A) and the shelves (B). Rip and crosscut these parts to size.

A cardboard prototype helps with planning

Before cutting wood it's often a good idea to build a full-scale prototype using corrugated cardboard (available free from appliance stores) and clear packing tape. This technique lets you better visualize the project's proportions and scale in its intended location. By hanging a model on the wall for a few days, you might choose to trim several inches off its depth to get the look you want. By the way you don't have to make your cuts with a utility knife and straightedge. Use your tablesaw or bandsaw for fast and easy results.

Drawing 1 Exploded view

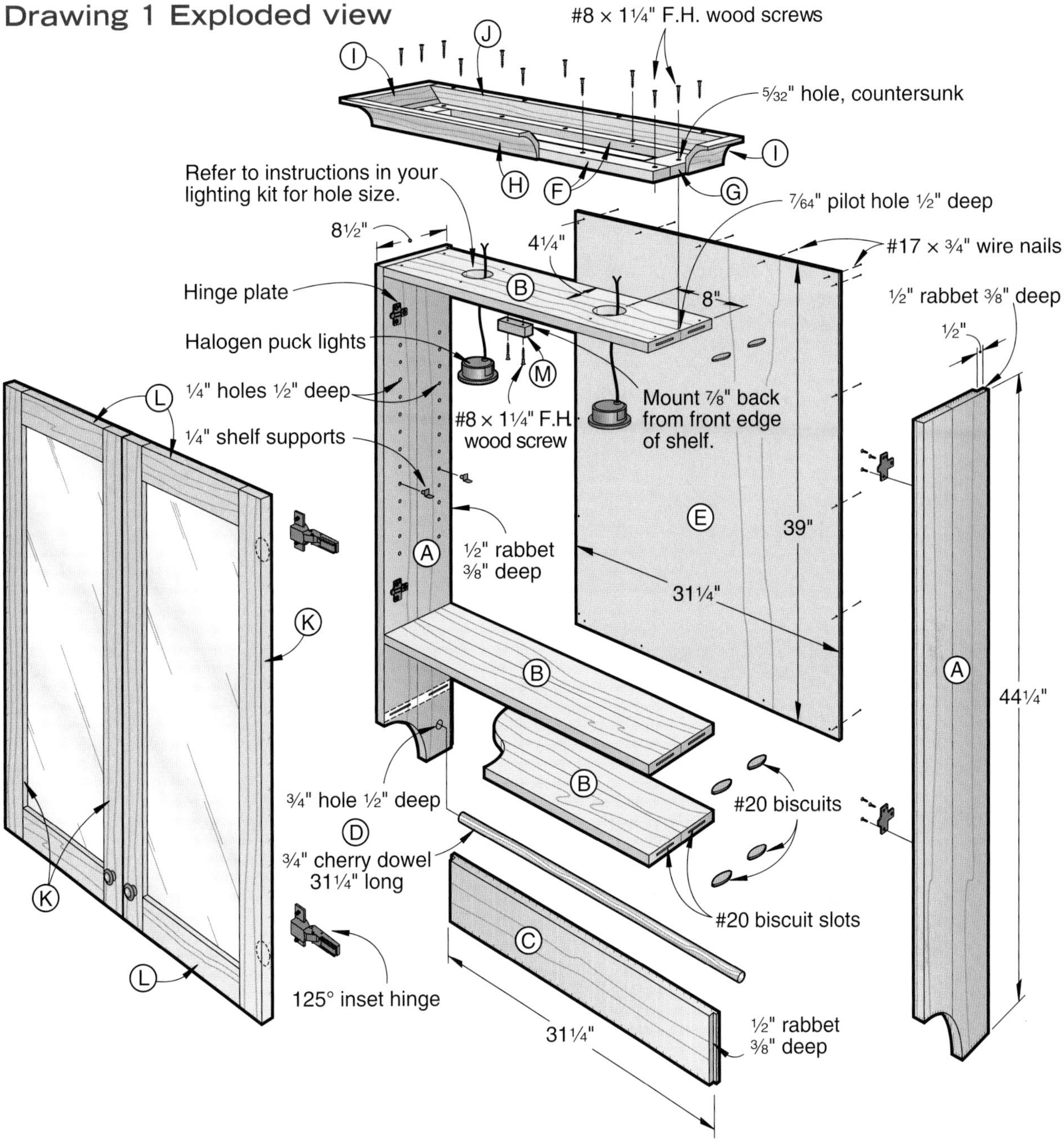

#8 × 1¼" F.H. wood screws

⁵⁄₃₂" hole, countersunk

Refer to instructions in your lighting kit for hole size.

⁷⁄₆₄" pilot hole ½" deep

#17 × ¾" wire nails

8½"

4¼"

Hinge plate

½" rabbet ⅜" deep

½"

Halogen puck lights

8"

¼" holes ½" deep

¼" shelf supports

#8 × 1¼" F.H. wood screw

Mount ⅞" back from front edge of shelf.

39"

½" rabbet ⅜" deep

31¼"

44¼"

¾" hole ½" deep

¾" cherry dowel 31¼" long

#20 biscuits

#20 biscuit slots

125° inset hinge

31¼"

½" rabbet ⅜" deep

Labels: I, J, H, F, G, Y, B, M, A, E, L, K, D, C

---

2 BORE HOLES FOR THE HALOGENS. Following the instructions furnished with your lights, use a Forstner bit or circle cutter in your drill press to make suitably sized holes into one of the shelves (B) where shown on **DRAWING 1**.

3 CONSTRUCT THE JIG shown in **DRAWING 1A** (page 224) to help you accurately drill the shelf-support holes into the inside faces of the sides (A). To use the jig align its top end with the upper end of each side and butt the jig's fence against the edge of the side. Chuck a brad-point bit into your handheld drill, add a depth stop, and drill the holes using the jig's holes as guides. Remember that the sides are mirror images of each other, not identical.

4 POSITION THE HINGE PLATES where shown in **DRAWING 2** (page 224) and drill their pilot holes but do not attach these plates yet. Drill the ¾" towel-bar hole near the bottom end of each side (A).

DISPLAY CABINET (CONTINUED)

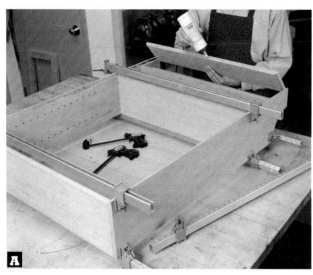

A

To fasten the lower back, apply glue to the rabbets and also along the upper edge of the lower back. Clamp against the lower shelf.

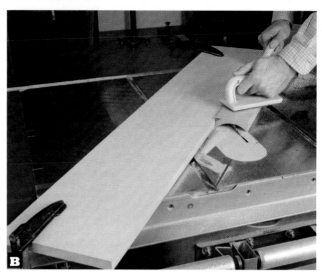

B

Securely clamp an angled fence to your tablesaw to cut the cove in the molding blanks. Push blocks are a must.

Drawing 1A
Hole-drilling jig

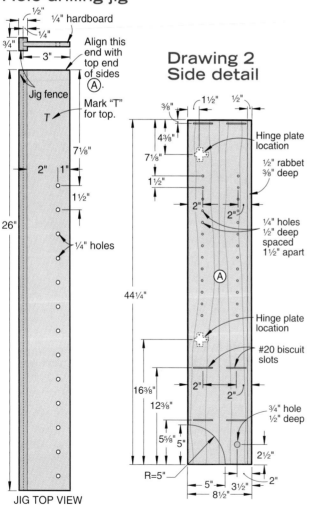

JIG TOP VIEW

5 **TEMPORARILY ATTACH** the two sides, inside face to inside face, with cloth double-faced tape, flushing the ends and edges. Using a compass draw the arc at the lower front corner where shown. Cut and sand the arc and separate the pieces.

6 **CUT THE RABBET.** With your table-mounted router, cut the rabbet along the rear inner edge of each side (A) where shown, making several passes, raising the bit after each pass.

7 **MARK WITH A PENCIL** the locations of the biscuit slots in the sides (A) and the shelves (B), making certain that each shelf's front edge is flush with the front edge of the sides.

8 **RIP AND CROSSCUT.** Referring to the Materials List, rip and crosscut the lower back (C) to size. Adjust the fence on your router table to cut a ⅜" rabbet ½" deep. Referring to **DRAWING 1** rout a rabbet along each end of the lower back.

9 **CUT THE TOWEL BAR.** Cut a ¾" cherry dowel 31¼" long for the towel bar (D). Referring to the Materials List, cut a piece of cherry plywood to size for the back (E).

10 **ASSEMBLE THE SIDES.** Applying glue to the biscuits, assemble the sides (A) and the shelves (B), making certain that their front edges are flush. Also apply a drop of glue to each end of the

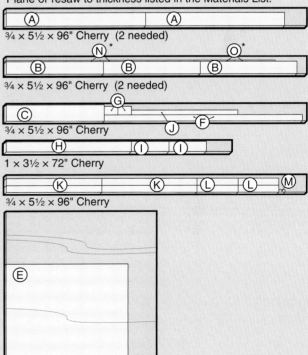

C

Make a custom sanding block by tracing the cove molding's profile onto a piece of scrap and bandsawing it to shape.

MATERIALS LIST

Case Part		FINISHED SIZE			Matl.	Qty.
		T	W	L		
A*	sides	¾"	8½"	44¼"	EC	2
B*	shelves	¾"	8"	30½"	EC	3
C	lower back	¾"	5¼"	31¼"	C	1
D	towel bar	¾" diameter	31¼"	N/A	CD	1
E	back	¼"	31¼"	39"	CP	1
F	front/back fillers	¾"	2"	31¾"	C	2
G	end fillers	¾"	2¾"	4⁵⁄₁₆"	C	2
H*	front molding	1"	3¼"	36¼"	C	1
I*	end moldings	1"	3¼"	10⅝"	C	2
J	top back rail	¾"	1½"	34"	C	1
K	door stiles	¾"	2¼"	30½"	C	4
L	door rails	¾"	2¼"	11¹⁄₁₆"	C	4
M	doorstop	¾"	¾"	2"	C	1
N*	side stops	¼"	⅜"	28¾"	C	4
O*	top/bottom stops	¼"	⅜"	11⁵⁄₁₆"	C	4

*Parts initially cut oversize.
Material key: EC–edge-glued cherry, C–cherry, CD–cherry dowel, CP–cherry plywood.

Supplies: #8×2" flathead wood screws; #8×1¼" flathead wood screws; #20 plate-joiner biscuits; #17×¾" wire nails; #17×¾" wire brads; 2-lamp halogen lighting kit; 1" knobs, (2); ⅛" glass; ¼" glass; glue; ¼"×3" lag screws (2), 125-degree inset clip hinges with mounting plates (2 pair).

towel bar (D) and insert its ends into the holes in the sides before clamping the assembly.

11 GLUE THE CARCASS. Referring to **PHOTO A** apply glue to the rabbets and upper edge of the lower back (C); clamp it into place, applying pressure against the lower shelf. To check that the assembly is square, measure the diagonals of the carcass. When the measurements are equal, the assembly is square. Remove any glue squeeze-out and let it dry overnight.

BUILD THE TOP ASSEMBLY

1 CUT THE FRONT/BACK FILLERS. Referring to the Materials List, rip and crosscut the front/back fillers (F) and the end fillers (G).

2 CUT BISCUIT SLOTS into the fillers (F, G) where shown on **DRAWING 5.** Glue and clamp the assembly.

3 DRILL PILOT HOLES. Unclamp when the glue is dry and drill countersunk ⁵⁄₃₂" screw-shank holes through the assembly where shown. Position the rear edge of the assembly flush with the rear edge of the top shelf and center it side to side. Holding the assembly in position, use the holes as guides to drill ⁷⁄₆₄" pilot holes ½" deep into the top shelf. Do not attach the assembly to the top shelf at this time.

Cutting diagram

*Plane or resaw to thickness listed in the Materials List.

Ⓐ   Ⓐ
¾ × 5½ × 96" Cherry (2 needed)

Ⓝ*   Ⓞ*
Ⓑ   Ⓑ   Ⓑ
¾ × 5½ × 96" Cherry (2 needed)

Ⓖ
Ⓒ   Ⓕ
Ⓙ
¾ × 5½ × 96" Cherry

Ⓗ   Ⓘ Ⓘ
1 × 3½ × 72" Cherry

Ⓚ   Ⓚ   Ⓛ Ⓛ   Ⓜ
¾ × 5½ × 96" Cherry

Ⓔ
¼ × 48 × 48" Cherry plywood

DISPLAY CABINET *(CONTINUED)*

Drawing 2 Cove-cutting setup

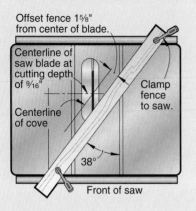

Offset fence 1⅝" from center of blade.

Centerline of saw blade at cutting depth of ⁹⁄₁₆"

Centerline of cove

Clamp fence to saw.

38°

Front of saw

Drawing 3 Bevel-ripping setups

¼"

STEP 1

Fence

H/I

Saw table

Blade at 45°

Fence

STEP 2

¼"

Saw table

Blade at 45°

CUT THE COVE MOLDING

1 RIP BLANKS. From 1"-thick cherry, rip blanks 3¼" wide for the front molding (H) and the end moldings (I). You'll cut these pieces to final length later but for now crosscut one blank to 40" and two at 12".

2 PREPARE THE TABLESAW. Put a blade with 60 to 80 sharp carbide teeth into your tablesaw, then raise the blade so ⁹⁄₁₆" projects above the table. Referring to **DRAWING 4** clamp an angled fence to your tablesaw where shown. Make all measurements from the blade in its raised position. Before you lower the blade to make the first cut, make a note of the position of the handwheel's handle. Then count the revolutions of the handwheel as you lower the blade. This procedure eliminates guesswork as you raise the blade toward its final position.

3 FORM THE COVE by making a series of cuts, raising the blade in ⅛" increments. Referring to **PHOTO B** use push blocks to move the molding blanks over the blade. Keep the edge of the blank against the fence and advance it with both consistent downward pressure and steady forward motion. To reduce blade marks in the final pass, remove ¹⁄₁₆" or less with that cut and make the pass nonstop at a slow but steady rate.

4 CUT MOLDING. Referring to **DRAWING 4** make four cuts on each molding blank to complete its profile. Make two cuts with the Step 1 setup, then change to the Step 2 setup for the final two cuts.

5 CROSSCUT THE MOLDING. Crosscut a 1½" piece from one of the front molding blanks as a pattern to make a sanding block. As in **PHOTO C** trace the shape of the pattern onto the end of a 1"×3¼"×4½" scrap wood block. To safely hold the block on end while bandsawing, we used double-faced tape to temporarily attach it to the end of a scrap 2×4 on edge. Bandsaw just to the waste side of the line.

6 SAND PROFILE. To make the sanding block fit the molding perfectly, rub it against adhesive-backed sandpaper that you place on the molding's profile where shown in **PHOTO C**. Then apply sandpaper to the block and smooth all of the molding blanks.

MITER THE COVE MOLDING

1 BUILD THE JIG. First build the jig shown in **DRAWING 6**. After screwing the jig to your tablesaw's miter gauge, angle the setup to miter an end of one of the blanks for the end moldings (I), as shown in **PHOTO D**.
*Note: **PHOTO D** shows the mitering of the front molding (H). Use the same process for both parts H and I.*

2 MARK MOLDING. The molding is placed upside down in the jig. To avoid confusion put a pencil mark on each blank to clearly identify the molding's upper edge. Let the square-cut end of the molding blank run long for now. Rotate your miter gauge to the opposite 45-degree setting and miter-cut the other end molding (I).

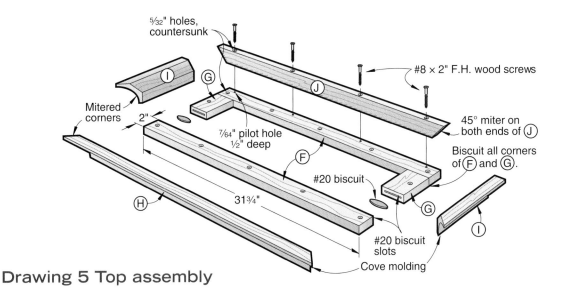

5/32" holes, countersunk

#8 × 2" F.H. wood screws

Mitered corners

2"

7/64" pilot hole 1/2" deep

45° miter on both ends of Ⓙ

Biscuit all corners of Ⓕ and Ⓖ.

#20 biscuit

31¾"

#20 biscuit slots

Cove molding

Drawing 5 Top assembly

3 **MITER-CUT** one end of the front molding (H), then dry-clamp it and one of the end moldings (I) with a mating miter to the top assembly (F, G). After adjusting the pieces for a tight miter joint, use a sharp knife to mark the cutline for the opposite miter on the front molding, as shown in **PHOTO E.** Make the cut, then again clamp the front molding against the top assembly. Add the other end molding to check the joint. If you need to make adjustments, you'll still have enough length on both end moldings to recut the joints. When you're satisfied mark the square-cut ends of the end moldings and cut them to length.

4 **GLUE AND CLAMP** the front and end moldings (H, I) to the top assembly (F, G). You can use masking tape to hold the joints closed while the glue dries. We didn't use any fasteners, but you could add a few #17×1" wire brads to prevent the pieces from slipping.

5 **CUT AND FIT TOP BACK RAIL.** Referring to the Materials List and **DRAWING 5,** cut the top back rail (J) to fit onto the top assembly. Drill the shank and pilot holes for the mounting screws, then glue and screw this part into position.

6 **POSITION THE TOP ASSEMBLY** on the carcass assembly and drive screws through the mounting holes. Make certain that the rear edge of the assembly is flush with the rear edge of the top shelf and is centered side-to-side.

MAKE GLASS-PANELED DOORS

1 **CUT DOOR STILES.** Referring to the Materials List, rip and crosscut the door stiles (K) and the door rails (L) to size.

2 **MORTISE THE STILES.** Chuck a ¼" Forstner bit into your drill press and drill a series of overlapping holes to form the mortises in the stiles (K) where shown in **DRAWING 7A.** Use a chisel to smooth the walls of the mortises and to square the corners.

3 **PREPARE FOR TENONS.** To set up for cutting the tenons, screw an 18"-long 1×4 extension to your tablesaw's miter gauge. Then put a ¾" dado head into your tablesaw and raise it for a ¼"-deep cut. See **DRAWING 7B.** Clamp a stop block to the miter-gauge extension and make test cuts in scrap lumber to check the thickness of the tenon in the mortise. After you cut the cheeks of all the tenons, raise the dado head to make the ⅜"-deep cut at the top and bottom of each tenon.

4 **DRY-ASSEMBLE, THEN GLUE.** Check the joints with a dry assembly (no glue), then glue and clamp the door assemblies. Make sure that the doors are square and flat.

5 **ROUT A RABBET.** Chuck a ⅜" bearing-guided rabbeting bit into your table-mounted router and rout a rabbet around the interior perimeter of each door's back. To help prevent chip-out, rout the ⅜"-deep rabbet in a series of ⅛"-deep passes. Use a chisel to square the corners of each rabbet.

6 **CUT THE DOORSTOP.** Rip and crosscut the doorstop (M) to size, then drill two 5/32" countersunk shank holes through it. Referring to **DRAWING 1** screw the doorstop to the underside of the top shelf (B), centering it.

DISPLAY CABINET (CONTINUED)

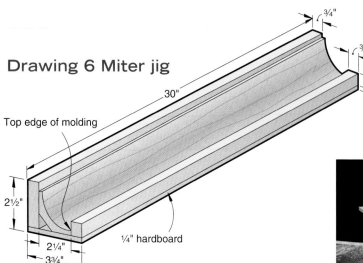

Drawing 6 Miter jig

Top edge of molding

30"

3/4"

3/4"

3/4"

1/4"

2½"

1/4" hardboard

2¼"

3¾"

7 **INSTALL THE HINGES.** Referring to **DRAWING 7** drill the hinge-cup holes, using a 35mm or 1⅜" Forstner bit, following the hinge maker's instructions. Install the hinges, test-fit the doors, and remove the hinges.

8 **BUY GLASS.** Take the doors to a glass shop and have ⅛"-thick glass cut ⅛" undersize for the openings.

9 **CUT BLANKS.** Rip and crosscut four ¼"×⅜"×30" blanks for the side stops (N) and four ¼"×⅜"×13" blanks for the top/bottom stops (O). Chuck a chamfering bit into your table-mounted router and rout a ⅛" chamfer along one edge of each blank. For safety use featherboards and push blocks when routing.

10 **MITER THE SIDE STOPS** (N) and the top/bottom stops (O) to fit the door openings. Set these parts aside for now.

FINISH BEFORE FINAL ASSEMBLY

1 **APPLY YOUR CHOICE OF FINISH** to all of the wood parts. Four coats of an oil/urethane wipe-on finish were applied with a cloth. Between coats we sanded with 600-grit wet/dry sandpaper and removed the dust with a tack cloth.

2 **FASTEN THE BACK TO THE CARCASS** assembly with #17×¾" wire nails.

D The jig cradles the cove molding, preventing it from rocking while you make the miter cuts. Screw the jig to your tablesaw's miter gauge.

E Want to know how pros get nearly invisible miters? Just use a sharp knife to transfer the cove molding cutline from the top assembly.

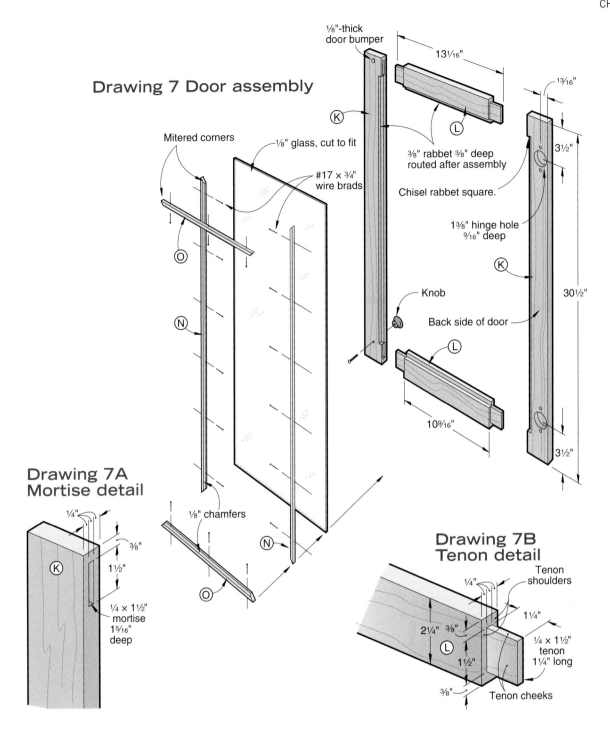

Drawing 7 Door assembly

⅛"-thick door bumper

13¹⁄₁₆"

13⁄₁₆"

Mitered corners

⅛" glass, cut to fit

#17 × ¾" wire brads

Ⓚ

Ⓛ

⅜" rabbet ⅜" deep routed after assembly

Chisel rabbet square.

3½"

1⅜" hinge hole ⁹⁄₁₆" deep

Ⓚ

30½"

Ⓞ

Ⓝ

Knob

Back side of door

Ⓛ

10⁹⁄₁₆"

3½"

⅛" chamfers

Ⓝ

Ⓞ

Drawing 7A Mortise detail

¼"

⅜"

Ⓚ

1½"

¼ × 1½" mortise 1⁵⁄₁₆" deep

Drawing 7B Tenon detail

Tenon shoulders

¼"

1¼"

2¼" ⅜"

Ⓛ

1½"

¼ × 1½" tenon 1¼" long

⅜"

Tenon cheeks

3 **FASTEN THE GLASS IN PLACE** by using #17×¾" wire brads to attach the side stops (N) and the top/bottom stops (O) to the doors.

4 **MOUNT DOORKNOBS.** Referring to **DRAWING 1**, drill centered mounting holes for the doorknobs and attach them. Reattach the hinges and mount the doors.

5 **BUY GLASS SHELVES.** Have ¼"-thick glass shelves cut to size and ask to have the edges seamed (sanded to remove sharpness). Don't

forget to allow for the thickness of the inset doors when you measure for the shelves. Our shelves measure 7"×30¼".

6 **INSTALL THE LIGHTS** following the manufacturer's instructions.

7 **HANG THE CABINET** on your wall by drilling holes and driving two ¼"×3" lag screws through the top back rail (J) into wall studs.

INSTALLING CABINETS

CAREFUL MEASUREMENT AND PLANNING MAKE FOR A TROUBLE-FREE PLACEMENT.

The preceding sections showed you how to build goodlooking, durable kitchen cabinets. Here's how to install them dead-level and solid enough to survive anything your family can throw at them. If you measured carefully during the building phase, you're halfway to a smooth installation. Pay the same attention to setting the toe-kicks and make sure the screws hit the studs, and your cabinets will give you years of satisfaction.

After you've taken care of any electrical, plumbing, or heating and cooling work, mark on the walls the height of your toe-kick, base cabinets, and wall cabinets, as shown in **DRAWING 1**, to help keep everything on target during installation. Be sure to measure up from the floor's highest point; work your way around the room with a 4' level to find it.

START ON THE WALL

Start the installation with the wall cabinets rather than working over the base units. Enlist someone to help you hold each cabinet in place. Your installation starting point depends on the room layout. Often it's best to start with a cabinet that must be centered over a stove or sink.

If your cabinets won't contact a soffit above, install temporary supports as shown in **DRAWING 1**. Otherwise locate the cabinets by holding them firmly against the soffit. Raise the first cabinet into place and check it with a reliable level. Place shims between the wall and cabinet to make slight adjustments. Drill pilot holes into the wall studs and attach the cabinet to the wall with white 3" pan-head screws. Ideally each cabinet is held by four screws in each stud, two near the top and two near the bottom.

Use a ¾" divider made of the same wood as your cabinets positioned to protrude ⅞". A ¾" spacer between each pair of cabinets goes near the back edge and can be made from scrap, because it won't be seen. (Refer to **DRAWING 2** on page 213).

Raise the second cabinet into place beside the first one and drive two screws through its back and into the studs but don't snug them tight yet. Clamp the two cabinets together with handscrew clamps, as shown in **PHOTO A**.

Again check the installation with your level. For a cabinet that's adjacent to a wall, place shims between the cabinet and the wall, as in **PHOTO B**, to help snug it into place. A piece of scrap material placed behind the shims will protect the wall from damage.

While your assistant holds the cabinet in place, put two more pan-head screws through the back and into the wall studs. Use a level along the front edge of the cabinet and drive two 1¼" flathead wood screws, one near the top and one near the bottom, from the first cabinet into the second, as shown in **PHOTO C.** Place these screws where they'll be hidden by the hinge plates. Now tighten the screws in the cabinet back.

In many situations your row of cabinets will run from one wall to another, as in the case shown here. We sized our cabinets to allow a 1¼" gap at each end of the installation, then covered it with trim as shown in **DRAWING 1.**

From matching solid wood cut two boards 1½" wide and the length of the cabinet side. Temporarily attach the filler block with screws located inside shelf-pin holes. Hold the trim piece vertically in place and check to see whether it sits flush against the wall. If any gaps show use a compass to scribe a line on the face of the trim and cut it to fit. (See the box on page 232 for scribing information.)

After cutting the other side of the trim so that it sits flush with the outside edge of the cabinet, remove the filler block and glue the two pieces into an L shape. After the glue dries screw this assembly in place so that it extends ⅞" beyond the cabinet side. That measurement will make it flush with the ¾" doors after they're mounted on their hinges.

BUILD A FOUNDATION

Position the toe-kick frames on the floor, then use shims to bring any low spots into alignment with your mark on the wall. To raise a given spot on a frame, start one shim under the nearest crosspiece with a

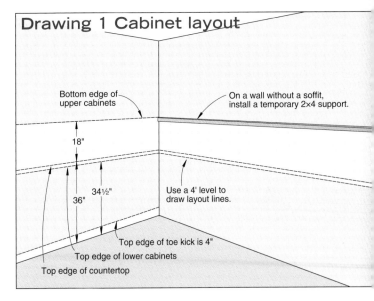

Drawing 1 Cabinet layout

Bottom edge of upper cabinets

On a wall without a soffit, install a temporary 2×4 support.

18"

34½"

36"

Use a 4' level to draw layout lines.

Top edge of toe kick is 4"

Top edge of lower cabinets

Top edge of countertop

B Protect the wall with a board when you use shims like this. Remove the shims after screwing the cabinet to the wall.

A Use clean, smooth handscrew clamps to align cabinets. You can apply adequate pressure this way without damaging the wood.

C There's no need to clutter up the inside of a cabinet with lots of screw heads. Fasten adjacent cabinets with screws placed inside hinge or shelf holes.

hammer, then start a second shim on top of the first, driven from the opposite side of the crosspiece. Two wedge-shaped shims together create a flat, square support.

Use your level to check the toe-kick from the wall to the outside edge, as shown in **PHOTO D**. Use shims in several spots along each gap so that there's no flex in the completed installation.

When everything is level screw the frame to the wall studs with #10×3" pan-head screws. Finally screw the toe-kick to the floor by driving two 3" screws through each horizontal piece. Wherever possible locate the screws so that they also pass through shims.

DRESS UP THE TOE-KICK

From stock that matches your cabinets, cut a board to the length of the toe-kick and wide enough to reach from the floor to the highest point on the toe-kick. Scribe a line on the backside of this board by running a pencil along the top of the toe-kick. Place the board on supports and carefully cut along that line with a circular saw. Attach the board with #8×1¼" wood screws driven from inside the toe-kick frame.

You're likely to need a heating-and-cooling register somewhere within the toe-kick. To make the grille place the board on a tablesaw, set a stop on the fence, raise the blade to make a slot, then reposition the fence and repeat the procedure. Cut six ⅛" kerfs, with ¼" spaces in between. Keep the kerfs 1" away from the top edge and 2" away from the bottom. The kerfs are longer on the backside because of the curve of the saw blade, but the appearance of the exposed side is all you have to consider.

Leave an open space in the toe-kick frame during assembly to allow for airflow or cut it out now with a handsaw. After installing the face board, use construction adhesive to seal the bottom edge inside the toe-kick. This step makes sure the heated or cooled air flows directly into the room.

PLACE THE BASE CABINETS

Start placing your base cabinets with a unit that must line up with an architectural feature. For example traditional kitchen design centers the sink cabinet under a window.

Speaking of the sink cabinet, you'll have to cut holes in the back of that unit to accept the plumbing pipes. Mark the position of the cabinet on the wall, then measure from one end mark and the toe-kick to locate a given pipe. Measure from the same end on the cabinet and from the bottom. Cut the hole just slightly oversize, using a jigsaw.

Place the first base cabinet on the toe-kick frame and check it with your level. If it's off adjust the frame.

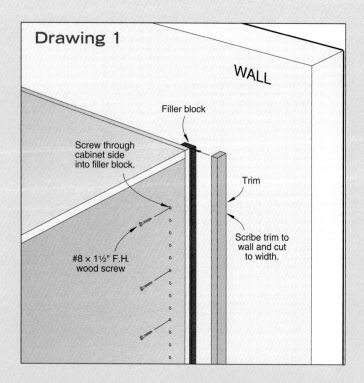

Drawing 1

WALL

Filler block

Screw through cabinet side into filler block.

Trim

Scribe trim to wall and cut to width.

#8 × 1½" F.H. wood screw

Scribing described

If a wall is out of plumb, your perfectly square cabinets will leave an unsightly gap wherever the cabinet-to-wall edge is exposed. Eliminate that problem by "scribing," shown in the diagram opposite.

To scribe a trim piece, place it against the wall, then use a level to hold it vertically. Adjust your compass to span slightly farther than the largest gap. Lay the point of the compass against the wall at the top of the trim piece. Put the pencil point on the trim and pull the compass carefully down, keeping it perpendicular to the wall.

Set a circular saw or jigsaw at a slight angle to create an undercut. Cut along the line you've made on the trim piece, leaving a sharp edge to fit against the wall. This technique reduces the problem of small gaps caused by wall texture.

D Screw the toe-kick to the wall, then adjust it horizontally with a level and shims. Later trim off any protruding ends of the shims with a handsaw.

E If you build your base cabinets carefully and set the toe-kicks perfectly level, this step is easy. Clamp adjoining units together and attach them with screws.

Set the first cabinet in place. If the top edge sits flush against the wall, drive at least two 3" pan-head screws through the backer board and into the studs. Because most of the top was left open on these base cabinets, you can work from a standing position and reach down into the cabinet to attach it to the wall. The countertop goes on later.

If the bottom sits flush against the wall but the top shows a gap because the wall isn't plumb, insert shims over the wall studs. Then drive screws through the

cabinet back and the shims and into the studs. The bottom of the cabinet must sit solidly on the toe-kick frame.

Clamp the adjoining cabinet to the first one with handscrew clamps, as shown in **PHOTO E.** Attach the rear spacer with screws from the inside of each adjoining cabinet. Again place the screws where they'll be hidden by a hinge plate or inside one of the shelf-support holes. Continue in this way to the end of the run.

ADD DOORS AND DRAWERS

When all of the cabinets are set, install the drawers and doors. The doors are ready to snap into the hinges. However we built the basic drawer boxes without their fronts, so we'll do that now.

First locate the center of the drawer front. Place a piece of masking tape in the approximate center, then use a ruler to mark diagonal lines from opposite corners. Drill through the intersection of those lines, peel away the tape, and you have a hole for the drawer-knob screw.

Slip the drawer into its slides. Lay a 1/8" shim on top of the cabinet door below the drawer opening. Set the drawer front on the shim, align its ends with the door, then drill through the knob hole and drawer box. Install the knob, then drill four screw pilot holes from inside the drawer, making certain not to go clear through the front. Countersink the holes and drive the four #8×1" flathead wood screws. Repeat that procedure with all of the drawers.

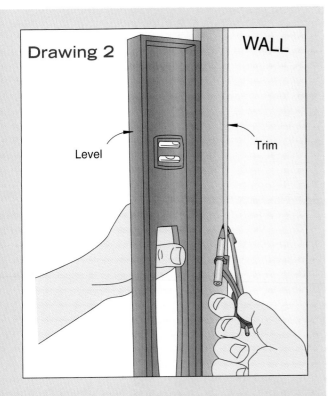

Drawing 2

WALL

Level

Trim

GLOSSARY

Apron: The bottom piece of window casing that finishes the window frame beneath the interior sill. (See also Stool.)

Astragal: A molding that looks similar to some symmetrical chair rails. It was originally used as an attachment to one of a pair of cabinet doors so that when one was closed, it kept the other from opening.

Baseboard: Trim running along the bottom of a wall to cover gaps between the wall and floor.

Bevel: A cut that runs at an angle through the thickness of a board or piece of trim.

Board foot: One board foot of lumber is 144 cubic inches. To calculate board feet multiply a board's thickness by its width and then by its length. If length is in inches, divide by 144; if length is measured in feet, divide by 12.

Bow: A defect in which a board is warped along its length when viewed along its narrow dimension.

Butt joint: The joint formed by two pieces of material cut at 90 degrees when fastened end to end, end to face, or end to edge.

Casing: Trim that lies flat on the wall surrounding a door or window opening to conceal the gap between jamb and wall.

Countersink: To drive the head of a nail or screw so that its top is flush with the surface of the surrounding wood.

Cripple stud: A short stud, typically used above headers in door and window openings and below sill plates in window openings.

Crosscut: To cut a board to length across the wood's grain.

Dado: A groove in the face of a board into which the edge of another board can be fitted.

Fibonacci gauge: An adjustable design tool that holds constant the Golden Mean ratio even if it's compressed or expanded. It is named after 13th-century Italian mathematician Leonardo Fibonacci.

Framing: The structure of the house, including all the wooden (or metal) parts of a house's frame—wall studs, headers, joists, rafters, etc. The term "frame" is sometimes also used to describe the jambs surrounding a window or door.

Golden Mean: A ratio of 1:1.618, which produces a pleasing proportion when applied to the length of the long side of a rectangle in relation to the short side.

Hardboard: A type of sheet good made of wood fibers soaked in water and then pressed. The natural glue that holds wood together—lignum—binds the fibers together. Tempered hardboard is treated with an oil such as linseed or tung oil and then heat-treated for strength.

Header: The part of a house's frame that spans the top of a door or window opening, often made from two pieces of 2x lumber with a spacer of ½-inch plywood.

Jack stud: One part of the pairs of studs that frame a door or window opening. Jack studs, sometimes called trimmers, are cut to match the height of the opening. The header rests on top of the jack studs. (See also King stud.)

Jamb: The wooden frame, usually ¾ inch thick and as wide as the total thickness of the wall, that surrounds a window or door opening.

Jamb extension: Wood applied to the edge of a jamb to make it the same thickness as the wall.

Joist: A horizontal part of a house's frame that supports the floor and/or ceiling.

King stud: One part of the pairs of studs that frame a door or window opening. King studs are cut to the same length as other wall studs. Jack studs are nailed to the king studs.

Level: Perfectly horizontal with no part higher or lower than another. Also a tool used to assess this condition.

Medium-density fiberboard (MDF): This type of sheet good is made of strands of wood fiber mixed with glue and pressed to form a flat sheet. The pressure produces an almost perfectly smooth surface that is somewhat harder than the core.

Miter: A corner joint between two pieces of wood where the adjoining ends are cut at matching angles (usually two 45-degree angles that meet to form a 90-degree angle). Also the process of cutting these angles.

Mortise: A shallow recess cut so that a piece of hardware, such as a hinge leaf or a strike plate, can fit and be flush with the surrounding wood surface.

Mullion: A narrow vertical piece that divides glass sections in a single window or door.

Muntin: A narrow piece of wood that divides glass openings in a window sash or a door with lights.

Ogee: An elegant elongated "S" profile found on many crown moldings.

On center (OC): A phrase used to designate the distance from the center of one regularly spaced framing member to the center of the next.

Parting stop: A narrow strip of wood that separates the sashes of a double-hung window.

Penny: This designation of nail size comes from the abbreviation of the letter "d," which stands for denarius, a Roman coin. The "d" is used to designate the cost of a nail, with larger nails being more expensive.

Pilot hole: A hole bored before driving a screw or nail to ensure against splitting the board. A pilot hole is slightly narrower than the fastener being driven through it.

Plate: A horizontal piece of lumber to which the wall studs are attached. The bottom plate is anchored to the floor. The top plate is usually double in thickness to tie walls together and to help carry the load from above.

Plumb: Perfectly vertical. This can be determined using a level or a plumb bob.

Rabbet: A groove cut across the width of a board at its end, into which a crosspiece is fit for a secure joint.

Rail: A horizontal piece on a panel door or on a window sash.

Return: When used with regard to trim, a piece of molding that completes a run by turning into the wall.

Reveal: A narrow flat area on a molding or board (usually a jamb edge) left uncovered for visual effect.

Rip: To cut a board along its length in order to trim it to the desired width.

Rough opening: The opening in the framing made to accommodate a door or window's jambs.

Sash: A frame containing a piece of glass.

Shim: A wedge, usually made of wood or composite material, used to align jambs and other materials in a rough opening.

Sill: A trim piece at the bottom of a window or door, sloped so water can run away from the house. Or the framing piece at the bottom of a door.

Square: A 90-degree angle.

Stile: A vertical piece on a panel door or a window sash.

Stool: A horizontal piece of trim installed at the bottom of a window inside the house, often called the sill.

Stop: A narrow strip of wood installed inside a door jamb that keeps the door from swinging too far inward when it closes.

Stud: A vertical member of a house's frame, often made from 2×4s or 2×6s.

Threshold: Also called a saddle a wood or metal piece that lies on the floor at the bottom of a door and spans the flooring materials of adjacent rooms.

Toenailing: Driving a nail at an angle through one framing member so it can penetrate a second framing member.

Torque: The twisting force used to cause rotation. Measured in inch-pounds it is useful in evaluating power tools, especially drills.

Wainscoting: A layer of solid wood applied over the lower part of a wall and topped with nosing, panel trim, or chair rail.

Warp: A surface that is not true or flat.

This section will help you find specific tools, hardware, and materials used in the projects presented in this book. In most cases the manufacturer is listed. However the product might also be available from the following online and retail woodworking suppliers: Amazon.com (www.amazon.com); BPWay.com, llc (www.bpway.com, 877/462-7929); Cabinetparts.com, Inc. (www.cabinetparts.com, 800/857-8721); Hartville Tool (www.hartvilletool.com, 800/345-2396); Lee Valley Tools Ltd. (www.leevalley.com, 800/871-8158); Rockler Woodworking and Hardware (www.rockler.com, 800/279-4441); Woodcraft (www.woodcraft.com, 800/225-1153); Woodhaven, Inc. (www.woodhaven.com, 800/344-6657).

Page 10:
Hardware kit for making a Fibonacci gauge from Schlabaugh & Sons (www.schsons.com, 800/346-9663).

Page 37:
Computer holder from Lee Valley Tools Ltd. (www.leevalley.com, 800/871-8158). Keyboard tray, cable organizers from Rockler Woodworking and Hardware (www.rockler.com, 800/279-4441). Desk drawer from Woodworker's Hardware, (www.wwhardware.com, 800/383-0130).

Pages 50–51:
The tools described on these pages can be purchased from Garrett Wade (www.garrettwade.com, 800/221-2942); Lee Valley Tools Ltd. (www.leevalley.com, 800/871-8158); McFeely's, (www.mcfeelys.com, 800/443-7937); MLCS (www.mlcswoodworking.com, 800/533-9298); Rockler (www.rockler.com, 800/279-4441); and Woodcraft (www.woodcraft.com, 800/225-1153).

Page 55:
Self-centering doweling jig and Kreg pocket jig kit from Woodcraft (www.woodcraft.com, 800/225-1153).

Page 62:
Router table, Rockler Router Table with PC690 Router Combo Package; circle jig, Rockler Ellipse/Circle Router Jig; both available from Rockler, (www.rockler.com, 800/279-4441).

Page 71:
Feather-Loc Multi-Purpose Featherboard from Bench Dog Inc. (www.benchdog.com, 800/786-8902). Miter Hold-In item #242 from Woodhaven, Inc. (www.woodhaven.com, 800/344-6657). Magnetic featherboard from Grip–Tite (www.grip-tite.com, 800/475-0293).

Page 75:
Jointer from Grizzly Industrial Inc. (www.grizzly.com, 800/523-4777). Planer from Ridge Tool Company (www.ridgid.com, 800/474-3443).

Page 84:
CenterPoint® Center-Finding measuring tape from U.S. Tape (www.ustape.com, 800/472-8273).

Page 85:
Marking knife #127680 from Woodcraft (www.woodcraft.com, 800/225-1153).

Page 93:
Wolfcraft Dowel Pro #3751 from Wolfcraft North America (www.wolfcraft.com, 630/773-4777). Veritas doweling jig #05J08.01 from Veritas Tools (www.veritastools.com, 613/596-1922); Dowelmax from O.M.S. Tool Co. (www.dowelmax.com, 877/986-9400).

Page 99:
Dado-cleanout bit from Woodline USA (www.woodline.com, 800/472-6950). For a wide selection of cutter bits, check MLCS (www.mlcswoodworking.com, 800/533-9298).

Page 119:
Tabletop fastener #34215 from Rockler (www.rockler.com, 800/279-4441).

Pages 122–123:
Early American water-base stain from General Finishes (www.generalfinishes.com, 800/783-6050). Dark walnut oil-base stain from Varathane (www.varathane.com, 800/323-3584). TransTint black dye #128490 from Woodcraft (www.woodcraft.com, 800/225-1153). ZAR Ultra Max water-base satin finish from United Gilsonite Laboratories (www.ugl.com, 800/845-5227). Olympic Pearlessence from PPG Architectural Finishes (www.olympic.com, 800/441-9695. Also available at Lowe's stores nationwide.)

Page 125:
Some synthetic bristles, such as Purdy's Syntox, rival natural bristles for bristle size and flexibility. Available from Purdy (www.purdycorp.com, 800/547-0780).

Page 149:
For further help get the DVD "Conquering Crown Molding" from Gary M. Katz OnLine (www.garymkatz.com).

Page 150:
Miter clamp pliers and miter clamps from Collins Tool Company (www.collinstool.com, 888/838-8988).

Page 172:
Hollowood, the manufacturer of the columns shown in this project, is no longer in business. There are hundreds of alternatives, including PVC and aluminum columns that can be covered with a wrap of thin wood slats. Columns can be ordered online or special ordered from home centers. To cut the groove that receives the column, consider purchasing a circle cutter (#16N41) capable of cutting 8" circles available from Woodcraft (www.woodcraft.com, 800/225-1153).

Page 173:
A ⅜" radius cove-and-bead router bit was used to make the profile around the base and capital. Order tool #178-3345 from Eagle America (www.eagleamerica.com, 800/872-2511).

Page 175:
Bookshelves used in this project include one BILLY series W31½ × D11 × H79½ and two BILLY series W15¾ × D11 × H79½ available from IKEA (www.ikea.com/us, 800/434-4532).

Page 177-181:
Hardware used in this project includes Mission-style hinges. Hardware Hut.com has several hinge and door pull options (www.thehardwarehut.com or 800/708-6649). The low-profile double magnetic catch (item #27H04) is available from Woodcraft (www.woodcraft.com, 800/225-1153).

Page 181:
For a low-voltage, cooler option to the halogen lights shown in this project, consider a Xenon Pocket® light kit, item #39668, available from Rockler (www.rockler.com, 800/279-4441).

Page 195:
For multiple wide-swing inset clip option, ⁷⁄₁₆"-diameter-thick door bumpers #02S82, shelf supports #27I20, contact Woodcraft (www.woodcraft.com, 800/225–1153). Knobs are from Amerock. available at many home centers and hardware stores, or at Woodworker's Hardware (www.wwhardware.com, 800/383-0130).

Page 200:
Each pair of tall sides (A) requires 20 cam housings and screw studs, each pair of short sides (A) requires 12 cam housings and screw studs. Each door box requires 8 cam housings and screw studs, 2 hinges and hinge plates, 1 knob, and 4 bumpers. Each drawer box requires 12 cam housings and screw studs, 2 undermounted drawer slides, 8 1" washer-head screws, 2 knobs with 1½"-long knob screws, and 4 bumpers. The cam housings are available in almond, brown, and white. When ordering specify the color that best matches your plywood. Hardware available from Woodworker's Hardware (www.wwhardware.com, 800/383-0130).

Page 209:
Cabinet hardware from Woodworker's Hardware (www.wwhardware.com, 800/383-0130).

Page 210:
Veneer edging in various species is available in 8' rolls. To trim both edges of the veneer at the same time, consider purchasing a double-edged veneer trimmer #02286821. Edging and trimmer available from Van Dyke's Restorers (www.vandykes.com, 800/558-1234).

Page 229:
The 1" knobs are from Amerock. Amerock hardware is available at many home centers and hardware stores. To locate a dealer visit the company's website at www.amerock.com or check the wide selection at Woodworker's Hardware (www.wwhardware.com, 800/383-0130).

Page 225:
Cherry dowel ¾"×36", #50B04; Blum inset clip hinges; self-adhesive door bumpers, #02S82; glass-shelf supports, #27120: order from Woodcraft (www.woodcraft.com, 800/225-1153).

METRIC CONVERSIONS

U.S. UNITS TO METRIC EQUIVALENTS			METRIC EQUIVALENTS TO U.S. UNITS		
To Convert From	**Multiply by**	**To Get**	**To Convert From**	**Multiply by**	**To Get**
Inches	25.4	Millimeters	Millimeters	0.0394	Inches
Inches	2.54	Centimeters	Centimeters	0.3937	Inches
Feet	30.48	Centimeters	Centimeters	0.0328	Feet
Feet	0.3048	Meters	Meters	3.2808	Feet
Yards	0.9144	Meters	Meters	1.0936	Yards
Square inches	6.4516	Square centimeters	Square centimeters	0.1550	Square inches
Square feet	0.0929	Square meters	Square meters	10.764	Square feet
Square yards	0.8361	Square meters	Square meters	1.1960	Square yards
Acres	0.4047	Hectares	Hectares	2.4711	Acres
Cubic inches	16.387	Cubic centimeters	Cubic centimeters	0.0610	Cubic inches
Cubic feet	0.0283	Cubic meters	Cubic meters	35.315	Cubic feet
Cubic feet	28.316	Liters	Liters	0.0353	Cubic feet
Cubic yards	0.7646	Cubic meters	Cubic meters	1.308	Cubic yards
Cubic yards	764.55	Liters	Liters	0.0013	Cubic yards

To convert from degrees Fahrenheit (F) to degrees Celsius (C), first subtract 32, then multiply by $\frac{5}{9}$.

To convert from degrees Celsius (C) to degrees Fahrenheit (F), multiply by $\frac{9}{5}$, then add 32.

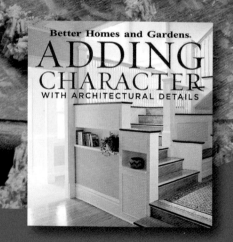
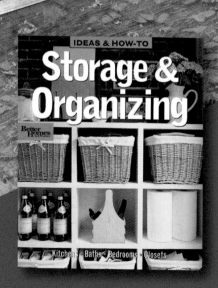
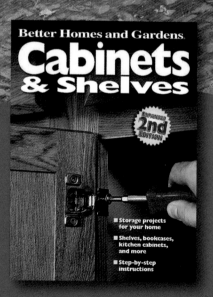